Praise for
The Fat Lady Never Sings

"Readers have a dugout view and perspective, almost as if they were sitting on the bench or on the top steps. It brings to life and depicts legendary figures who unfortunately often get forgotten, ignored and not fully appreciated. From Coach Big Lou DeFilippo to Derby's No. 1 fan, Mike Regan, we get a birds-eye look with no detail left out during this special group of players, and long-lasting diamond memory. It's a mammoth home run for generations to come."

—Mark Jaffee,
Waterbury Republican-American sports writer, formerly of the *New Haven Journal-Courier* and *New Haven Register*

THE FAT LADY NEVER SINGS

THE FAT LADY NEVER SINGS

◆

How a Football Team Found
Redemption on the Baseball Diamond

Steven Reilly

iUniverse, Inc.
New York Lincoln Shanghai

THE FAT LADY NEVER SINGS
How a Football Team Found Redemption on the Baseball Diamond

Copyright © 2006 by Steven M. Reilly

All rights reserved. No part of this book may be used or reproduced by any means, graphic, electronic, or mechanical, including photocopying, recording, taping or by any information storage retrieval system without the written permission of the publisher except in the case of brief quotations embodied in critical articles and reviews.

iUniverse books may be ordered through booksellers or by contacting:

iUniverse
2021 Pine Lake Road, Suite 100
Lincoln, NE 68512
www.iuniverse.com
1-800-Authors (1-800-288-4677)

The events in this memoir occurred.
Some details have been changed or added.
The name Pat Rosino is fictitious.

ISBN-13: 978-0-595-39467-8 (pbk)
ISBN-13: 978-0-595-83864-6 (ebk)
ISBN-10: 0-595-39467-1 (pbk)
ISBN-10: 0-595-83864-2 (ebk)

Printed in the United States of America

To my wife, Sue; my parents, Robert F. Reilly Sr. and Nancy Reilly; my brother Robert F. Reilly Jr.; and his wife, Rachell J. Reilly. And in memory of my late brother Fred M. Reilly.

Contents

CHAPTER 1	Thanksgiving Day 1992	1
CHAPTER 2	Big Lou's Reign	6
CHAPTER 3	Gino, Donny, and Ben	10
CHAPTER 4	The End of the Streak	15
CHAPTER 5	The Fat Lady Prepares to Sing	18
CHAPTER 6	John D and Bethlehem Days	21
CHAPTER 7	Return to Derby High	27
CHAPTER 8	5–15	31
CHAPTER 9	Seven Straight with Lou's Hat	36
CHAPTER 10	Struggling to Return to the Tournament	55
CHAPTER 11	The Sad Season	64
CHAPTER 12	Return to the Tournament 1991	72
CHAPTER 13	Team Meeting 1992	84
CHAPTER 14	The Season Begins	93
CHAPTER 15	Battling for Ten Wins	102
CHAPTER 16	Pete and Joey G's Triumph	116
CHAPTER 17	Winning Two while Missing Home Plate	128
CHAPTER 18	Losing Two Coin Flips	132
CHAPTER 19	Rounds One and Two	137

Chapter 20	Triumph at Fort Courage.	146
Chapter 21	Nobody Remembers the Runner-Up	153
Chapter 22	Benanto's Advice	163
Chapter 23	Riding Bus Number Seven	168
Chapter 24	The Game	179
Chapter 25	Extra Innings	196
Chapter 26	The Parade, the Clubhouse, and the Evergreen	209
Acknowledgments		215
Endnotes		217

1

Thanksgiving Day 1992

Ben, Donny, and Gino sat together on the red wooden bench on the sideline in the last football game they would ever play for Derby High School. With his right hand, Ben squeezed into his mouth the little water left from the green plastic bottle. The fingertips of his left hand barely held on to his red helmet; a dirty plaster cast covered his arm—wrist to elbow.

Gino and Donny just sat there with their helmets off, their heads between their hands, and their elbows on their knees. Mud obscured nearly every inch of their red and white uniforms. Their war paint, or eye black, as it's more accurately called, was smudged under their eyes and down their faces. Although the three had left everything they had on the field, they knew that it wouldn't be good enough, not in Derby. Nobody would remember this game's score, but no one would ever forget they lost. In a few short minutes, they would be labeled losers forever, and there was nothing they could do about it.

I leaned on the silver chain-link fence near a back corner of the end zone. I could hear the scoreboard clock behind me slowly and painfully clicking down the time. The Game was about to be finally and officially over. It was the annual Thanksgiving Day game against rival Shelton High School in 1991. Although the weather report predicted a 30 percent chance of snow, the game ended up taking place on a fall morning that was too warm for a heavy coat and too cold for a Windbreaker. The sun glared in my eyes, but I liked where I was standing; it allowed me to make an easy exit from the park whenever I wanted.

Most of the nearly six thousand fans were continuing to make their way out Derby's Leo F. Ryan Memorial Field to beat the traffic. Almost all of the people leaving before the game clock reached four zeros were Derby fans. Many were trudging through the open gates wearing red, making their way to their cars without ever looking back at the field. They couldn't bear to watch Shelton's players and fans celebrate on their field. Soon the Shelton faithful would drive through

Derby's streets with their horns beeping, orange and black pompons waving out their decorated car windows, screaming that Shelton is number one.

The chain links atop the fence bar dug through my red jacket into my forearms. The metal barrier and the cinder track prevented me from getting any closer to the uncovered bench. Twenty feet away from the fence that surrounded the field, assistant coaches, police officers, and others lucky enough to obtain a red field pass walked past the three players on the bench without saying a word. I wondered what I would say to them if I were on the bench with them, but it was not my time, not my season.

People want to remember success, forget about failure. Even a child knows he does not want to be the one holding the wonder ball or the one without a chair when the music stops. Perhaps we feel that way as children because winners are admired and accepted. Perhaps it's because it makes them feel they've achieved a bit of immortality—to gain something nobody else has. Or perhaps it's because winning makes the pain of life go away, even if only for a moment. When you're part of a team, if you put the team's goal ahead of your own, the reward can be everything that's good about life: friendship, comradery, loyalty, a connection that lasts forever.

The outcome of a single event can change a person forever. It isn't the losers who are remembered; it's those who make a monumental effort that go down in the annals of history. Dorando Pietri is remembered for the way he finished the 1908 Olympic marathon: collapsing after entering the stadium, getting up, taking a wrong turn, collapsing again, and finishing—only to be disqualified for being helped across the line. I remember Gabriella Anderson-Schiess's stiff right leg and limp left arm as the exhausted marathon runner lurched past the finish line in the 1984 Olympics. We admire most, however, the loser who persists and finally wins against the odds. He is most extraordinary.

I turned from my thoughts back to the players on the bench. These three seniors had been taken out of the game to allow the underclassmen, who mostly sat on the bench, a reason to get their uniforms washed. Sometimes I think it's a strategy coaches employ in hopes that the team that's killing you will follow suit, remove its regulars from the game, and have mercy on you. They usually don't until you take the first step and take your starters out. That's the risk a loser has to take. This strategy sometimes makes the final score look closer than the game actually was. In this game, it wouldn't have mattered how close the final score was.

It was the ultimate disgrace for the three seniors. It was bad enough they were losing to Shelton on their home field, but now they would be on the bench when the final whistle blew and the siren from the red and white ambulance parked below the scoreboard blared, marking the end of an era. You see, in Derby, the smallest town in Connecticut (only 5.3 square miles), football was life.

Every boy in this blue collar town dreamed of playing football for the Red Raiders of Derby High School. The city didn't have much else going for it, only the pride in its successful high school football program. Most years, unemployment in Derby was higher than the state average, and what was left of Derby's manufacturing base was slowly waning out. For years, small downtown stores were closing in favor of department stores in larger cities. The City's downtown buildings were decaying; reconstruction was prone to politics and wasn't well planned. If Derby lost one of its rival football games, the mayor would worry he might not get reelected. The townspeople would have to blame somebody.

For many years, the football games were played before a few thousand people, except for games against rivalries, in which the crowds reached nearly ten thousand fans. For a town of just more than twelve thousand people, everybody who read an *Evening Sentinel*, bought his smokes at the United Cigar Store or the Bridge Smoke Shop, sipped cappuccino at Durante's Market, ate breakfast at Connie's Cucina, or ordered a pizza by delivery from a Derby phone attended the games. Those who couldn't attend listened as the local radio station, WADS, broadcast the games.

Whenever Derby scored a touchdown, someone lit the wick of a small red and white cannon in the back of the north end zone near the scoreboard. If you attended a game and didn't realize Derby scored, you could be startled off your gray pine bleacher seat. White smoke, along with the pungent scent of black powder, crept across the field for the next ten minutes, constant reminders to the visiting team that they had given up a touchdown.

During most home games, a short, stout man dressed as an Indian with an authentic red, white, and brown war bonnet and wearing red, yellow, and black war paint made a grand entrance. With one hand gripping a dry leather rein and the other a turkey-feathered lance, he rode down a hill behind the adjacent baseball field's rusted backstop on a horse with a frayed blanket on its back. The brown and white spotted stallion clopped its way to the cinder track before Derby's stands, and its silent rider raised the lance to acknowledge the raucous cheering of Derby fans. The horse stopped behind the team's bench, and the Indian warrior motivated the team.

I glanced toward the baseball field, behind the opposite end zone. Traditionally while the high school game carried on, younger kids played their own tackle football game. They played on the diamond during each football game until the day they were able to play on the big field. Until last year, nobody had seemed to care that these games chewed up the baseball field's infield. The city finally resodded the infield and roped it off during football games. But that didn't stop the game-during-the-game from taking place; it just moved the game into left field. As I looked across the field, I noticed the kids were already dispersing to go home with their parents.

I turned around and noticed month-old campaign flyers with black-and-white pictures of smiling candidates littering the tarred entranceway leading from the north gate to the Ryan Field complex down the path behind me. Derby fans followed the same path to reach the gray wooden bleachers supported by aging concrete that covered the side of a pine and maple tree-filled hill for the football field's entire length. Several flyers whipped up against the double gate portion of the chain-link fence the ambulance used whenever it traveled on the cinder track surrounding the field to get to a team's bench. At the north entrance, candidates for state or municipal office sometimes passed out campaign literature and shook hands. Fans sometimes grumbled as they walked past them, as if the politicians violated the game's sanctity and hindered them from securing a good seat.

Twenty minutes before the annual Thanksgiving Day game between Derby and Shelton kicked off, each town's politicians, along with each school's representatives, gathered at midfield as if they were at a summit. After they shook hands and returned to their respective sides of the field, the warm-up began. Derby's mascot, an alumnus or student dressed in full Indian garb waving a wood and stone axe, would have at it with the Shelton mascot on the home team's emblem, painted on what was left of the midfield grass after a long season. Since Shelton's nickname was "the Gaels," it was always someone dressed in a Viking outfit. The mascots warmed up the cold crowd before the main event. The Indian tackled the ox-horn helmeted Viking and then the Viking tackled the Indian or vice versa, so each team's fans could alternately cheer. They terminated the ritual after the fights became real, not staged.

From 1967 through this game in 1991, Derby's winning football tradition amassed three overall state championships, seven undefeated seasons, and multiple Housatonic League championships. After the Connecticut Interscholastic Athletic Association instituted divisional state championship games based on a school's enrollment in 1976, Derby won two of those as well. For a school of Derby's size, the number of all-valley, all-Housatonic League, and all-state players as well as players who excelled at Division I and II colleges and universities was an astounding accomplishment for such a small high school in the Northeast. But the most important record achieved was that—since 1963—Derby had never had a losing season. The torch had been passed each of the past twenty-eight years to Raiders who had endured the sacrifices necessary to ensure the continuation of the "Streak."

2

Big Lou's Reign

Derby's coach, Charlie DiCenso, finally stopped pacing up and down the mud-laden sidelines between the forty-yard line markers. He removed his red cap with a white D and ran his left hand through his curly light brown hair. With puffed cheeks and tightened lips, he let out a long breath while squeezing his cap's bill. He put his cap back on, revealing the half dollar-sized gold ring with the ruby red stone on his right hand he had received last year when he brought the city another state football championship. He adjusted the cap with both hands, leaving the bill just above his metal-rimmed glasses.

Although Charlie tried to pull off another miracle underdog upset against the orange and black of Shelton High School, it wasn't going to happen today. A 5–6 season would be the best he could do. One year ago to the day, he had used a dirty white towel to wipe the Gatorade off his face before speaking to reporters about the upcoming state playoffs. Tomorrow he would be known as the coach who couldn't carry on the Streak.

The Streak had started just before the arrival of legendary coach Lou DeFilippo. Prior to Coach DeFilippo's reign, a winning tradition had already been in its infancy with Coach Ron Carbone, then with Bill McAllister. After four years, Ansonia, an adjacent city and another of Derby's archrivals, stole Carbone, and the rivalry hardened. The following year, Carbone left Ansonia to coach at Hamden High School and Ansonia stole McAllister after his undefeated 8–0–1 first year. After McAllister left, Derby searched for a new football coach who would continue the winning ways of his two predecessors. When the search began, Derby learned an overqualified coach named Louis DeFilippo was interested. Derby had gotten lucky.

Big Lou was a giant of a man as well as a giant of a person. He had been a lineman for the New York Giants from 1941 to 1947, with a stint in between with the navy during World War II, and had been an assistant coach with the Baltimore Colts. He had also been an assistant coach at Purdue, Fordham, and Columbia universities.

Before his professional playing days, he had snapped the ball from center for the Fordham University Rams. In 1941, he was the team's captain and played in the Cotton Bowl with—as legend has it—one of the versions of the famous Seven Blocks of Granite. Years later, he was inducted into the Fordham University Athletic Hall of Fame. The legendary Green Bay Packer coach Vince Lombardi had played at Fordham on the 1937 version of the Seven, and it was sometimes rumored that Big Lou was on it with him. It was more than rumor; he had been Vince Lombardi's friend, and was acquainted with many professional football players and coaches.

Prior to coming to Derby, Big Lou had coached football at East Meadow High School on Long Island. While coaching East Meadow from 1961 to 1968, he compiled a 46-9-1 record and won five straight league championships from 1963 to 1967. In 1964, his team won the Long Island Championship, and he was voted Coach of the Year by the Long Island Press. In 1967, the East Meadow Kiwanis Club honored him as its Citizen of the Year.

While at Derby from 1968 to 1982, his teams had compiled a record of 116-30-8, with undefeated seasons in 1968, 1969, 1972, 1973, and 1975. The 1969 and 1973 teams had earned recognition as Connecticut's overall champion. Honored as Coach of the Year by the National Football Foundation in 1972 and by the Connecticut Interscholastic Athletic Conference (CIAC) in 1973, he was also inducted into the Connecticut Coaches Hall of Fame. He received the Gold Key Award from the Connecticut Sports Writers' Alliance, and was their High School Coach of the Year in 1975 as well as the New Haven Grid Iron Club's Coach of the Year in 1982.[1]

Lou was loved not only by the football players and coaches who knelt in pews together at an early morning mass at St. Mary's Church before each game, but by everyone else in town. He didn't demand respect, but commanded it. His knowledge of the game of football was unsurpassed among his peers. On the high school level, only a handful of coaches in Connecticut could come close. Big Lou's personality could motivate anyone to do better than they would ever think possible. Lou's credo was simple, yet powerful: never quit. Whenever he voiced those words, you would think he had made the phrase up. Maybe he had.

Besides coaching football at Derby High, Big Lou was the boys' gym teacher. During phys ed classes, he pounded that same phrase into the young minds who wore the required DHS white gym shirts and red shorts. Even those who didn't play football still called him coach. Some students got jealous of the treatment football jocks received. On Fridays before each game, they were allowed to wear their game jerseys in school. Every other male had to wear a collared shirt and tie.

Those on the team were exempt from taking gym; instead they were allowed to go into the weight room and lift. If a football player was nursing an injury, he could spend the class in the cylindrical stainless steel whirlpool in the windowless ten-by-ten room adjacent to Lou's office. Exemption from one of Coach's gym classes was no small reward; sometimes the students were lucky to survive the forty-two-minute session. Unless you were on the football team, there was no excuse good enough to miss his class. If you told him you forgot your jock, he would tell you to go get a peanut shell and rubber band. If you told him your jock had broke, he simply grabbed a stapler and clicked it back together for you.

In addition to the usual sports, phys ed included everything from tumbling, wrestling, and gymnastics to marine drills. In the gymnastics segment, one of the suicidal events we had no choice but to line up for was to bounce off a spring board, leap over a set of oak parallel bars with a light blue mat laid over them, then tumble and roll on a floor mat 1.25 inches thick. Though spotters always stood by with their hands spread, you wouldn't count on them to save you from being carried to your next class.

We even played the traditional sports in gym class, such as softball, under rules designed to make your spine tingle if you didn't hustle. Under Coach's rules, each team used their own pitcher. After the team at bat made three outs, the other red and white team sprinted off the field and tossed one to their hitter; they didn't have to wait until the new fielding team was ready. If you didn't hustle onto the field, you could get nailed off the head by a line drive, but nobody ever did. You only got one pitch. You either got a hit or made an out. It was that simple. Unlike normal baseball rules, a foul ball was an out. In a forty-three-minute period, teams could get a full seven-inning game in before heading to the showers.

Despite the fact you might talk about gym classes while circling an index finger around your ear, there was something about the way you felt after surviving a class without barfing your lunch. Lou toughened you up. You weren't allowed to quit.

If a male student got into trouble at the school, they didn't suspend him; they simply made him see Coach. A visit to Coach was worse than a suspension. Lou's voice sounded like a drill sergeant's. As you stood in line for attendance on the wooden gym floor before jumping jacks commenced, he always barked, "If you quit at anything, you'll quit at everything. You'll quit on your team, your school, your friends. You'll someday quit on your wife and family, and you'll quit on yourself. Nobody quits in Derby!" Sometimes he emphasized the point. "They may quit in Ansonia, they may quit in Seymour, they may quit in Shelton, but nobody quits in Derby!" I attended Derby High School from 1969–1973 and only played baseball, but I never forgot those words. Big Lou wouldn't let you.

Next to Shelton High School, the high schools of the neighboring towns of Ansonia and Seymour were Derby's biggest rivals. The day before each of those three games, Derby's students piled whatever crates, skids, and junk wood they could find in town. The pile towered as high as a gooseneck goal post. At night, the pile was torched as players, cheerleaders, and students roared before it. The orange-yellow glow could be seen from the hills of neighboring towns. Shelton and Ansonia High School built their own bonfires to stir their fans into pandemonium. On a clear night before the Shelton game, you could see Shelton's bonfire as you rubbed your hands together near Derby's. I'm sure Gael fans also espied Derby's flickering flames. On one year, before one of those rival games, Derby students even lit the Red Raider bonfire on the adjacent baseball field's uncovered mound.

Even the cannon that boomed at home games whenever Derby scored was called Little Lou. Although Little Lou eventually surrendered to safety and health codes, the football field remains named after Big Lou. Following Big Lou's retirement, Charlie DiCenso, a longtime, loyal assistant, continued Lou's legacy and started one of his own, achieving one overall state championship in 1990 as well as two Class S state championships. Despite declining enrollment at Derby High after Lou's departure, the winning tradition and the Streak lived on with Charlie.

3

Gino, Donny, and Ben

In 1991, under Coach DiCenso, Gino, Ben, and Donny were not going to escape the tradition or the duty of continuing the Streak. Gino DiMauro III, a senior at the school, was the son of the city's mayor, Gino DiMauro Jr., and the grandson of Gino DiMauro Sr. He grew up on Eighth Street, which was in a small Italian neighborhood on Derby's west side. He hung out near a street corner that, for many years, had a bicycle repair shop in the front of an apartment building's red brick foundation that sold Red Hot Dollars, Pixy Stix, and Atomic Fire Balls for a penny.

Gino's father had played football when he had been at Derby High. Gino's grandfather had been the Indian chief on the horse until he got too old to ride without a saddle. By the time young Gino played, Papa Gino had been elevated from mascot at the football games to membership on the city's board of education. In Derby, I think that was considered a demotion.

Gino III, with a blond flattop and sideburns to the bottom of his ear, could barely touch the top of the doorway into the locker room. He couldn't catch many runners from behind, so he was a lineman. In Derby, a player's physical size didn't matter as much as his heart; most years Derby was outsized and outnumbered by its opponents. If you weren't athletic enough to play a skill position, such as a running back, defensive back, or wide receiver, or if you couldn't remember the plays, you'd better be able to block. Gino wasn't all that good at any of it, but at least he didn't disgrace the family.

Gino also played baseball. Until his senior year, the highest level he had reached was playing second base on the junior varsity team. Second base is where a coach grooms the following year's shortstop. Gino could block a ground ball like a hockey goalie, pick it up, and throw it to first base. He struck out more times in batting practice than the rest of the team combined, but at least he swung at strikes.

When Gino did play second base, though he didn't wear glasses for his vision, he wore plastic protective eye goggles. Nobody ever heard of a second baseman who wore eye goggles. The light-skinned Gino took a lot of ribbing when he donned them, as their dark edges surrounded his eyes and made him look like a raccoon. I guess he wanted the goggles in case he had to knock the ball down with his round-cheeked face.

Gino's nickname was Pizza Box Maker because he, along with Ben, bused tables and sometimes assembled white cardboard boxes at a small Italian restaurant called Roseland just below Ryan Field. Roseland still had wooden booths and an old-fashioned Seeburg jukebox inside. It often had customers waiting out the door. Sometimes, from the fields above, I could smell the garlic from Roseland. Traditionally, the football coaches met there and ate after the games.

Like Gino, Ben Bartone was a senior. Ben's father, Ralph, had been an all-Housatonic League guard on Derby's football team and had been known in his high school days in the 1960s as one tough hombre. Ralph had tried to play basketball, but he had just been the comic relief during many of the junior varsity games he played in, even as a senior. I had attended the junior varsity and varsity basketball games when I was in grammar school. They were played back-to-back in the evening on a local grammar school's slippery linoleum floor. I can't recall Ralph ever tapping the scorer's table to get buzzed into a varsity game. But in Derby you could be a senior and still get away with playing on the junior varsity basketball team. The other teams not only didn't notice but didn't care, as it never created any mismatches on the court. Despite the fact Ralph was not all that talented at shooting hoops, no other team's players ever messed with him on the court.

Ralph raised his family on Lakeview Terrace. Lakeview was a tight-knit neighborhood on Derby's far west side off Route 34. Route 34 was known as the River Road since it was adjacent the Housatonic River. Lakeview contained identical two-floor duplexes. On its south side, kids could scratch out four bases with sticks on a small, weed-strewn field. In the summer, Lakeview residents crossed Route 34 to grab a cheeseburger at a snack shack named the End Zone or swim at the Recreation Camp on the river. Lakeview Terrace's north side outlet was at Hawthorne Avenue, adjacent to 350-acre Osborndale State Park. In its inception, occupancy at one of the duplexes in the Lakeview community was limited to those whose income didn't exceed bureaucratic guidelines. When Lakeview was built, that was the majority of Derby's population.

Ralph's son Ben was a different kind of athlete. At 5'10" and about 165 pounds, he had been Derby High's quarterback since his junior year. Like many of Derby's past quarterbacks, he also played defense as a cornerback. Earlier that season, Ben had shattered his left wrist while making a tackle against North Haven. The Raider faithful had been stunned. The question among the coaching staff had been whether Ben would ever return as the quarterback.

After Ben's injury, the team began to lose. Although Derby's backup quarterback gave it his best, he was not nearly as good as Ben Bartone. As each week passed, the coaches questioned Ben's desire to return. Only in Derby would that question ever have arisen. Ben watched each game from the sideline with his wrist still encased in the plaster his surgeon had formed over the hardware he implanted. The team was in trouble, and, more importantly, the Streak was in trouble.

The coaching staff had to decide how to approach the difficult games ahead without Ben. In hindsight, the concern about whether and when Ben might return distracted the team. Without him, the team never got into a rhythm. When Ben did return for the last two games of the season before the Shelton game, they changed the offense when they realized it was still too soon for him to free his wrist from the bone brace. In high school football, it's hard enough to teach a team one style of offense, let alone two. The coaches implemented a shotgun-style offense for Ben. But he still had to catch the football with one hand in a cast, grip the ball in his right hand, and throw it or hand it off.

Despite Ben's return, the team continued to lose, in part because Ben couldn't control the snap or play defense. With a 5–5 record, they needed to beat three-touchdown-favored Shelton to keep the Streak alive. The Gaels were coming into the game having already wrapped up the Housatonic League championship with an 8–0 league record.

In addition to playing quarterback, Ben was an infielder and a pitcher on the baseball team. Most quarterbacks in Derby ended up pitchers, but Ben was more than your average high school pitcher or infielder. In fact, he was far better than average. Besides having pitched ever since he was in Little League, Ben played for a Mickey Mantle summer league team for thirteen to sixteen-year-olds. Many Mickey Mantle team participants paid significant entry fees to play just about every day in a given summer. Some Mantle teams required their players to buy their own uniforms. Similar to Babe Ruth leagues, they had their own state and regional tournaments and World Series.

As a fifteen-year-old freshman, Ben played third base and pitched on Derby's American Legion team for sixteen to eighteen-year-olds, which I coached. When Ben pitched, he averaged only about one walk per game, which in high school baseball gives your team a chance to win, since you can't defend a base on balls. Nothing bothers a high school baseball coach more than a walk.

When he didn't pitch, Ben played third base. His swing was smooth, short, and compact—a clinician's dream—and he possessed good baseball instincts. His junior season, Ben made the Class S all-state team as a third baseman. He also liked to cast a fishing pole for rainbow trout at Picket's Pond in Osborndale State Park. He was not your typical Derby football player.

Donny Shepard was also a senior. He lived two blocks from Gino in a single-family house adjacent to some three-floor apartment buildings on Hawkins Street's south side. The section was about four football fields from where I lived as a kid on Hawkins Street's northern end. Hawkins Street's south side was a one-way street until it reached its intersection with Eighth Street. As a kid, I had learned the game of baseball in the crowded neighborhood by playing with taped-up Wiffle balls in small backyards, alleyways, or streets not far from Stork's Tavern and the Over the Hill Tavern.

Donny hadn't played football until his senior season; he had only played baseball. When Lou was the coach, that might not have been possible. If you didn't play football from your freshman year on, you wouldn't be allowed to overtake somebody else who had already paid his dues. No one else in Donny's family had ever played football for Derby High. With declining enrollment, the coaches couldn't afford to let an athlete like Donny walk the school halls and not play football. They finally persuaded Donny to play.

The coaches told Donny he could be a wide receiver. Along with another receiver, he would be responsible for bringing the plays voiced through his red helmet's ear hole by the offensive coordinator into the huddle on every other down. But, because of his athleticism, Donny became far more than an alternate receiver. By the time of the Shelton game, he was a defensive back, punter, and returned punts and kickoffs. He dug his spikes in the field for every other play on offense, every play on defense, and every play on special teams.

Although he nearly separated his left shoulder while making a tackle, Donny never missed a game. The weightlifting preparation for football strengthened his throwing arm and the rest of his body. He was bigger, stronger, and faster, and that improved his baseball skills. Football made him a tougher competitor.

Donny was also a pitcher most high school batters preferred not to face. He was a tall and limber kid, about 6'3", with a strong cleft chin. Donny's fingers wrapped farther around a baseball than most pitchers. He was a right-hander who caused a catcher's glove to pop about as often as Ben.

Like Ben, Donny also played in the summer on my American Legion team. His biggest drawback when I coached him in the summer was that he was sometimes temperamental—not a good trait for a pitcher or a hitter. Donny had also pitched since Little League and had once pitched a no-hitter in a Little League championship game. His nickname was Rocket Man. His baseball dream was to someday play in Yankee Stadium. He didn't own a fishing pole, but, like Ben, he was a competitor and hated to lose.

4

The End of the Streak

As the game against Shelton wound down, Derby managed to score a couple of late touchdowns to make the score a respectable 27–14 from the 20–0 halftime score. Some of the Derby crowd—in the middle section of the stands under the glass-faced press box—kept holding out for a miracle. But the chances of that happening had disappeared with the chance of snow before this game ever began.

As I stood behind the sideline fence near the corner of the end zone, another baseball player, Peter Chrzanowski, approached me with a wide, dimpled grin. His crimson windbreaker blended with the crowd behind him. "Hey, Riles, you're coming back, right?" Riles was a nickname a former baseball player I coached had pinned on me. Pete asked me that same question more times than Donny Shepard punted in the past couple months, but I didn't mind. I think he kept asking it because, although I was a volunteer assistant baseball coach at Derby from the1986 season through the 1990 season, I hadn't helped out last year until the week before the state tournament's start. Because of my profession as a lawyer, I was never sure if I would be able to work my schedule to coach. At the end of each season I coached, I always warned the team that, while I hoped to return, I couldn't commit until I knew what my schedule would be like the following spring. I should have never told that to Pete.

Like Donny, Ben, and Gino, Pete was also a senior and their close friend. He was a catcher and an outfielder on the baseball team, but he didn't play football. The football coaches envisioned Pete as a defensive back, running back, or receiver but couldn't coax him to play. Pete was always in the front row of a team picture, but was quicker than a scared jackrabbit, was baseball savvy, and packed power in his five foot six or seven frame. Pete lived on Derby's east side, where there were bigger lawns to water and places where a kid could toss a hardball without shattering windows or having someone chase you off their property.

Pete played baseball virtually year round, playing both on a Mickey Mantle league team as well as for my summer American Legion team. Pete knew the game and was easy to coach. Having Pete around was like having another assistant coach in the dugout. His talent had moved him to varsity his sophomore year. For some reason, Pete wasn't planning on playing baseball his junior year until a close female classmate died in a car crash. The experience convinced him not to waste any opportunity to enjoy his high school years. Although Pete could be on any high school league's all-star team, he thought he was better than he was, which is sometimes a big advantage in baseball.

The baseball season was still a winter away, but, as Pete stood beside me with both hands shading his eyes, he started talking about this year's season. "I don't know where I'm going to play this year," he said, resting his elbows atop the fence. "I may play center field or catch again, unless this freshman kid Lizza coming up can catch. Everybody tells me how good he is, but he only played on a Sandy Koufax league team."

Sandy Koufax was a league for kids between Little League and Babe Ruth. The field's dimensions were halfway between Little League and a regulation high school field. Like Mickey Mantle league teams, Koufax teams play virtually every day in the summer.

"The kid is huge, Riles, but who knows if he can catch on a varsity level. He doesn't have as good an arm as I do. If he can't catch, maybe he could play first base."

"I've never heard of the kid."

"We know Ben and Donny can pitch, but we've got to put the rest of the team together. Hopefully, Gino can play second base and Joey G. can play third. Joey G. went to a camp this year at Old Dominion University in Delaware."

I don't want to burst your bubble," I said, "but we still have to hope Ben can bat or, if not, he can at least pitch."

Joey G. was a nick name for Joe Guion. The light brown-haired senior lived in a small traditional house off New Haven Road, which, although technically on Derby's east side, was not far from where Route 34 crossed the Housatonic River to the west side of town. He never put on a red helmet with a face mask or tied on shoulder pads for Derby High, but I don't think that mattered to the coaches.

As a junior on the baseball team last year, he was mostly a JV player. In Derby, if you're a junior and you're on the JV team, it means either there aren't enough players to field a JV team that year or you aren't good enough for varsity.

Joey G. was a decent fielder but wasn't much of a hitter. Ben was the third baseman when he didn't pitch; I didn't know where Joey would fit in. He didn't have enough range to play shortstop and wasn't fast enough to play outfield.

He was one of the harder kids to coach because he was an eternal pessimist. No matter what you said to Joey G., he would say something negative about it. If he rapped a line drive right at somebody who closed his eyes and caught it, Joey G. would think somebody upstairs didn't like him. If you're a baseball player, a negative attitude results in a self-fulfilling prophecy. If you think you stink, you will. Even the best baseball players must be able to deal with failure. If you bat .300, you're quite good, but that still means you failed seven of every ten at bats. If you're a high school baseball player batting less than .300, you better know how to bunt. I was hoping Joey had learned how to bunt at the clinic in Delaware.

As the game clock neared the end of its countdown, I couldn't help think that thankfully—at least in football—the players had a clock. If there wasn't one in basketball, Derby High might never get to the baseball season. In baseball, you have to get three outs. If a team couldn't do that, it would be losing forever.

When the final whistle blew, the stripe-shirted, white-hatted referee held the game ball up in the air, and the ambulance siren wailed. Ben, Donny, and Gino were now officially losers. The Streak was over.

I began to wonder what these guys would face for the rest of their lives—unless they moved out the Valley. The remnants of the Streak resonated everywhere in the school. When the lunch bell went off each day, they would have to walk by the eight-foot-high walnut trophy cabinets lining the gray walls leading to the cafeteria. If they looked up at the walls on the boys' side of the gym, they would see a sea of white-edged fire-engine red rectangular banners hanging high and proud, commemorating all of the championship football teams. Could any one of them ever walk into a store, restaurant, or bar in Derby without hearing a whisper that he had played on the team that had blown the Streak?

"I'll catch you in the spring, Pete," I said as I pulled my jacket's zipper higher, straightened my baseball cap, and tightened my shoe laces.

As Pete walked away, making his way toward the team's bench to console his friends, he couldn't resist saying to me again, "You are coming back this year, right? D needs you, Riles."

I reiterated to Pete for the umpteenth time: "I will be helping out D again this year, Pete."

5

The Fat Lady Prepares to Sing

Six months later, it was the top of the seventh. We were losing by two runs. Pete flew out to shallow right for the second out, and now there was one strike on Ben in what could be his—as well as our team's—last at bat for the season. On Friday night, June 9, 1992, under the towering lights of Palmer Field in Middletown, we were playing Terryville High School for the 1992 Class S state baseball championship. The crowd of about 3,500 people, most of them Derby fans, was so loud that, from my third base coaching box, I had to cup my hands around my mouth and yell my instructions to Joey G., who was only a few feet away from me on third base and Richie Calvert, who was on second. Richie had entered the game to pinch run for Gino when Joey G. advanced to third and Gino to second.

I was afraid for Richie. Although he had some speed and was a junior, he didn't get in varsity games much, except as a pinch runner. In high school baseball, nobody wants to be a pinch runner. Pinch runners don't make the Baseball Hall of Fame. When your coach calls your name to run for your team's slowest player, there is no glory. In the wiffleball games in the backyards of Derby, kids use an invisible man; nobody pinch runs.

In football, however, it's different. Even if you only return punts or kickoffs or are the "headhunter" on the kickoff team, you still receive the looks from teachers, fellow students, and administrators that tell you they know who you are. In baseball, unless the song "Wild Thing" is playing when you enter the field, nobody wants "role player" written under their yearbook picture. If they're just a pinch runner, they often quit.

At least Richie had experience pinch running. He was the sort of kid the older cafeteria workers tried to push to buy a double lunch and one of the few kids on our team who didn't play football. Before the baseball season started, Richie competed on the wrestling team—not that wrestling prepared him to run the bases well, but at least he was used to fierce competition. Like baseball, in wrestling your ego is on the line. If you don't want to win, you could have your face squished into a sweat-filled floor mat and be humiliated as the referee's hand bangs the mat three times. Competitiveness aside, Richie was at least faster than Gino, whose high-top brick red Nike spikes made him look even slower than he was.

Richie represented the tying run, but, if he didn't get a long enough lead, he might not score on a base hit. If he took too many steps off the base, he might get picked off. If he did, he might as well walk back to Derby. The Terryville pitcher had already picked someone off first base in the sixth inning. I was also afraid for myself. If Richie got picked off second base, it would have been considered my fault.

"Richie!" I yelled with my hands cupped around my mouth. "Just get a good primary lead and sit. Get a good secondary lead on the pitcher's delivery. Don't jump around. Watch the pitcher!" I didn't know whether he heard me. I wasn't concentrating as much on Joey G. on third since his run would be meaningless if Richie didn't score. Joey G. had to score standing up, or there was no point sending him toward home plate. Joey G. knew that, so I had faith enough in him not to get picked off or to do something stupid. I didn't have that faith in Richie.

Despite the screaming, cow bell clanging, and horn blaring coming from the stands, I had no trouble hearing the echoey words of the faceless public address announcer behind the reflection in the press box glass. "Ladies and gentlemen-*gentlemen* at the conclusion-*clusion* of tonight's-*nights* game-*game* please do not-*not* go-*go* onto the playing-*playing* field-*field*." I wished I couldn't hear those words. They hit me from every direction and rang through me like a funeral bell. Reality started to sink in. Although we had made a great run at the title, this team was about to lose a state championship game.

Our team was standing on our dugout's edge on the third base side of the field. They all had their red hats on inside out, screaming at the top of their lungs. You may wonder why they were wearing their hats inside out. Baseball has many funny superstitions. One of them is that the players in the dugout on the team that's losing wear their hats inside out, hoping for a comeback. They call them "rally caps." I knew what rally caps were, but in eighteen years of coaching I only saw a team rally to win once while wearing them. I wondered who on our team had thought that up as a last resort. The only one in our dugout who wasn't standing was Reegers. He couldn't stand. He was a quadriplegic. Reegers, like everyone else in the dugout, however, was shouting words of encouragement to what could be our last batter.

I paced up and down the confines of my lined, rectangular coach's box. Forty feet away, D was on one knee, encouraging Ben. Until now, I hadn't noticed the older version of our team's red hat atop D's head. I stopped and stared at the word *Raiders* scripted in black across its crown.

6

John D and Bethlehem Days

I first met John DeFrancisco, or Coach D as he was known, when I was in high school from 1969 through 1973. I hadn't had him as a teacher, but I knew he taught English. If a caricature artist drew John D., you would think he was Kelsey Grammer with gold metal-rimmed glasses that extended beyond his brown eyebrows. His infectious smile would be the same, but he would be about four inches shorter with wavy hair on the sides of his head. Even though John wore glasses, he looked imposing. Whenever he hobbled past you, you wondered what was wrong with his knees.

He wasn't the kind of guy who could sneak up on you in the hallways of Derby High outside his classroom or on the loading dock behind the cafeteria to share a smoke with a fellow teacher. When I bumped into him on the way to the cafeteria or gym, he hadn't been somebody I was afraid of, but I had still kept my distance. Whenever he spoke loudly or emotionally—which was most of the time—he might spray some words on me. If I visited his angled-ceiling classroom, I might be lucky enough to see him play Iago's role in a reading of *Othello*, but I wouldn't be allowed to leave before it was over.

He was also one of Big Lou's younger assistant football coaches. He was a freshman coach and a varsity assistant, mostly a scout. A scout had to attend the next opponent's game and miss Big Lou's halftime speeches, unless the next opponent played on a different day than Derby did. Until they had paid their dues, scouting duty fell on the younger assistant football coaches at Derby.

John D. participated in the pep assemblies that took place the day before big football games. Whenever it was his turn to stand before the microphone on the stage of the six-hundred-seat auditorium, the band beneath the stage and the students hushed. They knew they were about to be entertained.

His popularity extended beyond football. Some years, he was the public address announcer at home basketball games. He grabbed the microphone before the tip-off and introduced players as if he were Marv Albert in Madison Square

Garden. He was involved with several after-school activities that did not involve sports, including the drama club. His peers and the students thought everything about John D. was high drama.

Whenever anyone asserted John D. was an English teacher at the high school who had graduated from Fairfield University, he or she was met with a dropped jaw or raised eyebrow. His diction outside the classroom never matched up with his Jesuit education. When I attended Derby High, I was a student of Anthony DeFrancisco, John's father. He had been known as Tony D., and I had sat in the first row of one of his English classes.

While Tony D. was good-natured, he had been an old-school type of teacher. The short, thin, black-haired educator had demanded a lot from his students but was easy to get along with as long as you did your work and what you were told. He was critical if a student was absent for only one day. He didn't believe in the mystery of the one-day illness that could keep you from school. Out the corner of his mouth, he called it the "galloping crud." I had heard that years ago Tony D. had been the varsity baseball coach, and John D. had played first base for him. Although I was a cocaptain of Derby High's baseball team in 1973, Tony D. had retired from coaching some years before; I heard few stories about his coaching days.

In 1973, my senior year at Derby High, the football team was undefeated again. They had won the Housatonic League championship and were ranked as the fourth best team in the *New Haven Register's* poll.[2] The undefeated season was preserved on Thanksgiving Day when they beat Shelton on a last-second field goal by a soccer-style place kicker named Billy Gonzalez. Billy was escorted off the frozen field by the police and a circle of Derbyites standing face out trying to protect him from the orange-black Shelton mob, who wanted to see to it that Derby's hero didn't make it to the bus.

When the baseball season came around, Tom Fahy, a sociology teacher and my JV coach, became the varsity coach. Mr. Fahy, as I always addressed him, was nearly bald and looked like an erudite professor. Before his teaching and coaching career at Derby High, he had been a star pitcher for Quinnipiac College in Hamden, as was our former varsity coach, Bob Martino. Since the CIAC had created a postseason baseball tournament, Derby High had never qualified, but we had seven seniors and several juniors who were sick of losing. When our rookie coach didn't want to start practicing as early as the players did, as one of the cocaptains, it fell on me to take up a petition to protest his decision. It didn't work.

Despite the preseason turmoil, Mr. Fahy used his superior pitching knowledge and experience to our full advantage. More importantly, he just let us play. As a result, we made the CIAC state tournament for the first time in school history, entering the tournament with a 9–8 record. To qualify for the tournament, we had to win at least as many games as we lost. On the cutoff date, we were 8–8, but we had a game scheduled for that afternoon. We had to win it, or else we wouldn't qualify. The pressure on us to win the game subsided when it rained and the game was canceled. I'm still not sure whether the opposing coach had cooperated—I don't recall it raining that hard.

To avoid the claim that we'd backed into the tournament, before the state tournament started we defeated a more-talented North Haven team in a makeup game. Although we won our first game in the tournament, we lost our second, and for that accomplishment the city had actually thrown us a four-course banquet at the Actor's Colony Inn in Seymour.

Nobody had ever thought baseball could do anything in Derby. I thought we had started our own tradition. The next year they regressed to 3–17 when several veteran ballplayers were kicked off. They had been caught switching red Velcro letters on the backs of other players' pin-striped white game jerseys to create embarrassing names. Traditions are not easy to start, let alone a baseball tradition in a football-manic town.

In 1976, at the age of twenty, after playing some baseball during my first two years in college, I decided to coach a city-sponsored Senior Babe Ruth team. That summer, I managed a wild bunch of guys, most of whom had played baseball at Derby High. They had some talent but couldn't win more than four or five games a year for Mr. Fahy. I knew these guys were sick of losing. I was sick of watching them lose, so I tried to schedule as many games as I could outside our league, against teams I thought we would be capable of competing with. The expanded schedule gave us a reasonable chance to finish with a winning record. I hoped to keep the players interested for the entire summer season and to let them learn the game while having some fun. That way, when the following spring came around, they would have a better chance of having a successful high school season. Looking back, I think I had just wanted to take them outside Derby, where nobody could critique their performance.

Sometimes, I carpooled the team to the farm country of Litchfield County, to a small town named Bethlehem, which most everyone only learned existed around Christmas time. The town was about a forty-five minute drive north from Derby, through some farm areas where, even on a hot summer day, I rolled up my windows. We went there to play against a team coached by an enthusiastic—albeit a bit unorthodox—young coach named Gregg Hunt. I had learned from some other coaches in my division that he managed Bethlehem's Senior

Babe Ruth team and was looking to schedule some games, so I scheduled a couple against his team.

Playing Bethlehem was an experience no baseball game played in the Valley could provide. Some of their players swung a round point shovel with a five-foot-long ash handle in the on-deck circle. The ones who didn't swung a few bats between their hands like baseball days of old. They didn't possess a lead donut, normally used by the on-deck hitter to warm up. One of their players held his pants up with what looked like a clothesline cord wound through the belt loops. I had to restrain myself, as well as my players, from chuckling at some of their players' appearances.

The umpires were just as unique. In one of our games, on a sweltering day, the alarm went off in the town's firehouse, just beyond center field. The home plate umpire, the only umpire who showed up, removed his mask, black chest protector, and beat-up shin guards, and dropped them on home plate.

"Where are you going?" I asked.

"I'm sorry," he replied. "I'm one of the town's firemen, and I've got to go." He started to jog through the infield. After he passed the pitching rubber and second base, he kicked up the infield dust.

"Are you coming back?"

"Probably a false alarm. If it is, I'll be back in about twenty minutes."

As he rushed across the yellow patches of burnt outfield grass, I cupped my hands around my mouth. "What if it's not?" I asked, raising my voice.

"Then the game's over."

He ran to the field's end, past a sandpile that a jeep would have had trouble climbing, until he reached the four-garage-door firehouse. The red fire truck exited the firehouse with our umpire driving, lights flashing, and sirens blaring. As the sun reflected off its chrome, the six-wheeler exited the gravel driveway, past the brick-sided, square town hall, and disappeared from sight. The game was delayed until the ump/fireman returned forty-five minutes later, telling us it had only been a false alarm.

Although we were a far-superior team (talentwise) to Bethlehem and won most of the time we played them, they always hustled on and off the field and never dogged it. They left us on the field once, when we got overconfident. You would have thought Bethlehem had won the World Series, as their players mobbed the jubilant runner coming across the plate with the winning run. The lesson for me and our players had been never to take anyone lightly. We had learned the game is never over until the fat lady sings—even if the fire alarm goes off and the umpire leaves. Although we didn't win our league that year, I had kept the players interested for the entire season. Nobody had quit. Between league and nonleague games, the team had ended up with a winning record, so I considered the short summer season a success.

The next spring, the same bunch of kids who had played for me in the summer played for my old coach Tom Fahy at Derby High. After a 9–9 season, they won five straight in the tournament to capture the CIAC class S state championship. Coach D. was the freshman coach then. I didn't attend the championship game played at Quigley Stadium in West Haven, the former home of the minor-league West Haven Yankees. I hated to watch a baseball game I couldn't have an impact on.

I was jogging around Derby's cinder track, adjacent the football field clubhouse, when the team's yellow school bus returned from that final game. Before they entered the clubhouse the baseball team borrowed in the spring, the players decided to take a victory lap. Like track stars in the Olympics wrapped in their country's flag, the team paraded around the oval track with their plaque before the empty football field stands. Some of the players who had played for me in the summer approached me during their lap and thanked me for helping them learn how to win. Some didn't. That summer, a banquet was held honoring the state championship team, but I wasn't invited.

The following summer, with mostly the same players I had coached the year before, our Senior Babe Ruth team won our district championship in a three-game playoff against Torrington. I remember that John D. supported us with his presence at the third and final game played at Fuessenich Park in Torrington.

I never forgot that he had gone.

Throughout the twilight game, Dave "Nud" Derosa—who wore uniform number 3 on his red mesh jersey with a white Old English letter D on it—was playing first base. After a ground ball was fielded and thrown to first for an out, Torrington's player bumped Nud as he went by the bag. An argument ensued. The announcer in the press box above the run-down gray concrete stands on the first base side of the field blared over the speaker system, "The game should be played with better sportsmanship, not like you, Number Three." The announcer continued to razz Nud as D witnessed the controversy.

As the game continued, Torrington's fans taunted and harassed Nud. The announcer came down to my third base dugout to justify himself.

"If you get on that microphone again," I said in a threatening voice, "to criticize one of my players publicly, I will shove the microphone up your ass."

Although I regretted losing my cool, it apparently got the players going. We proceeded to get seventeen hits and buried Torrington to capture the best-of-three series and the district crown.

After the game, D extended his hand and congratulated me as well as the players he had coached as Derby High's freshman coach.

After winning the district, we reached the semifinals of the state tournament before we were eliminated. The city's recreation department rewarded us with a pizza party in the small basement party room of The River Restaurant, a local Italian restaurant on lower Main Street, to celebrate our league and district titles. The party turned out to be a cheap way of getting the uniforms back; the entry fee for each player had been their uniform. One player claimed he forgot it. I drove him home to get it, or else I never would have retrieved it.

The recreation director, Pete Adanti, had invited the mayor, Ed Ceccarelli, who had shown up. That was a municipal mistake. Mayor Ceccarelli, a stout man in his sixties with a full gray mustache who looked like Wilford Brimley, spoke at the celebration. Before he spoke, we presented Mayor Ceccarelli with the two-foot-high championship trophy, which we were told would be displayed behind glass in city hall.

Near the end of his election-year speech, the mayor adjusted his thick glasses. He spread his hands on the edge of the eight-foot-long head table, covered with a tomato-sauce-stained white tablecloth, and added, "I just want to let you fellows know that if any one of you ever need my help in any way, just ask, and I'll help in any way I can."

Billy Schwab, one my less-bashful eighteen-year-old players, raised his right hand. With his black eyebrows lowered and his neck stiffened, he said, "Mr. Mayor, there is something you can do for me."

"What is it, son?"

"I'm going to college next year and don't have enough money. Is there any way you can lend me the money?"

The mayor folded his arms, gulped, and replied, "I can't do that."

The rest of the team laughed. Pete Adanti coughed until veins appeared in his face. I removed my summer-seasoned red cap, covered my eyes with my right hand, and shook my head.

7

Return to Derby High

Years later, in 1985, I was a lawyer without any gray hair on the sides of my head yet, working for a firm of four lawyers at the corner of Golden Hill Street and Main Street in downtown Bridgeport. The firm included my younger brother, Fred, who followed me through Quinnipiac College and the University of Bridgeport School of Law to the firm. I was married, underpaid, and overworked, but still coaching summer baseball in one capacity or another. Coaching gave me a respite from the pressure of trying to make a living on four hundred dollars a week and half of what I brought into the firm. Although 1985 was only my fifth year of getting up at 6:00 AM to defend and prosecute car accident and workers' compensation claims, draw estate plans, and handle real estate closings, I was burning out rapidly. Some weeks, I worked more than eighty hours.

One morning, another lawyer in my firm attended a 9:30 AM roll call of civil cases exposed for trial in superior court in Bridgeport. He was supposed to inform the judge handling the call that the senior lawyer in our firm responsible for a case was actively engaged in another court, awaiting a jury's verdict, and would be available to begin the case on the calendar as soon as the verdict was returned. Instead of telling the court those facts, he told the court we were ready for trial. He left the seven-story Main Street courthouse and didn't return to the office.

Later that day, while I was the only lawyer in our office, the judge's clerk called. The judge desired to see a lawyer from our firm pronto, concerning a certain motor vehicle case, or the case would be dismissed. I grabbed the three-pound file and hurried to court.

When I walked into the sixth-floor courtroom, I wondered why a panel of jurors entered at the same time as I. I thought another case must be starting.

The judge had already taken the bench and opposing counsel, who I immediately recognized as a defense lawyer who awaited verdicts in the courthouse every other week, sat at one of the six-foot-wide tables with his file spread out as neat as a solitaire board.

Looking at me, the judge announced, "Counselor, jury selection is about to begin in the trial of your case."

My heart stuck in my throat. I knew little about the file other than that it concerned an accident involving a car stopped in snow on the side of a highway. The car had been struck by another vehicle, injuring my client. I knew that my client had been a passenger, and his wife had been the stopped car's driver. We had been forced to sue the wife in addition to the other driver. I realized my fellow lawyer had bagged me. Despite my pleas to the court, the judge ordered me to commence jury selection, or my client would lose his case. Luckily, the trial started in the afternoon and limited the time I could look like a fool. The clock on the wall behind me gave me an idea: if I could delay jury selection long enough, it would give me time for my boss's jury to return a verdict, allowing my boss to handle the matter.

Although I had tried many courtside controversies, handled a jury trial, and had experience in voir dire, as lawyers call it, this situation involved a plaintiff's personal injury case. My only experience in selecting juries had been from the defendant's side.

When I returned to the office that evening, I had learned that the cavalry wasn't going to rescue me from the trial. I needed to pull an all-nighter just to continue the trial half-prepared. Luckily, the case settled the next morning during the recommencement of jury selection. I had had enough. I had decided that this would the last trial I would ever be involved in. After I returned to the office, I received a call from the judge's clerk, who said the judge had learned of my decision and asked that I return to his chambers.

"Come in, Counselor," the judge said, no longer wearing his black robe. He opened his hand and motioned toward a chair. "Sit down." The afternoon sun beamed through the sealed window in the room onto one of two brown, padded arm chairs in front of the judge's beige desk. I chose it without knowing why. Ceiling-to-floor brown bookcases filled with tightly packed tan casebooks surrounded me. Two-foot-high stacks of manila court files were piled on the credenza behind the middle-aged judge, adjacent his framed family photos.

"I heard you were considering ending your legal career. I'd like you to reconsider." He glanced at the square red message light on the phone on the desk. For a moment, he considered retrieving the message but didn't as he looked back at me.

"I'm tired, Judge," I replied as I wiped my left eye with my thumb. "I've been working eighty hours a week with little pay. For what? To get put into a position of having to try a case for someone who doesn't want me? To stay up through most of the night? The client wanted my boss. He didn't hire me, but yet he was forced by the court to take me. The case was supposed to be marked over, but for some reason wasn't. I graduated second in my class at law school for this?"

"I know sometimes we have to be bastards...but we have to move justice along." He shuffled an inch-thick pile of pink message slips on his desk into a neat pile.

"Why?" I asked as I raised my eyebrows and turned my head. "It doesn't have to be that way. Judges don't have to be bastards. We mark a case ready in a system where we're put on one hour's notice. No matter where we or our clients are, we're forced to stop what we're doing and show up, regardless of the consequences. This case could have easily waited until my boss returned. Other lawyers around here get continuance after continuance, but I'm forced to go forward on a case that's not mine, and the attorney handling it is on trial somewhere else."

The judge was persistent. "I just don't think you should allow this experience to be the end. There are other areas in the law you could practice in."

"Judge," I said as I moved to the edge of my seat. "When I left your courtroom this morning and made my decision, I felt free—finally free of all this. My life was starting over. I appreciate your concern. I'm considering going back to law school for an LLM or perhaps get into teaching."

"Well, my door is always open, Counselor, if you ever want to talk about this again."

"Thank you, Judge."

I stepped onto the elevator and pushed the round clear plastic button for the first floor. As I waited for the door to open, I laughed as I thought, *Why would I want to talk to a bastard again? No motivational speech? No, you can do it, Steve, just hang in there?* But I knew the judge was a decent and honest man and acted as sincerely as the system let him. He was not an administrative judge, and was under pressure to move cases along or face the consequences himself.

After I left the courthouse and strode up Main Street, a message from my past crept into my mind. I didn't know exactly what it was, but I did know I couldn't quit. Before I returned to the office, I had decided to apply to a law school for an advanced law degree and ask my boss if I could work on a part-time per-hour basis. The pay would help cover the bills while I determined in what direction I wanted to go in law.

In March of 1987, I received a phone call from John DeFrancisco. After coaching seventeen years at the freshman and junior varsity levels behind Tom Fahy, John had finally gotten the varsity baseball coach's job. He asked me if I would be interested in coaching an American Legion summer team he had been organizing with the help of some veterans at the American Legion in Derby. If I was agreeable, John wanted me to attend his first team meeting at the high school; he could introduce me to the same kids I would likely be coaching in the summer. John told me he remembered the last time Derby had been successful, their players had gained experience on a summer league team before the high school season. I had never forgotten that John attended my *Senior Babe Ruth* team's district championship game. I told him I would attend the after-school meeting.

Standing off to the side of John D.'s classroom wearing my navy blue suit, white shirt, and maroon tie—trying to avoid leaning against a blackboard—I listened to what John D. said to the team. Though much of what I heard sounded like fodder for a training film on what not to say to your team on day one of your high school baseball coaching career, the players smiled, laughed, and kidded with D. I knew the spring season would be an adventure, and wanted to get involved. I began thinking of how my schedule might allow me to help with the team during the afternoons. After the players left the meeting, I approached John, standing behind his teacher's desk. The brown veneer-topped desk seemed small for a man his size.

"Thanks for coming, Steve," he said. He aligned the edges of some hard cover books on his otherwise-barren desk and opened his middle drawer. "I appreciate your willingness to get involved with this Legion thing."

"I meant to ask you, do you mind if I come around to help?"

"You can come around whenever you want," D replied as he walked out into the hallway with a pack of Carlton Menthols in his hand.

"No. What I meant was, do you mind if I come around every day and help out? My schedule is such I think I can work it out."

D froze. "Huh…You mean you're willing to help every day?"

"Yeah."

"Sure. You kidding me? I'd love to have you every day. That's great."

As the saying goes, such was the beginning of a beautiful friendship.

8
5–15

My first year assisting John D. started with promise. We won two of our first three games. But in one weekend, everything changed. Our most experienced pitcher, Chris King—a hard thrower who was also the football team's quarterback—jumped off a water tower on a whim, wrenched his left ankle, and ended his season. Our first baseman, Frank Pecheco, put some bronze tokens into an arm-style pitching machine at the Milford Recreation Center's batting cages and was nailed by a dimple ball that broke his wrist. After Frank's injury, we had warned everyone else on the team not to go to Milford Recreation. On that same weekend, Greg Pettinella, a tall rubber-armed pitcher, ignored our warning and broke his foot there while fouling a ball off it.

Without our two pitchers, we were in deep trouble. We had to give a flash card course in pitching to anyone else willing to take the hill. But even though we worked each practice until the headlights on the cars on Chatfield Street turned on, the possibility of us having a successful first season record was minimal.

For a while, our losses were by statistically improbable scores worthy of a *Twilight Zone* episode. We lost five games in a row, by one run, with successive scores I didn't want to remember. The countdown was something like 7–6, 6–5, 5–4, 3–2, and 2–1.

As strange failure can attract the press, a *New Haven Register* reporter called the school. After the receptionist transferred the call to John's classroom, the journalist questioned whether the scores were some sort of record. John pulled the phone away from his ear, bit down on his lower lip, and stared at the receiver as a distant voice was repeating the word *hello* like a parrot. A few moments later, John barked into it, "I just want to win!" and banged it back on the wall hook. John and I grew closer as friends with each close loss. In baseball, misery certainly loves company.

While each time we lost, I went home and replayed the game in my head, John lost a part of himself. He couldn't eat or stop thinking about what went wrong. He had convinced himself he couldn't gain the other Derby High coaches' respect if he didn't win. He had been yearning to find a niche where he could coach baseball while not bucking Derby's football tradition. I didn't have that problem. John soon found out football was still king at the school when the city's public works department left the white gooseneck goal post, which stood near second base, standing until nearly the start of the baseball season. That oversight had nearly caused John to breathe in a brown paper bag. Although the losses were hard to deal with, at least we were competitive.

During that first year, I learned about John's competitiveness, which sometimes was near maniacal. John had two preschool-age daughters, Jessica and Jennifer. He freely admitted to the team that he wouldn't even let his daughters beat him at checkers or tic-tac-toe. Whenever he spoke to the team about his own competitiveness, he pointed out, "If they're keeping score, I'm winning." I knew John played for several years for a local slow pitch softball team named Kasden Fuel. They played in many out-of-state national tournaments and had players who would send a teammate home if he hadn't worn the correct color stretch socks. I had once seen John toss up an arch for them from the pitching rubber, then grab his own neck before the ball reached home plate to taunt the batter. But I had never known the full extent of his competitiveness.

John's wife, Nancy, his mother, and his father attended most games along with his daughters. At one game, John's daughters were with Nancy, and a foul ball spun up. Five seconds later, it drifted within a baseball bat's distance of Jessica as she played in the sand of a long-jump pit in between a silver chain-link fence and the first base stands. The fans, players, and umpires screamed, "Look out!" They were concerned the small girl with the long golden brown hair might be whacked in the head by a hardball falling from the sky.

John shouted, "Jessica…catch it!"

Not only did parents and fans constantly second-guess John, but even his own mother questioned his baseball coaching ability. During the games, John's mother, Lala, a thin woman with short coal black hair, sometimes yelled to John to take the pitcher out or to make some other move she thought was best. John searched for his coffee or cigarettes whenever his mother fed him advice or criticism, but he didn't do anything except to sometimes explain his decisions. I heard she had subjected John's father to that when he had been the baseball coach at Derby High.

John's father attended games, but he wasn't as critical of John as his mother was. He only offered his experienced advice when John asked him for it. I think John's father was just happy he wasn't being criticized anymore. When Lala wasn't yelling to John, she was yelling at or holding her nose toward the ump whenever he made a call that went against her second son.

I also learned about John's smoking habit. John simply couldn't stop smoking. He smoked during practice, he smoked on the school bus to and from games, and he smoked during the games. Some of the other coaches kidded us about having smoke signals.

Umpires constantly warned him that he faced ejection if he continued smoking, but nothing stopped him. He just went behind the dugout and satisfied his nicotine urge between innings. Sometimes he would leave a lit cigarette behind the dugout; sometimes he would leave it on the ground before him or have a parent hold it during the game. Taking a drag from it, he insisted it wasn't his cigarette. Even if D had been the Invisible Man, an umpire would have still known he was there. D's teacher's mailbox bulged from the warnings—"bullets" as he called them—stuffed inside by the athletic director, Ken Marcucio. None of it mattered, John simply couldn't help himself.

In addition to cigarettes, John had an insatiable desire for coffee during games. Before the games, someone always picked up coffees for all the coaches. If D had drunk all his coffee, he would hunt yours down, drink it, then deny he had done it. You had to practically camouflage your coffee whenever you were not near it, so he couldn't take it.

I found out the hard way to avoid getting into any vehicle D was driving. The first thing I looked for when I got in his navy blue Chrysler van was the seat belt clasp. He often wandered over double yellow lines while picking up and putting down a cigarette in his overflowing ashtray in the console. D hardly ever avoided pot holes. His skills were near the level of Mr. Magoo. Whenever D's daughters went with him to practice, they clicked their seat belts and said, "Hold on, Daddy's driving."

D never understood why other drivers raised their arms in the air at him as he veered off into their lane (while his front seat passenger gripped the ends of the arm rests). The van was equipped with a gauge for the level of windshield washer fluid in its plastic reservoir. The yellow light flashed empty that entire first season. In his van, D discussed strategy or just about anything else going on in his life or those of our players. While I enjoyed the discussions, I wondered whether the risk of life and limb as a captive passenger was worth it.

D used his van to pack equipment and move it between our fields. The baseball field didn't have a batting cage, but a Little League field above the steep, tree-filled hill behind the baseball field did. Each day we moved equipment from the clubhouse or the school to both fields or between them with his van. D sacrificed his van for the good of our team, as the equipment gouged the blue vinyl inside it. We used it to haul pitching machines, canvas ball bags, bat bags, catchers' equipment, and, whenever it rained, shovels, mud-caked metal rakes, and coarse-haired brooms. The fact that transportation of equipment in his van might ruin it never entered his mind. He just traded the van in and leased or bought a new one. He was that passionate about succeeding as Derby High School's baseball coach.

I discovered that whenever we lost, John couldn't sleep. Sometimes I visited his white cape-style house, and we commiserated over what we could've done better. D and I would stay up late into the night discussing what we had done wrong or what we should've done that would've given us a better chance to win. Nancy sensed which nights I was stopping over and would have coffee and something to eat ready for us before she went to bed. On the night before the day of a game, we discussed ways of beating the other team. Our obsession with winning consumed us, although at least I could go home and sleep most of the time.

The day after one loss, John told me he hadn't slept. He revealed that at 3:00 AM he had driven to a local Dunkin' Donuts. He sat on a round black-cushioned stool at the counter and studied the wire-bound brown scorebook from the previous day's game. A scruffy-looking unshaven middle-aged guy entered and dropped onto a stool near him.

After a few minutes, he asked John, "What are you looking at?"

"It's the scorebook from my game," John replied as he held his head up with his right hand, his half-smoked cigarette still burning in the clear glass ashtray. "I coach high school baseball for Derby. We lost."

The man took a slow sip from his white ceramic mug. "Do the numbers in that scorebook change if you look at them long enough?"

John finally saw the illogic of what he was doing and went home. He then got up at 6:30 AM, taught English classes, and met me at practice in the afternoon at Ryan Field. I asked John once why he deprived himself of sleep. He said his father once told him a person only needed so much sleep to survive, and that when you die, you are going to sleep for a long, long, long time.

Although I learned about many of John's bad habits that first season, I also learned a lot about the way Tony and Lala raised him. He was one of those teachers and friends who didn't just tell you his door was always open for you. Players and former players stopped by 15 Bluff Street any time they wanted in the evening hours. If a player or student needed extra help or a letter of recommendation for college, John was eager to do it. When an extracurricular activity at the school needed a teacher to sponsor it, he never refused a request. If he saw a player walking on the street from school, he pulled over and asked him if he needed a ride home. Another friend of John's had stayed at his home for several weeks while going through a crisis. John never turned anyone away who needed his help.

Every time we parted after a practice, a game, or a meeting at his house, John thanked me for helping him and held out his hand. Whenever we held a team meeting, he told the team that they should appreciate the volunteer coaches' presence.

There wasn't a player on the team John didn't like. He respected that a baseball player put his ego on the line during each game. Many a time he told the players, "While a football lineman can make a mistake and nobody knows, if you strike out or make an error, even my daughters can tell you blew the game."

John was also protective of his players. Whenever an umpire chastised a ballplayer, John intervened. He told the ump if he had a complaint with one of his players, he should address his complaint to him, not his player, and he would deal with it. After all, most of them were just sixteen and seventeen-year-old kids.

Although we ended up 5–15 that first season, we never quit. We even won the last game of the season on the road with a pitcher who could barely break a pane of glass—or as John would say, "Throw a beach ball in the ocean." After that final game, John spoke to the team and told them he would rather die than go 5–15 again. The team believed him. I believed him.

9

Seven Straight with Lou's Hat

During my second year coaching with John D., we began to question ourselves as coaches. For the first fourteen games of the season, we had five wins and nine losses with a team we felt was talented enough to win.

An early season game with Cheshire High School typified how our season started. The Rams were loaded with talent, and we played them on their field. The bus ride to Cheshire involved traveling ten miles on Route 42, an old two-lane road with spiraling hills and tortuous curves. Without a better way to get there in an old school bus, most of the team felt nauseated by the time we arrived. For insurance reasons, cars were not allowed.

On the bench seat behind the driver, John and I discussed the lineup and how we would insert substitutes into the game if the need arose. The discussion continued from the conversation we had had the night before at John's house, in between watching ESPN. John didn't sleep much the night before a game; this game was no different.

As our bus was shifting, turning, and braking its way to Cheshire, John was discarding cigarette butt after cigarette butt out a driver-side window of the bus—without ever looking where he was flicking them. Most bus drivers didn't care that John smoked. Some even shared a few of their cigarettes with John whenever he forgot to bring his on the bus.

"John," I whispered. "Look at the bus driver and tell me what he's doing that's unusual."

John looked at the driver, an elderly, gaunt-faced man, and yawned. "What about him?"

"He's got the windshield wipers on."

"So?" D replied as the worn rubber wipers went back and forth, etching curved lines across the windshield.

"It's not raining out," I replied.

Holding his cigarette, D squished his lips together, blew through them as if he were trying to blow an imaginary bubble, and said, "We're in trouble."

John was superstitious about events that happened before games. If something happened that might be a bad omen, he would say to me, "We're in trouble." Even when the omen was a good one, he still told me, "We're in trouble."

When we finally reached Cheshire's parking lot, we lumbered toward the baseball field a quarter mile away. We aerated the tarred pathway with our straight-edged metal cleats as we neared our dugout. I looked up and felt scattered raindrops on my face. I thought perhaps it had just been me who couldn't see that it was raining on the way to Cheshire and perhaps nothing was wrong with the bus driver.

We approached the manicured field, but Cheshire's team was not there yet. When we had reached our angled-roof dugout with the tall pine trees behind it, we told the team to stretch and loosen up. After they dropped the equipment bags, they strolled behind our dugout. With our backs to the chain-link fence before our third base dugout, John and I talked about whether we should have the team take some batting practice when they finished throwing. I started walking alone along the left field line to check the visitors' warm-up mound. "Hey, Riles," John shouted. "Where's our team?"

The team was gone. It was as if someone had folded their arms, blinked, and they had disappeared. I trekked behind our dugout into the nearby woods. After I pushed some pine branches aside and slogged through some brush, I expected to find an open area, but didn't. Our mentally tough players were warming up under pine tree branches, so they wouldn't get wet. When I revealed to John where they were, he reiterated, "We're in trouble."

Cheshire arrived wearing their scarlet jerseys with a white Cincinnati Reds–shaped C on their front and white pin-striped pants. Fifteen minutes before game time, they began their infield and outfield practice. Our senior pitcher, Rob Altimarano, or Alto as we called him, began to warm up on the mound down the left field sideline with our catcher. As D studied Rob from near our dugout, he removed his glasses and wiped the scattered rain drops from them with his wrinkled handkerchief.

"Riles, I've got to take him out. I've got to take him out."

"How could you even think about taking a pitcher out of a game before the game starts?" I replied as D turned to face me.

With his back to him, D pointed over his shoulder with his thumb to Rob. "Look at him," he said with a look of disgust. "He hasn't thrown a strike yet in the bull pen. He's going to get rocked. If he can't strike anybody out when there's no batter, what's he going to do when he gets on the real mound?"

Although he started Rob anyway so as not to embarrass him, John's prophecy would come true. Alto hadn't even gotten three outs before D called time-out, plodded to the mound, and snatched the scuffed-up ball from him. The Cheshire leadoff hitter had walked. The second batter had ripped a line drive down the right field line that left a wind burn on Frank Pecheco's, our first baseman's, face. After the rocket left its trail of condensation, D had raised his eyebrows and said Pecheco should check his undies. The Rams went on to crush us by about ten runs. The Cheshire game was my first lesson into John's unique insight into a high school baseball player's mind and ability.

One sunny Saturday morning during the first half of the season, the junior varsity coach couldn't make a game. I agreed to coach the game with the freshman coach, Tony Lionetti. The varsity practiced before the game, and John hung around outside our first base dugout to watch. During the game, a sophomore player acted out of line after Coach Lionetti substituted for him. Loud enough for us to hear, the cleft-chinned player blurted, "I'm not coming out of the game for some f—king freshman."

John entered the dugout and scolded the player. "Hey, just shut up and do what you're told. If you don't like it, you can leave."

To my surprise, the kid started to walk across the infield—glove in hand—toward the clubhouse, interrupting the game.

After the kid reached the outfield grass, John bellowed, "Leave your uniform at the coach's room door if you're quitting!"

Soon afterward, John had to leave the game to go home. On his way out of the park, he walked around the thirty-foot-high backstop and the third base dugout so as not to interrupt the game. A mother of another player on our JV team, who stood under the shade of a solitary maple tree on the third base side of the field, confronted him. "You know, it's your job to mold the player's character, not to yell at him."

John sneered at the reflection in the unidentified woman's sunglasses. "No, it's my job to coach the game of baseball. It's the parent's job to mold the player's character."

The next day, the sophomore player's father telephoned John at home and revealed that his son had some emotional difficulty John had never been informed of. As a result of their discussion, John welcomed the player back on the team. The player's father was satisfied with the way the incident had been handled. John thought the incident was history. The parent who had confronted

John at the game, however, filed a formal complaint about John concerning the incident. As a result, John was called before the athletic director and the principal—with the complaining parent present—to defend himself.

At the meeting, the woman learned what her ears hadn't heard from the visitor's side of the field. She hadn't realized what the player had said in our dugout. Since the incident had occurred at a school function, it could have resulted in the player's suspension, something John had chosen not to enforce. Though the parent dropped the complaint, the incident distracted us for weeks, as John couldn't stop harping about it.

As painful as the incident was for John, it told me something about his character. To his credit, John never took the incident out on the sophomore player whose parent had complained or the player who had caused the incident. A lesser man might have, but not John. He knew the player whose parent complained was already embarrassed enough about his mother's interference with the team. Like his father, John was an educator first, a coach second.

During that same five-under-five hundred stretch, I learned about some matters concerning our teenage players that bothered me a lot more than they bothered D. Our junior first baseman, Frank Pecheco, and senior catcher, Jimmy Albert, had gotten into a fistfight at a local fast-food restaurant in Ansonia. Jimmy ended up with a purple welt over his left eye. I was concerned that he would have difficulty catching with only one good eye. The next day in the coaches' room at the clubhouse, I sprung the disturbing news to John.

"D, we have a problem," I said as I struggled to open my green locker, which somebody had kicked once too often before our season had begun.

"So what else is new?" D said as he sat and started lacing up his black coach's shoes.

"This is something to be concerned about. I heard there was a fight last night at Duchess between Albert and Pecheco."

"So." He bent over and pulled up his white-ribbed athletic socks. "Who won?"

"What do you mean who won? All I know is Jimmy got marked."

"What does that mean?"

"It means he has a black, partially shut eye, and he's our catcher. What are we supposed to do if he can't see?"

"He'll have to suck it up, that's all. You said it yourself, Riles. We can only play the hand that's dealt us."

On another occasion, a player was performing below his ability. He appeared to be taking in the beauty of the woods surrounding Ryan Field instead of preparing to react to a potential ball that might be hit toward him. I approached John about the kid's performance level dropping. John claimed he knew what was wrong with him. "Girls." He thought the preoccupied player might be learning about sex for the first time. When he called the kid into the coaches' room after practice, I thought John was probably right, although the distracted player wouldn't admit it. I couldn't believe John had talked to the kid about sex in the coaches' room. But then again, John was a teacher. I guess it came with the territory.

I also learned that John's knowledge of high school baseball players was more than unique, it was downright uncanny. With a game scheduled against Shelton, we were in a jam. Our best pitcher, Greg Pettinella, had just pitched the game before, and John had to decide whether to pitch Rob Altimarano again. A senior left-handed pitcher named Aaron Sill was just coming off a knee injury. He was finally back with the team, but he hadn't even thrown one inning during the year and only a few on the sidelines. Aaron had wrenched his knee during the wrestling season, and the injury had prevented him from playing baseball until more than halfway into our season.

Despite not having thrown for over a year, John wanted to pitch Aaron against Shelton. I disagreed. "I don't think it's fair to put that much pressure on Aaron. You're asking Aaron to try to pitch and win when the first time he even picked up a baseball was yesterday."

"Riles, let's make this decision the way Big Lou would. If you were in a foxhole, who would you want standing next to you, Aaron or Rob?"

"I might want Aaron if I was in a foxhole, but at least Rob has pitched this year already and has at least one win—when he shut down East Haven. You're asking too much of Aaron."

"Am I? Why don't we ask him?"

Despite my reservation, Aaron wanted the ball and went on to pitch a one hitter against a superior Shelton team that day. Though we ended up losing on a seeing-eye base hit in the bottom of the ninth inning, I knew John was never going to let me forget that his decision to start Aaron had been the right one.

After our ninth loss, John held a team meeting in the locker room, where he mapped out how we could still make the state tournament.

"OK, listen up, fellas. Here's our plan. The games we have left are all scheduled for Mondays, Wednesdays, and Fridays. From now on, on Mondays and Fridays, Pettinella is gonna pitch. On Wednesdays, Aaron's gonna pitch."

Sitting before John on one of the red wooden benches, Rob Altimarano raised his open right hand, as if seeking permission to go to the bathroom.

"Yes, Alto," D responded.

"Coach, when do I pitch?"

"Alto, it's not your time."

As we walked back into the coach's room, I asked D, "Where did you get that one from?"

D hung his red hat in his locker. "I'm trying to politely tell him he isn't going to pitch. It's similar to what Lou did. Whenever a player's parent approached him and asked about their son who wasn't in his plans, he never said anything bad, just politely referred to the player as a nice boy."

To John, Alto was a nice boy.

After we had four wins and nine losses, the season took a dramatic turn. After a practice, I traveled with a weary and dejected John to the annual all-you-can-eat picnic for the league's spring coaches at the Cheshire Holiday Hill. The smorgasbord was one tangible benefit I got from coaching at Derby. The school paid for my ticket. Although it was an event for only the spring season coaches, many other coaches, including retired ones, were invited out of courtesy. Even though Big Lou had retired from coaching, he was always invited.

Lou had been John's mentor and had influenced him to apply for the varsity baseball coach's position when it became vacant. Although Lou had never coached baseball at Derby, D courted Lou's coaching philosophy, especially after a difficult loss.

When we arrived at the picnic, we spotted Derby's coaches sitting at a round redwood picnic table. Under the shade of a beach umbrella, Big Lou had been joking with a group of Derby coaches. He smiled as John and I approached and moved his wooden cane from the spot next to him.

"Sit down, Johnny," Lou barked with his deep voice. "How's the team doing?"

Hiding the grime still on his palms from swinging a rubber-handled fungo bat, D bowed his head. "We've got some talent, Coach," D replied, "but, for some reason, I can't gel the team into winning."

"Here," Lou said as he removed his worn and weather-beaten red baseball cap—a single white letter D on its crumpled crown—and revealed his balding head. "Wear this hat. It's got at least seven more wins in it."

"No," John squeamishly replied. "I...I can't...Lou, I can't take it."

"Take it, John."

"Really, Coach?"

Lou nodded his approval. He wouldn't have to tell D again. With the speed of a man realizing he hadn't removed his hat before the playing of the national anthem, John removed his own sweat-ringed red hat. Revealing the rest of his balding forehead and his electrified brown hair on the sides of his head, he donned Lou's hat. On the way back from Holiday Hill, John couldn't stop talking about his new victory-broken-in, one-size-fits-all, red hat. He couldn't wait to show it to Nancy. I was just hoping I would get back from the picnic alive.

Amazingly enough, with John wearing Lou's hat, we started to win. With Pettinella pitching on Mondays and Fridays and Sill throwing on Wednesdays, we rattled off five straight wins to even our record at 9–9. We then had two rain outs, one of which was on the last day of eligibility for the state tournament. With an even record, the team qualified for the Class S state tournament—a first for John D. as a head coach.

Less than a week later, we learned what it was like to draw a low seeding in a single-elimination tournament. According to the rules, for the tournament's first two rounds, games would be played at the higher-seeded team's field. In the first round, we had drawn the Griswold Wolverines. The only thing we knew about the Griswold team was their location in the town of Griswold, near Norwich, in the sticks of northeastern Connecticut.

We also knew that, although Griswold's football team had been eligible to play in the 1985 Class S state football championship game, they had declined to attend, believing they were over matched. The declination had allowed Derby to play and eventually to win the championship. Knowing that fact gave us a psychological edge against Griswold, since we knew they had quit the football tournament. No Derby team would ever decline a chance—even a remote chance—at a state championship.

The bus ride to Griswold lasted about an hour and a half. Like our regular season games, the bus we rode in was an unair-conditioned, six-wheel diesel school bus. We had been lucky enough to get out of school around 12:30 PM for the extended ride. More than a dozen filtered cigarette butts flew out the open bus window and bounced off the pavement as we traveled on the congested I-95 to I-395.

We arrived at Griswold High a little after 2:00, and before their dismissal bell rang. We lugged our equipment to a dandelion-filled practice field just south of the school for batting practice, but there were no pitching screens anywhere, nor had we thought to bring one. I threw the pregame batting practice using two black garbage cans piled on top of each other for protection. Thus began "Garbage Can BP" at Derby baseball.

Like many Class S schools in the state, Griswold's field required unique ground rules. Several taut high power lines wrapped with rubber insulation extended from left to right center field. We learned before the game began that the obstacles in the outfield ozone would not be dead territory. Any ball that hit a wire would be played live, and you could catch a ball when it came down for an out.

After John introduced himself to the other coach, he asked him who was pitching. The coach told him he was throwing the "Caveman." Just then, a kid with bushy hair and a brown beard who was pounding his already-broken-in glove walked with a player wearing a chest protector and shin guards toward the right field bull pen. When the Caveman threw the game's first pitch, more Derby fans witnessed it than Griswold fans. Included among them was John's dad, who had been brought there by Nancy.

The game had its share of entertainment—as most our games did. Up to that point in his freshman, junior varsity, and varsity coaching career, D had never gotten thrown out of a game by an umpire, a fact which had always astonished me. I think it was because whenever John had expressed something derogatory to an umpire, it had been imbedded inside whatever else he had told the ump at the time. By the time the umpire had pulled his mask over his head, yelled "play ball," and realized he had been criticized, it had been too late for him to do anything about it. Such is the advantage for a coach who is also a teacher of English literature.

Once D had told an umpire that he (the ump) didn't know the rules and should read the Federation's (National Federation of State High School Association's) rule book. That hadn't been so bad until he told the ump how to accomplish reading the lengthy, small-print book quickly: "Put the rule book in your bathroom. That way it won't take you so long to read it." By the time the man in the royal blue shirt realized John had been telling him he was full of shit, it was too late for him to react, as the game was already under way again. If D ever would be chucked from a game, it would be more likely to happen in a state tournament game played on the road. Neutral umpires aren't provided in the tournament until you reach the quarterfinals.

When our first batter stepped to the plate to face the Caveman, the umpire raised his open right hand to the pitcher. The umpire's body appeared artificially pumped up, like Hans or Frans of *Saturday Night Live*, with protective equipment underneath his sky blue shirt and gray pants. With mask in hand, he walked toward D. "Coach, you can't stand there," he pointed out. "You're too close to the field."

Surprised, D leered at the ump. "What?"

"You have to back up," the ump added while putting his black, cushioned metal mask back on. "You can't stand there."

D took two giant steps backward.

"Is this OK?"

"No, Coach, you have to back up farther."

D turned around, took a few more steps back, and threw his hands up in the air. "Is this OK?"

The ump removed his mask again. Pointing to a spot close to our third base dugout, he said, "Coach, I'm just telling you to stay back near your dugout."

D stomped toward the umpire. "I didn't just take an hour-and-a-half bus ride to get screwed, did I?" he asked, aggravated. "You wouldn't be telling me that if I was Bob DeMayo," he added, referring to North Haven High School's legendary coach, who held the record for the most wins by an active coach in Connecticut. DeMayo, who had taught psychology at North Haven, had been known for standing close to the field in an effort to influence his team, as well as the other team and the umpires. Few, if any, umpires would ever tell the well-known Coach DeMayo he couldn't stand in his normal spot adjacent the field. I knew John was too sensitive to be told where to stand simply because he didn't win anywhere near as many games as DeMayo did.

The ump had slipped his mask back on again and, like a teacher scolding an unruly student, said, "I don't know what you mean, just stand near your dugout and be quiet. I don't want to hear anymore about it." Not to be outdone, D kept sarcastically asking the plate umpire whether it was permissible to stand where he was standing for the rest of the game.

Although this year was only D's second year coaching varsity, he already knew that some high school coaches could virtually stand wherever they wanted during a game. An umpire would never ask them to either move back or stay in the dugout, unless the coach blatantly abused the privilege. To D, it was an insult that this umpire had told him he couldn't stand in the spot he normally stood at during games. No other umpire had ever told him to step back.

The first base umpire was no better than the home plate ump. Whenever any of our players reached first base and Griswold's pitcher tried to pick them off, the first base ump wouldn't grant any of our requests for a time-out. Even after a player dove back into first base and scooped dirt under his belt, he had to stand while he kept a hand or foot on the bag. When we asked the ump why he wouldn't give our players a time-out when they requested it, the ump smugly told us that since he didn't have to, he wasn't going to. After that, each time one of our players dove back into first base, they wailed in pain while pleading for a time-out. The ump finally got the point and let us call time-out every time our players dove back into a base.

Despite our umpire difficulties, the Caveman didn't intimidate our players. We rocked him early, scoring six runs. But toward the game's end, D faced a crucial decision. Griswold threatened to tie the game when they got a couple of men in scoring position with less than two outs. D went outside the dugout and located his father, standing behind our dugout. Their eyes met. "Dad, what do you think, play the infield up or back?"

"Play it back, John," his father replied as he waved his right hand.

John followed his father's advice and told the middle infielders to stay back. The decision turned out correct, as an infielder caught a pop-up in short left field. Had he been playing up, he might not have been able to reach it.

In the seventh inning, we were still hanging on to a two-run lead. Greg Pettinella was pitching and had shaken off five signs in a row from our catcher, Jimmy Albert.

"D, I think you better go to the mound and talk to Greg," I said while squeezing a small button on the bottom of our orange Gatorade jug and holding a five-ounce green paper cup under the spout.

"Why, Riles? What's going on?"

"Greg just shook off five signs in a row from Jimmy."

"So?"

"He's only got four pitches."

D asked for time and walked deliberately toward the mound. He turned back to me before he reached the baseline. "I'll straighten this out," he added.

As he neared the mound, he stopped. He stared at Jimmy, who stood to give his knees a rest. D whipped his right arm across and pointed to the mound area. "Get over here," he barked.

While the three-way mound lecture continued, the umpire walked toward the mound, mask in hand. When the ump reached the dirt hill in the middle of the infield, D ended the conference with one last instruction to Greg and Jimmy. As D started to walk on the infield grass toward our dugout, the ump said, "I guess you told him in words he could understand, huh, Coach?"

D stepped over the foul line as if trying to avoid a land mine. "What was it all about?" I asked.

"You're right. Greg does only have four signs. Jimmy gave him all four. Greg shook off all four, so Jimmy gave him the middle finger."

"What did you say to them that the ump overheard?"

"I told them to cut the f—kin shit and let's just put Griswold away so we could get on the f—kin bus with a W."

D's terse words to our battery had the desired effect. We ended up winning the game 6–4. The victory was our sixth in a row with Big Lou's stretched-out, never-washed red hat atop D's head.

Forty-eight hours later, we traveled past the exit for Griswold to the last exit on I-95 before the Rhode Island border to battle the Wheeler High School Lions of North Stonington. Luckily, we had been let out of school earlier than we had at the Griswold game, as it took us two hours to get there. We didn't know much about our second round opponent—except that they were 15-5. Their coach had scouted us at our game against Griswold because Wheeler had received a bye and had been scheduled to play our game's winner.

The bus driver found Wheeler High easy enough, but we didn't see a field behind or adjacent to it. We pulled into a gravel parking lot across the street from the school to ask somebody where the field was. The bus circled the lot, and we saw what looked like two small, white, wooden open sheds across from each other. As we got closer, we realized they were dugouts with a baseball field between them.

After we exited the bus, D and I walked toward the infield portion of the field. The outfield wasn't surrounded by a fence. A ten-foot white foul pole stood alone at the beginning of a forest—another sprung from the ground twenty feet from the parking lot. A thin middle-aged guy wearing a pin-striped white baseball uniform and maroon hat was the only person on the field. With his back to us, he was lining the third baseline with a rolling lime-dropping contraption similar to what our city crew used. We approached the gentleman.

"Excuse me, sir," D said to the man, whose eyes were focused on the four-inch-wide white line he was creating with the motorless machine.

"Yeah?" he asked without raising his head.

D trailed behind him without stepping on the line, hat in hand. "Can you tell me where Wheeler High School plays their baseball games?"

"Right here," the uniformed man pointed out as he released his right hand from the waist-high lever and carefully stepped away from the line.

"It is?"

"Don't you remember me?" He removed his maroon cap and wiped the sweat from his forehead. "I watched you play the other day. We talked."

"Now I do," D said as he grinned and offered his hand.

Although it looked like some of our players might have to sit outside the dugout, at least Wheeler's field had dugouts. I couldn't stand fields that didn't have dugouts; a baseball game felt like a softball game without them. When you don't have a dugout, there is nothing separating you from your fans and parents and preventing them from telling you how they think you should coach the team or play their son.

"You always line the field yourself?" D asked as he began to follow the coach up the third baseline.

"Yeah. I rake the mound and mow the grass too. I'm tired of it. This is probably my last year."

"But aren't you guys like 15–5 or something?" D retorted.

"Yeah, we are."

"Geesh," D replied as he snapped a match across the top of a matchbook and lit up a cigarette. "I would line the field, mow the grass, and drag the infield before every game if I could go 15–5. By the way, you throwing a righty or a lefty?" D asked the question before every game. If our opponent's coach revealed it was a lefty, we would have a left-handed kid pitch batting practice instead of me.

"I'm throwing my Caveman," the coach responded.

"What, does everybody around here have a Caveman?" D asked.

When D came back from his conversation with the coach, he frowned and said, "He wouldn't tell me whether he was throwing a righty or a lefty."

"Yes he did," I replied.

"What do you mean he did?"

I laughed. "He must be a righty. Have you ever heard of a left-handed Caveman?"

"I was careful not to say anything bad about his lousy field," D said, lowering his voice. "I didn't want to give him another reason to want to beat us."

"I noticed. If he had to play the next game at home, he might want us to win."

The Wheeler coach pointed out we had the third base dugout, then walked into the outfield, bent over with the lining machine before him. D and I raised our eyebrows at each other. He was thinking the same thing I was and dropped his jaw. "You've got to be kidding me," I said. "They use a limed line as a fence to determine whether somebody hit a home run? What happens if the ball rolls past it?"

The coaches went over the ground rules with the two umpires at home plate. We learned if the ball bounced over or rolled past the limed line it was a ground-rule double, but if it went beyond the chalk in the air, it was a home run. If an outfielder tried to catch a ball and he stepped past the line, it would also be ruled four bases.

In the top of the first, our leadoff hitter was Greg Pettinella. The Caveman rocked back, then fired a fastball. Greg hit a tailing fly ball deep to left field. The umpire leaned to his right like Carlton Fisk in the 1975 World Series as our players bolted outside the dugout to watch the flight of the high fly. The ball went around the foul pole into a section of the dense woods behind it. The umpire motioned to the left with both hands and screamed, "Foul Ball!"

I got D's attention from my third base coach's box and told him if the limed line around the outfield was connected to the foul pole, the foul pole had to be considered the park's end. If a ball is fair when it leaves a park, it should be ruled a home run. D made a T with his hands and hollered, "Time-out!" He walked purposefully toward home plate. "I want a conference!" he demanded.

After D spoke to the diminutive elderly man in blue behind home plate, the two umpires huddled. After the huddle broke, the home plate umpire twirled his right index finger up in the air counterclockwise, signaling it was a home run. Greg gleefully sprinted out of the batter's box and around the bases before the umpires changed their minds. The Wheeler coach erupted on both umpires to no avail. We had just started the game, and we were already embroiled in a controversy. After Greg stepped on home plate and was high-fived by his teammates, D looked at me, turned his hat so the bill was on the side of his head like Max Patkin, and said, "Batten down the hatches, Riles, we're in for a doozy."

For the rest of the game, the Wheeler coach employed a strategy of removing the right-handed Caveman and bringing in a left-hander to pitch whenever either of our two left-handed batters came up. The left-handed pitcher, however, was already on the field, so each time they brought him in to pitch, Wheeler had to play musical positions with their fielders. Our scorekeeper flipped his yellow number two pencil to use the eraser with each position change he goofed up. D and I thought the Wheeler coach believed he was in the major leagues. Nevertheless, we soon learned there was a reason Wheeler was 15–5 as the game ended up going into extra innings.

In the top of the ninth, we finally got a man on second and third with one out. Since we hadn't been hitting the ball well, I thought it would be the perfect time for a suicide squeeze. The book on suicide squeezes states they are better tried with two men in scoring position. If the batter doesn't succeed in bunting the ball and the lead runner is out at home plate, at least you are left with the back runner on third.

Squeezes are also more successful with a pitcher in the windup. Third base runners are coached not to move for the plate until a split second before the ball leaves the pitcher's hand. That way, the pitcher can't throw a pitchout. With a pitcher in the windup, a runner on third can get further down the line before the squeeze play is suspected.

The strategy assumes, however, that if the batter can't get the bunt down, he will somehow psychologically recover and end up getting a base hit. Because the batter is still mentally dealing with his failure of not bunting the ball correctly, getting a hit is a long shot. D had apparently had the same idea as me, and gave the signal for a suicide squeeze.

Suicide squeeze signals are the riskiest ones. If the batter misses the sign, the runner on third has to escape the rundown that follows after his charge toward home plate. Worse yet, if the batter swings at the pitch, the runner trying to score could be pelted by a hit ball, and you'd have to hope a hospital was nearby. If the runner misses the sign and the batter bunts the ball, since he is not trying to get a base hit, the batter ends up out. As a result, coaches try to make suicide squeeze signs—as D would say—"as simple as the nose on your face." Most coaches require a return signal both the batter and the runner on third must give so that everybody knows, except hopefully the opposing team, the suicide squeeze is on.

Our signals were extremely simple. If they hadn't been, everybody in the park would have known what was expected to happen except our players. To put the suicide squeeze signal on, D would clap his hands like a madman while constantly repeating the words "come on" and adding the batter's last name. The batter would then whack his spikes with his bat, which presumably would only be seen by the opposing team as a ritual many batters use. At third base, I would tell the runner he had to "get on his horse," which I would only tell a runner if a suicide squeeze was on. My verbal signal gave the runner on third three signs: D's repeated clapping and yelling of the batter's last name, the batter hitting his cleats, and me telling him to get on his horse. Nothing could go wrong—or so we thought.

D started clapping his hands wildly and yelling, "Come on, Picirrillo…come on, Picirrillo…come on, Picirrillo!" (Picirrillo being the batter's last name.) But while the batter's name was Ed "Pokey" Picirrillo, our sophomore shortstop, the runner on third was Tony Peccirrillo, our senior center fielder. Both last names, when shouted, virtually sounded the same. Tony looked at me bewildered, and I realized we'd screwed up.

Pokey banged his worn metal cleats with his bat. "Get on your horse," I said, looking at Tony. But was Pokey banging his cleats because it's what ballplayers do, or was it because he knew the squeeze was on?

The pitcher rocked back and raised his glove. Tony made a mad dash for home in foul territory. The runner on second, Frankie Pechico, sprinted toward third.

As the pitch went toward Pokey, he was surprised, but he knew something was up. Before the ball reached him, he started to square his body, lower his bat, and slide his right hand down the metal barrel to bunt. Though the bat didn't make contact with the ball, Pokey moved his bat into the catcher's line of sight, temporarily blinding him or causing him to blink. The ball zipped right past the catcher as if through a hole in his mitt and scooted to the chain-link backstop. Not only did Tony score, but Frankie Pechico, flying around third, slid under the tag at the plate on the one-knee throw from the catcher to the pitcher. Frankie's score gave us a two-run cushion.

In the bottom of the ninth, however, Aaron was tiring. Wheeler had been hitting the ball hard and had scored another run.

"What do you think, Riles? Should I take him out?" D asked.

"I think Aaron's out of gas, but who are we going to bring in?"

"Pettinella."

"Well, if we're going to have to collect the uniforms when we get back to Derby, we might as well get beat with our best pitcher on the mound. You have to do it, D."

"I know."

Knowing when or whether to take a pitcher out is a skill no baseball book can teach—only experience can. The faint of heart will leave him in too long, and the analytical will take him out too soon. Success lies somewhere between the brain and the heart. Sometimes, it's just luck.

D knew Aaron's heart was bigger than his 145-pound body, but eighteen years of coaching had given him a sense of how the game would end if he left him in. Even though Greg had thrown a complete game against Griswold, D handed the ball to Greg on only one day of rest.

Aaron was livid. After D went to the hill, Aaron mouthed something to him that made D's eyes fixate on a space above and beyond the field. When D returned from the conference, he began looking for my white Styrofoam coffee cup. The inning before, however, I had seen D finish his coffee in a gulp and crush his cup like an empty cigarette pack, so I had hidden mine behind our dugout. I asked D what he was looking for. "Nothing," he said as he examined the tiny numbers on his black Timex wristwatch.

I knew whatever Aaron had muttered to D, he would deal with it after the game and not as Aaron sat on the bench disgusted. Fortunately, the game ended with a hard line drive to short that Pokey drove to his right and caught in midair. Dust flew up from his body as he raised his glove to prove the catch to the skeptical umps. Remarkably, we had beaten two Cavemen in three days, a first for Derby baseball.

Winning made the two-hour bus ride back to Derby a lot easier. Since it was already evening, we decided to stop at McDonald's before getting on I-95. When we reached the Golden Arches, the coaches sat together at a table with molded plastic chairs beneath the Hamburgler's picture on the wall. Another assistant coach, Tommy Donofrio, or Naugh as he was called, sat with D and me. Naugh was bigger than D. He was about 6'2" and 220 pounds with curly black hair. While he was much younger than D, they were close friends, as Naugh had also been an assistant football coach at Derby High and shared D's passion for the New York Yankees.

Before D went up to the crowded counter to order, he removed Big Lou's hat and flipped it onto our table. Naugh and I decided to see whether D would notice the good luck charm was missing when he returned with his Big Mac, fries, and Diet Coke. When D returned to the table, he said nothing about the hat. When we left the air-conditioned McDonald's, he didn't notice the wind blowing across the top of his bare head. We climbed the steps of the bus and eventually ended up on I-95 heading back toward Derby.

D sat across from me on the bench seat behind the bus driver's seat. Naugh settled into the seat behind D. We waited until the bus had traveled past a few mile markers and realistically couldn't back up.

"You know, D," I said, gazing at the diet soda spill spot on his red jersey, "I just can't explain the reason for our success. We were four and nine, and now we won seven in a row." D nodded and began to search for his cigarettes. "The only explanation I can think of is Lou's hat."

Naugh chimed in, "Yeah, D, it's definitely Lou's hat. There's just no other explanation...Lucky we have that hat."

D raised his hand to fix the bill of his hat, but his hand continued past his forehead.

He flung his red pullover jacket beside him in the air. The magic hat wasn't underneath.

After he looked under his seat, Naugh and I asked him whether it was possible he had left it at the McDonald's in Stonington.

D's eyes bulged from their sockets. He gasped for air. "Stop! Stop the bus!" he barked. "We have to go back!"

The bus lurched forward, and the hydraulic brakes squealed. Without giving it a thought, the driver proceeded to pull the bus over the unbroken white line and into the breakdown lane. But Naugh told the startled driver to keep going. He produced Big Lou's hat as if he was Harry Anderson, telling D he should be more protective of Lou's hat.

As D slumped in his bench seat, waiting for his heart to come back into his chest, the conversation focused on a real problem. The CIAC had previously scheduled our quarterfinal game to occur on the morning after the Derby High's senior prom; the affair had been scheduled to take place that Friday evening.

The next day, the school had tried to gain consideration from the CIAC, the governing body for high school athletics in Connecticut, to change the game's date but failed. The only concession we did receive was they moved the start of the game from morning to afternoon. Worse yet, we learned we had drawn our archrival—Ansonia. The neutral site selected was Fairfield University's field. Fairfield University was D's alma mater.

That Saturday morning, I turned on the Weather Channel. The local afternoon forecast had called for possible heavy rain. Most baseball coaches say they never pray for rain. We tell ourselves not to worry about the things we can't control, yet somehow our eyes are glued to the Weather Channel on game day like a child's to the Cartoon Network on a rainy Saturday morning. If you let the players know you're hoping for a rainout, they think you don't believe they can beat the team they're playing—a sure recipe for disaster.

D and I reached the clubhouse before noon. We sat in the coaches' room, waiting for the team to arrive. We worried about the possibility a player might not show. Everyone arrived, but most dragged into the clubhouse with heavy eyelids, as if they had spent the shortened night on a cheap mattress.

On the quiet half-hour bus ride south on Route 8 and I-95 to Fairfield University, D and I worried we had bad juju. For starters, the bus driver who had gripped the oversized steering wheel for our last seven wins was absent. Worse yet, our new driver was a woman—not that we didn't like women bus drivers per se, but they sometimes turned on their fm radio, played cassette taped music, or gossiped with the dispatcher on the two-way radio. D wanted our bus to be as dead silent as the football team's on the way to a game. He didn't want to hear conversation about matters other than baseball. He saw it as a sign of not caring about the ball game about to take place.

If a woman drove, the butterflies already in our stomachs on the way to a game would multiply. Worse yet, some female drivers told D he wasn't allowed to smoke. Most times, the men didn't say anything. They just drove and wished us luck as we departed. If D hinted we were late for a game, the men would fast-forward the trip. The women would just complain they were going as fast as they could.

When we reached Fairfield University, I thought the baseball gods had smiled on us. As the team departed the bus, it began to pour. The heavy rain hampered our ability to take batting practice in the netted cage fifty feet away from our first base side dugout. The Ansonia Chargers didn't take batting practice; I believed they must have taken it back at Nolan Field in Ansonia or chosen not to take it. The rhythmic rain pounded the field for about thirty minutes, then tapered to a soft sprinkle.

Our players splashed their spikes in puddles before our dugout. I thought they were going to cancel the game, until I saw a short-sleeved guy from the university's maintenance department emptying bags of Speedy Dry around home plate. Speedy Dry reminded me of kitty litter. Then the groundskeepers pushed, raked, broomed, and tamped the Speedy Dry mixed clay around home plate and the mound. The broadcast crew from WADS radio started to connect their wires. A blue and red line formed at the ticket booth at the main gate behind the chain-link backstop, telling me the officials were no longer considering canceling the contest.

As the "Star-Spangled Banner" played over the public address system, the team sensed we were in a big game. Although the national anthem is played before every football game, the anthem is never played before a regular season baseball game. After we put our rain-soaked caps back on, we huddled before our dugout. The pregame huddle is a ritual where players put their hands together and scream a word or sometimes two on the count of three. Most times, we would yell "win."

Ansonia had their biggest fan in the dugout with them, Matthew F. Shortell Jr., or Pop as he was known by everyone in the Valley. Pop was in his midsixties. A well-known baseball and basketball umpire, Pop had been an umpire when I had played in the Babe Ruth league and in high school. You couldn't forget him if he umped your game. With a limp caused by childhood polio, the gregarious 6'4", 275-pound umpire would hobble out toward the mound before the game began, turn toward the crowd, bark out the batteries of both teams, and scream, "Play Ball!" Whether there was one fan or five hundred fans, he would always do the same. But what Pop was most known for was his devotion to Ansonia sports, football in particular. Since 1946, Pop had been to every Ansonia High football game, all 578 of them.

While standing outside our crimson huddle, I looked at Ansonia navy blue one. They removed their hats, and Pop led them in the Lord's Prayer. I knew we were in trouble. Here we were, about to yell "win," while they were asking God for help. No comparison.

In the bottom of the first inning, a ground ball was hit back to our pitcher Greg Pettinella's right, normally an easy out. Greg snagged it in his glove, turned, and planted his back right spike to throw to first, but it slipped from under him. His butt slammed into the wet turf. Greg tried to make an accurate throw from his sitting position, but the runner was safe by two steps as the ball bounced to Frank Pecheco's outstretched mitt. D objected to the playing conditions, but the umps ignored him. The runner was safe, and, although the rain had stopped, the floodgates had opened. Nothing had ever gotten better after that, and Ansonia went on to crush us 9–0.

After the game ended, I stepped up to get on the bus behind some players. A tear trickled off the bus driver's face onto the black steering wheel as she held a crinkled pink tissue. I thought she was crying about our defeat until I learned she was sobbing because Greg Pettinella blamed her for the loss. As he got on the bus, Greg had apparently asked her why she had to be the driver today. Since we hadn't lost when the other male driver drove us, he told her the loss was her fault. She believed him. Jimmy Dugan was wrong, there is crying in baseball.

On the silent bus ride back to Derby, D and I both realized Big Lou had been right. At least seven wins had been left in his weather-beaten hat. But what Lou hadn't told us was that there had *only* been seven wins left in it. That was the last time I ever saw D wearing the hat.

10

Struggling to Return to the Tournament

In the pros, you can draft. In college, you can recruit. But in high school baseball, you have to coach the hand you are dealt. We lost six seniors to graduation. Gone were Greg Pettinella, who had been the winning pitcher in nine of our eleven wins, and was the shortstop when he didn't pitch; our outfielders, Dave Foley, Tony Peccirrillo, and Vinny Marulli; and our other pitchers, Aaron Sill and Rob Altimarano.

Junior Chris Gruttadauria, last year's backup catcher and designated hitter when Pettinella didn't pitch, contracted mononucleosis. We lost him for the entire 1989 season. We had also expected Chris to pitch. As a result, we had to mold a sophomore, Pat McMahon, into a varsity catcher and short one pitcher. To make matters worse, Pokey, our shortstop when Greg Pettinella pitched, had broken his left wrist during a game early in the season.

D and I banged ground ball after ground ball and fly ball after fly ball, day after day. Pat McMahon had been Pokey's friend, so he fit in well. Our workaholic sophomore catcher would catch a hundred foul pops a day launched by the JUGS machine and would tirelessly practice his blocking and throwing skills.

While D rocked in his favorite maroon living room chair the night before each game, we brainstormed ways to outcoach and outplay our next opponent until the baseball highlights came on the news. Fortunately for me, my wife Sue could always confirm I was at D's house, as my clothes always reeked of cigarettes.

John's dad came around for a few practices to help and to give advice. D enjoyed that. Mr. D, as I called him, even boarded the bus with us to some road games and sat on our bench. Wherever we went, John introduced his father to the umpires and opposing coaches; some were already acquainted with him from seasons past. Mr. D didn't last long coming to the practices; he couldn't tolerate kids who wouldn't listen. Sometimes in the batting cage he would try to correct a player's hitting flaw, but the hitter continued to swing his own way. D had told his dad that today's kids weren't the same as the players of yesteryear, but Mr. D hadn't bought it. Whenever a petulant player ignored his advice, he just told John, "I'm going home."

John's father's advice wasn't limited to the game's fundamentals. During an away game, Pokey watched the game from inside our dugout with his left hand in an ink-colored cast up to his elbow. Quiet as a shadow, he slipped behind our dugout teary eyed. Mr. D noticed and followed Pokey to learn what was wrong. He discovered that Pokey didn't know what to do with himself if he couldn't play. At the game's end, John's dad told D he thought we should allow Pokey to suit up and play in the next game, albeit we would need to DH for him. D was resistant at first, but then allowed Pokey to take some slow ground balls at short with his glove in the fingertips of his left hand.

The athletic director was skeptical about allowing Pokey to play but had known him since Little League and relented when Pokey's parents approved. Pokey was a gutsy kid who also played football, but only weighed about 150 pounds carrying our bat bags. The bottom of his brown leather glove covered the tips of his exposed fingers, but it looked like a ball hit hard at him would send the glove spinning into the outfield. At practice, Pokey took more than a hundred ground balls a day with his left hand and forearm encased in plaster.

But despite our tireless work, with eight games remaining in the season, we were 5–7 and had to figure out a way to get to the postseason tournament. Because of our experience with the 1988 team, which some current team members had been a part of, we were able to encourage the kids to believe it was possible to go 5–3 the rest of the way. Because of our schedule, D and I knew it was against the odds, but we had to stay positive lest the team lose hope of accomplishing the difficult task. We mapped our ambitious plan on the white dry-erase board in the locker room. The team was convinced it could work, but the plan didn't go as well as we had hoped. We were 6–10 and had to win four games in a row to make the tournament—but we would not quit.

Our final four games were against Cheshire, Sheehan, Lyman Hall, and Shelton—three of which had winning records. Making the task more difficult, the Cheshire game was on a Thursday, the day before our senior prom. Because of a prior rain out, the Sheehan game had been scheduled for Saturday afternoon, the day after the prom. Traditionally, the day after the prom had been reserved for the postprom picnic.

On the day of the Cheshire game, we told the players that if we lost and were eliminated from the tournament, anyone attending the senior prom would be exempt from Saturday's Sheehan game in Wallingford. If, however, we should upset the 14–2 first-place Rams, we would expect everyone to don their uniform and battle for the tournament Saturday. The team agreed with D's deal.

Cheshire arrived late and didn't take any pregame batting practice. Our players believed they had done it on purpose and had disrespected us, acting as if they didn't need BP to beat Derby. Cheshire's tardiness had probably been more a result of traffic than anything else, but we weren't going to tell that to the players. The motivation of disrespect can go a long way in high school baseball.

When junior first baseman Mike Mongillo stepped to the plate with runners on base, he overheard D remark to someone on our bench, "Mong can't hit for shit." The left-handed hitter proceeded to cream a fastball that hooked down the right field line, clanged off the metal fence, and rolled on to the adjacent cinder track for a standup RBI triple. When he reached third base, Mong yelled, "Can't hit for shit, huh, D?" D smiled and tipped his hat. I knew D liked Mike and wondered whether he had made the statement knowing Mike would hear it. With a few more timely hits and our pitcher, Frank Pecheco, keeping Cheshire's hitters off balance, we upset the mighty Rams. After the game, D handed Frank and Mike a game ball. The win was a giant lift for the team. The players now believed it was possible to make the tournament.

After the game, we had another team meeting in the locker room and discussed the prom situation once more. The team agreed that everyone would have to play against Sheehan. Each player was asked whether they would show up, and each pledged they would. Charlie DiCenso offered to help and got special permission to pick up the players attending the prom from their homes and to drive them directly to Sheehan's field to give them a chance to sleep later.

After the team left the clubhouse, Pokey's younger brother Rob, stood before the open door to the coaches' room. Rob, better known as Willow, was a sophomore second baseman. Rob's fellow teammates and D called him Willow after the diminutive movie character and title of the same name. Willow was no taller than 5'6" and weighed around 120 pounds soaking wet from lead-polluted water. He could have fooled an usher with a child's ticket at a Showcase Cinema, but he was as tough as Pokey.

As D hung his jersey in his locker, Willow gestured to me to come out into the hallway leading to the locker room. "Riles," he said in a half whisper, "Rosino ain't gonna be there tomorrow."

"How do you know?" I asked. The consequences of losing one of our better hitters in the lineup and a pitcher raced through my mind.

"Follow me."

I followed Willow into the empty locker room. He brought me to Pat Rosino's red wooden locker and pointed to the uniform hanging on a hook. I pulled the sweat-stained shirt off the hook and examined its stitched white number to make sure it was his. Pat was one of the players going to the prom, and everybody else going had taken their uniform with them so they could have it on when Charlie picked them up Saturday at their homes.

I returned to the coaches' room and gave D the bad news. His head dropped in disappointment. If Pat didn't show, D knew it wouldn't matter whether we beat Sheehan or not. The burden would fall on him to make a difficult decision. His heart told him that perhaps Pat had simply forgotten his uniform and would call him or a teammate to fetch it, but his head knew better.

Pat Rosino had already been straddling a fault line. In a previous game that year at East Haven, Pat had pitched and gotten rocked like a rubber raft in a hurricane. The outing had reminded me of the Bugs Bunny cartoon where Bugs pitched and the Gashouse Gorillas did the Rumba around the bases. Like the cartoon, one hit had been a line drive that screamed right past our center fielder. Pat was lucky not to get whiplash tracing the lasers going past him.

D finally decided to take the ball from him to avoid further embarrassment. When D strode straight to the mound and stuck his right hand out to take the battered ball, Pat just dropped it in the dust hole before the dirty, white rubber and walked off. D had to stoop and pick the ball up off the ground. D didn't remove him from the game but told Pat to take another position in the outfield, as Pat played outfield when he didn't pitch. I was incensed.

On the bus back to Derby, D and I sat on opposite sides of the aisle in the first row of bench seats. D stared out the front of the bus as it merged onto I-95 before the Q Bridge.

"D, I'm pissed."

"About what, Riles?"

"About Rosino," I replied as D turned in my direction.

"What about him?"

"You let him drop the ball like that on the mound when you took him out and still kept him in the game. He displayed a total lack of respect for you. You had to actually pick the freakin' ball up off the ground. He was getting rocked. You did him a favor taking him out."

D looked ahead again. He wanted to let the subject drop. I couldn't let it go. "I don't even want to be on the same bus with him. If something like that happens again, I'll walk home, take a cab, or ride with a parent before I get on a bus again with a player who does something like that to you."

D removed his gold metal-rimmed glasses and began to rub his forehead. "You're right, Riles," he said. "I'll deal with it when we get back."

D didn't want to think it was possible one of his own players would ever disrespect him like that. As a teacher he had experienced it, but not as a coach. After we returned to the clubhouse, D called Pat into the coaches' room. After Pat entered, D shut the door behind him. Ten minutes later, the door opened, and Pat walked out without saying a word. D had believed that Pat's indiscretion on the field would never happen again.

If Pat didn't show up to the Sheehan game with the tournament on the line, and D didn't tell him he was through, the rest of the team would. Because he was a chaperone, D saw Pat at the prom that Friday night, but Pat didn't say a word to him. D mentioned nothing to Pat either, as he wanted to give him the benefit of the doubt. That Saturday, although some team members kept peering outside our dugout inning after inning, hoping he would arrive, and another brought his uniform in case he did, Pat Rosino never showed. His absence meant we didn't have one of our starters in the batting order and couldn't pitch him.

No Derby team I had ever been involved with up to that point had ever battled more to try to win. Even before the game began, however, we knew we could be in for trouble when we saw the assigned base umpire for our most crucial game of the season.

The problem was not the home plate umpire, Ed Handy. A stout man who wore glasses behind his umpire's mask, Ed was a veteran Valley umpire who lived in Derby. D and I had dealt with Ed on many occasions. Ed's experience dated back to games D's father had coached. I had dealt with Ed a lot in summer league games. He was a gentleman and an easy guy to get along with. He was also a diehard baseball man. I had heard a rumor that when Ed was a young boy he had left home and tried to reach Yankee Stadium to see his favorite team. When he wasn't umping one of our games at Ryan Field, Ed sometimes watched us play. D and I knew our winning percentage with Ed Handy on the plate would be better than our overall winning percentage.

The base umpire, however, was a young guy in his twenties who—only a few days prior—had ejected D from a JV game D and I had attended. When one of our players hadn't swung at a pitch D thought was a strike, D had cried out, "Where was that pitch?" The comment had been directed to the batter, concerning his failure to swing. It had not been meant to criticize the umpire's judgment of the pitch as a strike or a ball. D had agreed with the ump that the pitch had been a strike. The umpire had refused to listen to our explanation, and D had been forced to walk out the gate of the park before the game could resume.

To D's credit, he didn't lost his temper over the incident. The ump had his own inflexible rule that if a coach uttered anything about his ball and strike calls, he automatically ejected the coach. I had first encountered the rookie ump while coaching on the Babe Ruth level. He carried with him a reputation of a quick-ejection trigger whenever any of his decisions were questioned, especially ball and strike calls.

After the JV game ended, I approached the young umpire as he strutted off the field and tried to convince him that high school baseball was not the major leagues. I advised him that he would presumably be around for many years doing Derby High School games, and, as a result, he should not be so quick to eject coaches until he has the full story—especially when no profanity had been involved or disrespect intended. I couldn't convince him to modify his approach to a high school game.

We played close to Sheehan, the superior team talentwise. Late in the game, Sheehan had a runner on second with one out, and the batter chopped a ground ball to our pitcher Jeff Owens's right. Jeff backhanded the ball, stepped as if to throw the ball to first, but then faked his throw, spun, and snapped it to third. Like Sheehan's runner on second, the rookie umpire bought Jeff's fake. He was staring at first base, expecting a ball to arrive as the confused Sheehan runner was sliding into our third baseman's glove, already on the ground with the ball tucked in it before the base.

The quick-fingered ump pointed to Ed Handy as if to say it was his call, but Ed just pointed back to him, silently telling him it was his call to make. Though Ed conceded the throw beat the runner to third base, he couldn't tell whether our third baseman had slapped the tag, and therefore left it up to the base umpire to make the final call on a play he hadn't even been looking at.

Because he had not seen the play, the rookie ump called the runner safe.

Like George Brett in the 1983 pine tar incident at Yankee Stadium, D rushed from our first base dugout toward the rookie ump. He screamed at the startled ump, a baseball-width's distance from his face. I had never seen D so incensed before. He sprayed his anger into the umpire's tight-lipped face. Worse yet for the young umpire, he was wearing dark sunglasses under his umpire's cap. Any umpire who wears sunglasses to work a game is only begging for a coach to say something about them whenever he dislikes a call.

I pushed my way between the red-faced D and the ump and threw my arms around D. As I held him, he tried to wrench his way free. Every muscle in his body tightened and he resisted my grip, but for his sake and the rookie ump's, I couldn't let him escape. A nervous Ken Marcucio rushed onto the field to try to help me get D off the field while the ump, with an ashen face and the afternoon sun reflecting off his hidden eyes, said nothing.

Ken and I pushed and pulled D away from the umpire, but not far enough. While I tried to persuade both umps to reconsider the call and Kenny tried to hold D back and calm him, the young rookie committed another cardinal sin for an umpire: he lied. Still within earshot of D, he tried to tell me the reason he had called the runner safe had been that from the corner of his right eye while he looked at first, he had seen that Ben Bartone, our sophomore third baseman, had not placed a tag. Hearing the stupid statement, I knew that an entire season's worth of frustration was about to erupt.

D's eyes misted with outrage. He yanked himself free from Kenny's hold and charged at the umpire again. Before D reached him, I bear-hugged him again. D snapped his left arm free and pointed his stiff index finger at the ump's face. Foam slipped out the side of D's mouth. "You saw nothing!" D screamed. "Now not only was that call awful, but you're a liar! You're nothing but a liar!"

Kenny and I continued to stand between D and the ump with our tired arms spread eagle. Like linesmen in a hockey game, we looked for our opportunity to grab him again. But D wouldn't let up. "These kids work hard every day only to be screwed by an umpire with sunglasses!" he added as he pulled away from me again. He mocked the fact the umpire had been quick to chuck him from the JV game. He embarrassed the ump by loudly challenging him, "Throw me out now! Throw me out now! You don't have the balls to throw me out now!" The umpire was frightened of D's anger and of our team's enraged fans and parents who let him have it from the portable aluminum stands across from first base. The Sheehan players, coaches, and fans stood silent and stunned.

Kenny and I finally tugged D back into our silent dugout, but we still couldn't contain him. D toppled the keg-sized orange Gatorade jug in the corner of our dugout onto the cement floor, causing the yellow-green liquid to spew everywhere, as if it had been shot out of Mt. St. Helens. He kicked the stack of paper cups lying beside the jug as if he were kicking a field goal. The cups exploded like buck shot against the cement dugout wall and careened to the bench before tumbling to the ground.

Mark Angelletti, an all-Housatonic League linebacker and all-state wrestler who sat in our dugout cheering the team on, was so frightened by D that he bolted from our dugout as if he were running from a bull during the Pamplona Festival in Spain. When the bedlam finally subsided, the umpires resumed the game in a dead silence. To make matters worse, the extra out proved costly, as the runner from third ended up scoring.

In the top of the seventh, we trailed by two runs. Before the inning started, an emotionally exhausted D huddled the team together. "No matter what happens in this inning," he said, "I am still proud of all of you. You didn't quit." His voice began to break. "I want to thank you for trying so hard to reach the tournament with everything we had to go through. I want to thank you for the way you came together as a team to try to achieve our goal, and I just want to thank you for the privilege of being associated with you." D and I walked away from the huddle, but it didn't break. Pokey exhorted them while the players put their hands together in the center of the charged huddle.

Although our fired-up team proceeded to load the bases, we only managed to muster one run. Our quest to return to the state tournament ended with the tying run only ninety feet away. Pokey was devastated. He refused to ride the bus back to Derby; he felt he didn't deserve to step on board. We sat together on a curb near our idling bus. I talked to him about how much he had grown as a man and couldn't turn back now. After a few minutes, he reluctantly got on the bus. After the driver pulled the folding doors shut, no one spoke until we reached the clubhouse.

When we got back to Derby, we met with the team in the locker room. Several members said if Rosino had been present we probably would've won, and then only need to win the two remaining games to make the tournament. The team was unanimous; they wanted Rosino off the team. One player revealed that he had spoken to Pat and learned that Pat's girlfriend had threatened that if he didn't go to the postprom picnic with her, they were through. To the team, Pat had chosen a picnic with his girlfriend over them.

To our surprise, Pat Rosino appeared in the clubhouse early Monday afternoon. He entered the open coaches' room as D and I sat on our gray, metal folding chairs. Three minutes later, Pat walked out of the coach's room and punched the plaster wall before the stairs on his way out the building. Although D had faced a painful decision, he never lost sight of the fact that Pat was just an eighteen-year-old high school kid. D knew that someday Pat would regret the mistakes of his youth. When Pat did, D's door would still be open to him.

After we failed to qualify for the tournament, for all intents and purposes the season had ended that Saturday afternoon in Wallingford. To the players' credit, they played hard in the last two games, but we didn't recover from our loss to Sheehan, and lost our final two games to finish 7–13.

The 1989 season was also the year I witnessed the demise of Walrus Man. One game, Pat McMahon had put a small plastic mint green character on the cement roof of our dugout for good luck. The game-board-sized figure was a

Viking standing with a sword and shield as if ready to do battle in some mythical war. The Nordic native reminded me of Thor, the main character of a Marvel comic book I had read as a kid. Pat called it Walrus Man.

After his batting average and stolen bases against ratio had improved with the amulet, Pat had brought Walrus Man to each game and put it on top of the dugout. If the park we were playing in didn't have a dugout, he had either put it in his pocket or on the bench.

After one of our tough home losses, our dejected team had walked toward our two-story clubhouse beyond center field. D and I stood before our first base dugout and began to discuss what had gone wrong. I noticed Walrus Man standing alone on top of our dugout, as if he were watching over his defeated kingdom. I pointed out the rigid synthetic figure to D.

Before my eyes, Pat's good-luck charm was transformed into D's bad-luck charm. He snapped up the mighty Walrus Man. "I'll show you what I think of Walrus Man," he said. D looked around to see whether anyone was watching, then flung Walrus Man spinning into the woods behind our dugout, never to be seen again.

11

The Sad Season

The 1990 season began with a shock. Mr. D, Coach's dad, took a bad fall on a small set of concrete stairs approaching the main entrance of Derby High while coming in to teach night school to GED students. No one knew what had caused John's elderly dad to tumble. But when they found him, alone and unconscious on the concrete stairs, they noticed a bulb missing in a light pole above the spot. Tragically, John's dad had sustained a fatal head injury; D was informed that it would only be a matter of days before his father died.

After the fall, John still tirelessly coached the team. Despite the other coaches and me telling him he wouldn't be doing any disservice to the players if he took some days off, John felt he would somehow shortchange them if he wasn't there every day. After all, they were part of his family too. He banged fly balls and ground balls until the calluses on his hands were black from swinging a rubber-handled fungo bat. He worked on defensive and offensive plays until his voice betrayed him. He then drove to St Raphael's Hospital in New Haven during the evening and stayed by his dad's side in the intensive care room, only leaving the room to pray and light a candle in the chapel.

A few days after John's dad went into the hospital, while D and I were hitting ground balls in the infield during practice, I spotted Nancy in the asphalt driveway that led up to the clubhouse beyond the center field fence. She took more time than it should've to reach the chain-link barrier. Nancy stood motionless behind the fence and didn't call out to us.

While I hit a ground ball with my fungo, I told John his wife was standing beyond the center field fence. After Nancy knew D had seen her, she turned around and slowly walked back down the driveway toward her car. After she turned, John slumped but used the silver fungo bat in his hands to keep from collapsing. His eyes started to water. The players turned to see what he was looking at, but only noticed a thin woman's back shrinking in the distance. After Nancy left the park, D raised his fungo bat and kept hitting ground balls for a short while, then told the team practice was over. With the quiet players ahead of us, we walked side by side to the clubhouse.

Inside the clubhouse's double doorway, John watched as the players lugged the equipment through the adjacent door, behind which was the football equipment storage room. With white shoulder pads and red helmets before them on unfinished pine shelves, the players pushed the overstuffed baseball equipment bags along the concrete floor to the corner of the musty room, under the bottom shelf. John pulled his circle of clanging keys from the right pocket of his gray sweatpants, banged the door shut, and turned the bent bronze key to the deadbolt. The team shuffled past us up the clubhouse steps without saying a word. I handed D a dime to drop into the pay phone on the wall adjacent the clubhouse doorway to call home. The worst was confirmed.

Although the apologetic doctors had informed John his dad suffered severe internal cranial bleeding and it would only be a matter of days, the news that Mr. D was gone hit D like a shot in the gut at point-blank range. D hunched over on the linoleum steps with his hands on his head. I sat beside him, not knowing the right words to say; I just listened and tried to be a friend. Law degrees didn't always help you come up with the right words to say.

D's dad had not just been his father, but his coach in high school, his mentor, and his best friend. Having played first base for him, D believed his father had never received enough credit for his accomplishments as the Derby High baseball coach. After D had been appointed the team's head coach, an *Evening Sentinel* reporter had interviewed both D and his dad in our gym for an article about a son following his father's path teaching English and coaching baseball. As soon as I saw D and his father pose for the photograph that was to accompany the article, I knew it was one of the proudest days in D's life.

John worried how his mother was going to cope with the loss. D's mom had fallen in love with his dad while he was in the army, stationed in Italy, and had returned to America with him. Though Lala did learn to speak English and was a feisty, opinionated woman, she had never driven a car, handled bills, or even drawn checks from her own checkbook. For those matters, she had relied on Mr. D.

After the players quietly squeezed past us on the steps and went out the gray double doors, they remained together outside in silence. They didn't want to abandon their coach. I went outside to let them know it was OK to leave, and to explain to them what to expect. After I returned, I continued to sit next to John on the worn linoleum steps until his older brother Bob, who had flown in from Alabama, arrived at the clubhouse.

The entire team went to the wake at the Adzima Funeral Home. The day after, they had were let out of school along with other students, teachers, and administrators to attend the funeral service, as well as the mass across the street at St. Mary's Church. It was the same church where D sat with his Nancy, Jessica, and Jennifer, every Sunday at 11:30 AM. The other Derby High football coaches were the pallbearers, along with me. Together, we carried Mr. D to his final resting place at Mount St. Peter's Cemetery on the east side of town.

I persuaded D to let me run the practices with the other coaches until he was ready to return. D was afraid he would be unable to make our next scheduled game, which was against Cheshire. I talked to Ken Marcucio about getting the game canceled, so D would not have it on his mind. Ken was already on it. The Cheshire coach, Bert Leventhal, readily agreed with our athletic director's request, under the circumstances. A couple days later, D returned, and our quest to try to make it back to the tournament began anew.

The season almost began without one of our elected cocaptains. I liked Pokey because he was one of the more dedicated players on the American Legion team I had coached the summer before this season. Pokey was a die-hard ballplayer, one of the few who would play the game every day if he could.

The summer before this season, I had also coached a Babe Ruth team in Derby along with the Babe Ruth league's all-star team. A few of the fifteen-year-olds on the Babe Ruth all-stars had also played on my Legion team, so they could play up a level. Near the end of the Babe Ruth season, the Babe Ruth all-star team had traveled to Wolcott for a Saturday morning/afternoon doubleheader in the Baseball Association of Wolcott's annual no-entry-fee tournament.

As bad luck would have it, my player-starved American Legion team had been scheduled to play a game that same afternoon in Naugatuck, halfway between Derby and Wolcott. My assistant would manage the second all-star game, while I returned to Derby to pick up some Legion team members and drive them to Naugatuck. I knew there was a chance I might be short players in the Legion game. Before I left Wolcott, I asked my assistant to determine whether any fifteen-year-old player who might not be starting the second game of the doubleheader wanted to play in the Legion game. If any all-star agreed, my assistant would have to try to persuade the player's parent to drive the fifteen-year-old to Naugatuck.

When I arrived in Derby, I learned we were one player short, so I drove straight through to Wolcott to beg a player to play in the Legion game to avoid a forfeit. If a team forfeited twice in the same season, it was automatically ejected from the league. If a team did get booted, they had to apply to get back in the league the following season, as well as pay a significant forfeit fee. Our high school team needed the Legion team, so I tried everything I could to prevent a forfeit.

I was driving on Route 8 from Derby toward Wolcott with Pokey and the team's bats, balls, helmets, and catcher's gear in my navy blue Renault Alliance when its four-cylinder engine began to buck like a bronco. White smoke appeared in my rearview mirror. I knew a quart of oil wasn't going to solve it and I wasn't going to reach Wolcott. A half mile after I passed Naugatuck, I exited the highway and headed back to Naugatuck's field on side roads when the car's engine clunked, clanked, and spit out dirty white smoke until it suddenly went permanently silent. So much for *Motor Trend* magazine's 1983 Car of the Year.

Since the team's equipment was in the car, an anxious Pokey and I had to tread the streets of downtown Naugatuck toward the field. We lugged the green canvas bags over our shoulders, shifting them from shoulder to shoulder, trying to avoid the curious stares of passersby. Despite our efforts, however, we were too late. By the time we had crossed the concrete arch bridge spanning the foul-smelling Naugatuck River and slid down the rock-filled path to the field below, the umpires had already ruled a forfeit in Naugatuck's favor. No one else had shown up from the Babe Ruth all-star game to prevent it.

Although Pokey was a dedicated baseball player, he wasn't much of a student. Problems at home left him disinterested in school. Before the season, D learned that eighteen-year-old Pokey had left home to live on the second floor of a two-story apartment house on Ansonia's west side and had been absent at school more days than he was present. One evening, I drove to the address D had given me with the other cocaptain, Mike Mongillo. The two-floor house's front door was wide open; the empty stairwell behind it lit up by a single uncovered bulb. The yard was covered with high grass and weeds, but it didn't look out of place for the area. If I had been trick-or-treating, I wouldn't have walked through the rusted gate at the street and knocked on the scratched wooden door. Mike jumped out of my car, but was back in less than thirty seconds. Lucky for Mike, nobody was home.

Eventually, D caught up with Pokey and advised him that if he wasn't going to attend class, he would be better off not playing baseball. The diamond would be worthless to him if he couldn't graduate from high school. D suggested Pokey attend evening GED classes to attain at least some type of diploma before he entered the workforce. But GED students weren't allowed to play sports. Faced with ineligibility, Pokey started attending classes regularly and passed enough of them to continue leading off and turning double plays from shortstop.

After Pokey became eligible to play and before the season began, D and I caught him in the clubhouse one night, along with Pat McMahon and Willow. They had slipped into the clubhouse by climbing up the wooden supports of the small rectangular roof that jutted from the building above the twin front doors and pushing the unlocked sliding glass window. They had set up a JUGS pitching machine in the elongated shower room at the back of the building's second floor and had taken batting practice with plastic balls until their window shadows had given them away to passing cars on Chatfield Street.

Although most of the season was somber because D was having a tough time dealing with the loss of his dad, he never shortchanged the team. Though I had to call Nancy once to help bring him home from the clubhouse because he was having a difficult time, he battled every practice and game. But even though the calluses on our hands had gotten thicker, we couldn't improve on last year's record and finished 7–13 again.

Despite everything difficult that happened that season, it was not without its lighter, happier, and sometimes even comical memories. After John's father passed away, John's mother, Lala, continued to come to the home games and became more vociferous than John's father ever had been. She sat near or sometimes stood behind the fence adjacent our first base dugout with John's wife, Nancy, and his daughters.

Lala was not one to mince words. She wasn't afraid to express her opinion about anything concerning the games or anything else going on in John's life. Whenever an umpire made a bad call, Lala bellowed to the ump with a broken Italian accent, "Youa stiiiiiiiink." Sometimes John would hunch his shoulders as if ice water had been poured down his back and yell over to her to keep quiet. His mother would just say, "Butta, Johnny, he dossa stink, so whya shouldn't I saya so?" After John would tell her to keep quiet, she would continue to hold her uplifted nose with her thin index finger and thumb in the umpire's direction.

During another game, one of our pitchers was throwing fastballs that weren't fast and curveballs that didn't curve. Lala was standing in her usual spot against the fence. After the pitcher gave up a hit, she cried out to D, "Heya, Johnny, don'ta you havea anyonea betta thana thisa kid. He stiiiiinks." When John pleaded with her to keep quiet, she wouldn't. "I can'ta believe that youa don'ta have anyaona better than thisa kid." John knew his mother's baseball instincts were right, albeit brutally honest. Although he wanted to tell her he didn't have anyone better he could put in, he had to remain silent, as the pitcher's proud parent was standing within twenty feet of Lala's caustic comments.

During a game with Amity High School in Woodbridge, their coach, Gary Rispoli, had found Willow remarkable. After we spun a double play, the Amity coach declared that from his third base dugout, he had never seen the second baseman because of the crown of his infield. Willow was that small.

D always had a unique way of getting his point across to players, and Willow was one of his frequent pupils. On a bus ride home from a game we had lost, John summoned Willow to the front to sit next to him. Willow obliged. John wrapped his left arm around him.

"Willow, you just got to be more patient at the plate."

Shifting his eyes to look at D's arm around him, Willow asked, "What do you mean, D?"

"Well, you can't be such a free swinger, trying to clobber everything thrown at you."

Willow bowed his head. "You mean you don't want me to swing?"

"Of course not. It's just that your strike zone is no bigger than a shoe box."

Willow remained puzzled. "Are you telling me you want me to try and get a walk instead of a hit?"

"No. I just want you to swing at pitches in your strike zone. Your zone isn't that big, that's all. You understand?"

Willow squirmed under John's arm. He had heard the speech before, but not by D. "Sure, Coach, I understand."

"Do you? It's not that I don't want you to swing," John explained as he patted him on the shoulder.

"I get it, Coach, really, I do," Willow said as he nodded.

"OK, Willow. I just want to make sure we're on the same page," he replied. He released Willow's shoulder.

As Willow stood up, the bus jolted, and Willow grabbed the top of the seat to keep his balance in the aisle. "We are, Coach. We are," he said as he waddled his way to the back of the bus. When he got halfway back, Willow spit out under his breath, "He doesn't want me to f—king swing." As I pondered the size of my own clay-stained white shoe, I realized D had gotten his point across.

Another afternoon, before we took the field for practice, D decided to address the team in the locker room on the subject of players who missed practice or asked to leave early. D shut the door behind him. He was in no mood for any interruption. But no sooner had D begun to lambaste the players for their lack of commitment than a familiar, repetitive beep resonated in the closed room. D raised his shoulders and clenched his teeth. Startled, Robert Ricciuti, a broad-shouldered outfielder, put his hand in his gray sweatpants pocket, grabbed his small square battery-operated device, and silenced it. The senior player stood motionless before D and awaited D's wrath as some other players chuckled. But D knew Rob worked part-time for an Ansonia funeral home and had applied to embalming school.

"Is that your pager going off, Rob?"

"Yes, Coach," Rob admitted, the device still out of sight.

"Does that mean somebody…?"

"It does, Coach. I have to help get the body and bring it back to the funeral parlor."

"Then you gotta go, Rob," D said as he flipped open his right palm toward the door. As Rob's spikes clicked on the hallway floor, I thought Rob rushed out with a little too much enthusiasm. D looked at me with raised eyebrows. "What am I going to do?" he said. "He's got to go. Somebody died."

We also had a senior manager and scorekeeper named Nick DiRubba. Whenever the coaches got depressed because of a loss, the round-cheeked Nicky brought us back to a positive outlook. In stature, Nick was a midget, but in heart Nick was Andre the Giant. The players liked the kind-eyed Nick so much they requested Nick be given a team uniform. As a result, we asked a parent to tailor one to fit him. Everyone applauded when D presented Nick with the uniform before the team in the locker room. Nick had been teary eyed and speechless.

I always had an affinity for Nick because of the positive way he approached life. Like D, however, Nick could scare you if you got into his car. I hitched a ride from him once from the school to the clubhouse. He drove with four-inch wooden blocks on top of the pedals, fast enough to make me search for the grab handle above my window.

When our first plan mapped out on the drawing board to make the tournament failed, Nick suggested we come up with a Plan B. Plan B became Plan C and then Plan D. Nick's nickname was Meat, but I never wanted to know why the team called him that.

After the twenty-game varsity season ended, Pokey's perseverance was rewarded, as the league's coaches voted him the shortstop on the all-Housatonic League team.

Although the varsity season concluded, the junior varsity still had a makeup game to play. The JV team was coached by my brother-in-law, Jacques "Jocko" Veillette. As D and I were up in the coaches' room, I was standing at the window, peering through the broken white plastic miniblinds at the game in progress.

"D, get over here," I said as I yanked the lift cord and slid one of the elongated windows open. "Check this out." D gazed out the open window at the game. "Who's playing second base?" I asked.

"I don't know, Riles. It looks almost like…it looks almost like…a midget. Oh my God, it is a midget, it's Nicky!"

We raced each other down the stairs to stand behind the center field fence to confirm what our eyes had told us from the coaches' room window above. Jocko had put Nick DiRubba into the JV game at second base.

We were afraid Nick was going to get hurt. If he did, how were we going to explain that to anyone? Nick hadn't been on the playing roster. D knew Nick shouldn't have been in the game, but he didn't say anything about it to Jocko while the game was going on. He let Nick live his dream. When Nick charged a ground ball at second base that looked like a softball heading toward him, scooped it up, and threw the runner out, we cheered loud enough for Nick to hear us. In his only time at bat, Nicholas DiRubba smashed a fastball which, for Nick, turned out to be a ground ball to second base. It wasn't in Nick to take a walk. After the JV game ended, D and I strolled out of the park together. Despite our disappointment about how the varsity season had ended, it was Nicky who showed us how to keep it in perspective.

12

Return to the Tournament 1991

At the end of the 1990 season, our program was dealt another setback. The Derby American Legion Post could no longer afford to sponsor a team. Entry fees, umpires, baseballs, liability insurance, and equipment had become too expensive. The loss of the team meant our players wouldn't be able to play summer ball unless they participated on another town's Legion team or in some other program. If players didn't make their mistakes and learn from them on summer evenings and weekends, it meant we would experience them next spring.

In some ways, I was relieved the Legion team disbanded, though I had sacrificed my car's engine the prior summer for a program that had folded anyway. The sacrifice I had made in the spring to attend every practice and game and the disappointment I had experienced with our lack of success made it easier for me to imagine a less-hectic summer. Juggling my law office schedule to attend each practice and game had been difficult. Most lawyers weren't sympathetic with a lawyer who coached high school baseball on sunny spring afternoons. I preferred to not let any lawyer who was my opponent in a case know I was a high school coach, lest they try to use it to their advantage.

During the season, I fought morning rush hour traffic on Route 8 and the Merritt Parkway to my office in Trumbull Center. In the afternoon, I rushed back to Derby, whacked ground balls and fly balls, pitched BP, showered, ate, and returned to Trumbull to finish the day's workload. While D thanked me daily for my sacrifice, I didn't know whether I wanted to return to go through it again. I needed a rest.

On most nights before games, I stopped by D's house to plan strategy. If we lost a game we should have won, I would go to his house after I returned from Trumbull to commiserate with him in our loss and keep his spirits up. He understandably missed his father's voice. He wanted to ask him how to cope with a difficult loss, how to deal each day with students who didn't want to learn, and how to be the husband and the father he wanted to be.

John's mother was a sweet woman who was protective of John, but she was rapidly turning him into the prodigal son. John's southern-accented brother Bob was a successful clinical and forensic psychologist with a busy practice 1300 miles away in Alabama, leaving John to help his mother, who didn't like to travel alone. John's mother lived less than a quarter mile from John. He visited her every night he could at 11:00 PM to make sure she was OK. If he didn't show up or at least call, she would leave him a message on his answering machine, saying that he might find her on the floor the next day. The guilt was his albatross; the cure was baseball.

A few days after the 1990 high school season ended and word got out of the demise of Derby's American Legion program, my summer sabbatical from baseball ended. I received a call from Bob Kelo, Seymour High's coach, who informed me that the Oxford American Legion Post had been searching for a new coach. Oxford's team had also been on the verge of folding, but not for lack of money, for lack of success. I told Bob I would be willing to get involved, but only as an assistant. I didn't want the responsibility of cutting players—from either Seymour or Derby if too many players tried out—or want anyone to think I was trying to take over a program designed to help Seymour High's program.

A few of our returning players at Derby were eligible to play and ended up making the Oxford team, including Willow; Pat McMahon; Donny Shepard, a lanky Sophomore pitcher who lived next door to Willow; and Brian Marcucio, our left fielder. The team also had one of our graduating players, Jeff Owens, who had turned double plays from second on the 1988 tournament team and had pitched for both our 7–13 teams. Jeff would soon play for Trinity College in Hartford. Two of our other players had been recruited to play summer ball elsewhere. Sophomore third baseman Ben Bartone and sophomore outfielder/catcher Pete Chrzanowski had hitched up with a Woodbridge Mickey Mantle league team.

That summer I overextended myself. My job pressure made it difficult to coach a rigorous American Legion season, which had more games scheduled than a high school season. In addition, while the Derby players attended most games, they lacked dedication. Their commitment level was far from what I believed necessary to return Derby High's team to the state tournament. When I learned that a few of them had skipped a Legion game to tan themselves at Milford Beach and escape the heat while I sweated with Seymour's kids on a dust-filled infield, it upset me. I hinted to the Derby players that I might not be around in the spring, as the sacrifice I had been making was too great, especially if the players were not going to reciprocate.

After the Oxford Legion season ended in August, I sat down several times with D. We discussed the fact that I was considering not coaching the next high school season to take some time away from the game. Each time the subject was approached, I sensed D thought he had something to do with my decision. I discussed the matter with him again during the fall, as I didn't want my decision to leave him without time to find other help. Before winter arrived, I told D I would not be returning.

Before the next season began, D kept asking me to reconsider. Telling him I would not be coming back and that he should seek out another volunteer was difficult. Eventually, three guys offered to help, and D thought he would be in good shape. One was George DeTullio, who had graduated with me from Derby, having played with me on the JV level. I had once caught a JV game at Shelton that George had pitched when our regular catcher had been absent. George didn't have many effective pitches. His best pitch had been a blood ball he had thrown after getting his right thumb caught in the clubhouse door on his way out of the building to board our bus. George was able to squeeze some time, as he worked nights for United Illuminating. When D was the freshman coach, George had been one of his assistants. I had heard George, or Tules as we had called him in high school, had had some problems with drugs but had gone through rehabilitation, straightened himself out, and had gotten married and had two children.

Another volunteer was Rick Lucarelli. Rick had been a pitcher/third baseman on Derby's 1977 state championship team. "Luke" had also played on the Senior Babe Ruth team I had coached and had become a Derby police officer. Another was Ron Luneau, who had played football and baseball for Derby High in the past and had been on the Babe Ruth team I coached. John was pessimistically optimistic before the start of the 1991 season. But when the season's first week rolled around, his help had been marked absent more than present and was not as dedicated as D felt he needed. D later recounted to me the result: One morning that week, after throwing an extra sweatshirt in his van, he contemplated how he was going to conduct the afternoon's practice alone. During his homeroom period, as he sat behind his desk, irrational thoughts raced through his mind.

What if nobody else shows up?

Without help, I can't hit ground balls and fly balls and still feed the pitching machine up top.

How am I going to coach infielders, outfielders, pitchers, catchers, and hitters all at once?

Without preparation, they won't be any good.
If they're no good, they can't win.
If they can't win, I'm a loser.

Not long after, he couldn't catch his breath and felt his heart racing. The 911 call was made, and two blue-shirted EMTs strapped D onto a stretcher and wheeled him out of the school and into an ambulance that rushed him to nearby Griffin Hospital.

Charlie DiCenso temporarily supervised the team's practices until D could return. Luckily, D had only suffered an anxiety attack. I visited D at his home the night of his episode and talked with him at length about what happened and everything he was going through. He was taking antianxiety medication as well as a couple other medications for a sometimes-rapid heart beat and was seeing a counselor to deal with his personal life as well as his coaching stress.

Charlie called D each day to find out how he was doing and to tell him what the team had worked on at practice. He kidded D that it wasn't hard to coach baseball. The reports only made D more uptight. He worried that the team was being shortchanged. D asked me to return for a few days a week in the late afternoon hours, but my schedule was such I couldn't. If I was going to take the time away from coaching, I couldn't return part-time. We both knew only full-time coaches can effectively teach high school players. If a coach isn't on the field with the team every day, the players notice and won't listen to what he has to say. I either had to coach every day or not at all, and I had already decided the latter. I talked with D at length about the fact that his team was comprised of experienced players, including two talented pitchers, Ben Bartone and Donny Shepard who had pitched in the summer. D decided he was going to return and try not to let the scenario get to him.

Although the team was winning in the first half of the season, the strategy wasn't working out well for D's health. I followed the team in the local newspapers and showed up at some home games when my schedule permitted. Whenever I went, I watched from behind the first base side fence. For some strange reason, several players never said hello either before or after any of the games I attended. I learned the reason from left fielder, Brian Marcucio. D had been using my absence as a motivation for the team. Brian and his twin brother, Scott, who also played, didn't agree with the silent treatment I was receiving as a result.

D had told the players prior to the season that I had quit on them and thought they were losers. Although I had been upset with some players in the summer, I didn't hold any grudge against them, and had never told D I thought they were losers. In fact, prior to the season starting, I had bought some new aluminum

Easton bats and red Wilson catcher's gear for the team. I knew the budget wouldn't cover much more than baseballs, umpires, and buses.

I never confronted D with what I had been told. From my observance of D's demeanor at games, it was clear that he was taking some sort of medication to get through them. He rarely got off the bench, didn't hit pregame infield or outfield, and was zombielike in coaching the team. George and Ronnie were doing a good job keeping the team from spinning out of control.

After the team won their tenth game and qualified for the state tournament, they planned a celebration with six-foot subs to take place after a future game. A few days later, the team lost that game but still had the Subway celebration anyway. It was unlike D to ever allow any celebration after a loss. I knew it was a sign of bad things to come. My prediction turned out accurate as the team went on a losing streak.

After the team experienced several more losses, I went to watch them play in Cheshire as my work schedule took me near their high school. I stopped at a local McDonald's on Route 10 to buy coffees for the coaching staff, as I knew it was difficult to find coffee when they had to ride the bus. As I walked into Cheshire's athletic complex and approached the right field fence, Derby took the field in the bottom of the first. The right fielder, Pete Chrzanowski, spotted me and sprinted toward me. He was running too fast to just want to say hello.

"Riles, you've got to go to our dugout right away. D is dying!" I knew from Pete's face he believed it.

"What do you mean he's dying? Has anybody called an ambulance?" In a flash, I recalled passing a pay phone on the side of the school, but it was at least a hundred yards behind me.

"I don't know. Mr. Marcucio is in the dugout. He might have."

I walked like a power walker down the right field sideline outside the fence, balancing the Styrofoam coffee cups in the recycled gray cardboard tray in my hand. I looked for D or Ken Marcucio but didn't see either. I passed Cheshire's first base dugout, but no one seemed concerned about anything happening in the other. I went around the pine-tree-shaded backstop to Derby's dugout.

Despite wearing a navy blue suit, I entered the dugout. D was hunched over, alone on the left side of the dugout; his head sagged between his shoulders. The rest of the team, all underclassmen, were crunched up on the dugout's right side, their wide open eyes fixated on D. If there had been a basement to the dugout, they would've been in it with the door securely locked. They acted as if D had a communicable disease. Sitting with his elbows on his knees, D's back rose only slightly as he fought for each slow breath. I bent over and put my head closer to him to try to determine the cause of the slight wheeze that followed. When I straightened, Ken Marcucio was standing beside me.

"What's happening, Ken?" I asked as I unbuttoned my jacket.

"John's having some sort of attack."

"Did you call an ambulance?"

"Not yet, but I may have to if he doesn't get any better."

I wiped off the bench with my hand and sat beside John. "What are you feeling, John?" I asked. Ken moved closer to catch the reply.

With his head still lowered, D replied, "I'm not feeling right. I'm having trouble breathing."

"Does the game have anything to do with it?"

"No."

I grabbed his cold left wrist and pressed my index and middle fingers over the underside, below his limp thumb. I counted to myself while I focused on the second hand of my watch. "Your pulse is OK, John. It's about the same as mine." I knew John was taking some sort of antianxiety medication. "Did you take your pills?" With his eyes closed, he shook his head from side to side as if his neck was stiff.

"Did you have anything to eat today?"

"No."

"You've got to take the medication and do what the doctor told you to do. How can you expect to get through a game without it, especially without eating?" I twisted one of the white coffee cups out of the cardboard tray, pulled the tab from the plastic lid, and handed the cup to him. "Here, John, sip some of this and take your pill."

He took a few slow sips and swallowed a tiny pill he plucked from under a cotton ball inside a small brown plastic bottle, then he leaned back against the concrete wall. A few moments later, his stomach contracted, and a burst of air shot out his mouth. "I'm still not feeling right."

"It's OK, I think you just burped the milk from the coffee."

After the inning ended and it was our turn to bat, John nudged me with his left shoulder. "Riles, go coach third base."

"I can't do that. I'm wearing a suit. I can't go on the field like this. Besides, Ronnie looks like he's doing a good job out there."

As the game continued, there came a point when I thought, *If he was feeling better, D would've gone to the mound and spoken to the pitcher, Ben Bartone.* Cheshire's hitters strung together some solid hits and threatened to burst the game open.

"D, you got to go to the mound," I said. D looked at me with heavy eyes but said nothing. "Ben needs you out there," I added. The players on the other side of the dugout looked as if I had asked D to walk across I-95 at 5:00 PM blindfolded. I thought if he got into the flow of the game, he might temporarily forget about anything bothering him. "Look at Ben out there, D. Look at him. He's battling out there, but he needs somebody to go talk to him now, and it can't be me."

To the bench brigade's amazement, D rose from the bench and crept around the fence before the dugout. He trudged up to the baseline and raised his right hand in the ump's direction like a tired traffic cop at the end of his shift. The umpire called time-out, but D had already crossed the limed barrier. Pat McMahon stood and lifted his catcher's mask. The ump removed his face mask and watched without saying a word.

Step by slow step, D labored up the crown of the infield grass to the center of all baseball attention to speak to Ben. As D left the mound, I saw a pink hue start to erase the paleness that had been on his face since I arrived. Ben looked into the dugout, shrugged his shoulders, and raised his black eyebrows as if to tell us he didn't know what the heck D was saying to him. Ben smiled as he acknowledged the sign for the next pitch. He didn't care what pitch Pat wanted him to throw; what mattered was that D was getting better.

With D feeling better, the team came back. In the top of the seventh, Derby got men on first and third with no outs. On a soft fly ball to right field, Tules had the runner on first tag up instead of going partway to second. The runner on third tagged and scored standing up, but the runner from first was tagged out trying to take second after the right fielder's throw to the plate was cut off by the first baseman. Tagging up from first base was a common move in slow-pitch softball, which Tules played a lot of, but rarely did you see it in high school baseball.

Derby got another chance to tie the score when there was a base hit to right with a runner on second, but the runner, Mike Smetana, slipped going around third when his right cleat had landed on the grass area outside the third baseline. Mike scrambled up and dashed toward home, but the bounced throw beat him to the plate. The catcher made a perfect one-knee tag. After the game, D and I strolled together to the waiting bus as if we had nowhere else to go after the game.

"It's too bad, D. You should have won this game," I said as we reached the outfield fence.

"If Smetana didn't slip going around third, we might've."

"Ben didn't pitch badly. He gave you a solid effort. Everybody did. You've got to be happy about that. I know a loss is a loss is a loss, but you can at least build on this one."

"Yeah, the kids played hard, that's all I can ask. We'll get better." D looked preoccupied as he stood with one foot in and one foot out the bus.

"How about you? You feeling better?" I asked. "Are you going to be able to take the bus back?"

"I'm OK. I just have to take my pills, and I'll be all right. I'm feeling better now."

"Good," I said. "I'll call you tonight."

The driver reached across and pulled the silver handle, shutting the double doors in front of me. As the bus rolled and roared away and I slid into the seat of my car, I realized that I missed the bus rides with the team and D, even the ones from Cheshire.

Although the losing streak continued, D became himself again. By the time the regular season ended, the team was 12–8 and waiting for their draw in the postseason tournament. Derby qualified for the tournament, but you would've thought they hadn't. When the time came to prepare, D's assistants were unavailable to help. Luke said he had somehow contracted severe poison ivy on his crotch, and Tules was having trouble switching his work schedule. Ronnie couldn't be there either until the week of tournament play.

John asked me again to help. He feared he might otherwise be alone. The team had a chance at a championship, and he didn't want the team shortchanged. I told him I might be able to take some time off from my practice as my schedule had temporarily freed up, but my return wouldn't work if the players didn't want my help. I didn't want to appear as someone who came around now that the team was in the tournament. John said he didn't care and that he wanted me there. I told him I didn't want to get involved if even one team member objected. The day after we spoke, John claimed the team unanimously desired me to assist, and I could start helping the team if my schedule permitted. I wondered if the team ever did vote.

As John had suspected, on the first day of tournament preparation, he and I were the only coaches present. The players were undisciplined, and even after twenty games still lacked leadership among themselves. Each time someone failed at a drill or a play, they bickered. To an English teacher, they were the modern-day baseball version of the *Lord of the Flies*. They ignored most of what D tried to get across. During one session of batting practice at the cage, Ben and Donny picked up old, waterlogged, and tattered baseballs from the dirty, white canvas bag and smashed them over a wooded embankment beyond the adjacent t-ball field. One of them was a coverless baseball, and they laughed as it flew across the field with its stringy tail.

I had seen similar behavior in Ben when he had been a freshman. Once, Ben had decided to skip practice. D had found out from some other players that Ben had been seen playing basketball at a friend's house close to Ryan Field. The next day at school, D had told Ben he had been suspended from the team indefinitely. He informed Ben that he wouldn't be able to participate until he had met with him and his father about whether Ben would continue playing baseball for Derby High. Ben's face turned whiter than a baseball fresh out the box. D knew Ben's worst fear was that Ralph would find out he had skipped practice and been suspended. Ben begged D not to tell his father and promised never to miss practice again. Since that day two years ago, Ben never had. But when D didn't react to Ben's juvenile behavior this time, I didn't think it was my place to say anything to Ben or Donny—except to try to convince them what they were doing was stupid.

Brian and Scott Marcucio and Pete Chrzanowski had been glad to see me return, and it felt good to be back with them to continue the quest for a championship. Despite the eighty-plus degree temperature in the end of May, I wore my gray sweatpants with four-pocket coaches' shorts over them and a red sweatshirt to practice. Pete guessed I had worn heavier-than-needed clothing to symbolically tell the team it was a new season—as if it were March 15 and everybody in the tournament had started out with no wins and no losses. Brian thought I was telling them that for me it was March 15, since it was my first day of the season, even though it wasn't for the rest of the team. Both Pete and Brian were correct.

During the preparation week, Tules appeared whenever he could. Each time he pushed a dimple ball through the JUGS machine, he challenged the players with his deep voice and livened up the practices.

With our 12–8 record, we at least were able to host our first round game against the Bacon Academy Bobcats of Colchester. The result wasn't the way the Bobcats had envisioned their postseason would end. They had endured an hour-and-fifteen-minute bus ride on a hot yellow school bus to get blown out and shut out, 11–0. Ben Bartone pitched six innings. In a moment of weakness, D let senior center fielder John Anroman pitch the last inning. Johnny was not one of the regular pitchers, but he had practiced as a pitcher during the preseason pitchers and catchers' week and had experience pitching when he played in the Babe Ruth league. Bacon Academy never knew they not only couldn't score against our best pitcher but also got zeroed by a senior who hadn't pitched since he was a freshman.

During the fall, John Anroman had been a running back on the football team. Before last season, Anroman's father had begged D to take his son on the baseball team. He had believed that if Johnny didn't play baseball he would get into trouble. Since D was an assistant football coach, Mr. Anroman knew D could keep his son on the right path. I knew Johnny from my days coaching Babe Ruth. Though he hadn't been on my regular season team, I had coached him on the all-stars. Johnny was an athlete, and, like most athletes, he could play almost any sport and excel at it. While his baseball skills were raw, they were still good enough for him to snag a starting spot in the outfield. Johnny's speed put him in center field, but his head always put him in D's doghouse.

Last year, before one practice began, Johnny had shown up barefoot. He thought he had escaped our workout. D had innocently told him to go to center field anyway and do his best. We whacked Shoeless Johnny fly balls and line drives, which coincidentally landed on the hot, black cinder track that cut across center field. Johnny got the message and had never come to practice without his spikes again.

In the second round of the tournament, we played the Nonnewaug of Woodbury Chiefs at their field. By virtue of their better record, Nonnewaug had earned the higher seed and home field advantage. Before we got on the school bus to travel twenty miles north up Route 8 and Route 67 to Woodbury, we decided to take batting practice on our field. We didn't want the Chiefs to know anything about our hitters. Also, whenever we played on someone else's field, we never knew whether our opponent would allow us to take batting practice or if there was anywhere to take it.

The last player to take batting practice hit a high fly ball to deep right. As the ball was in flight, a few players were walking together across right field toward our clubhouse and the street where our idling bus was parked. Among them was Donny Shepard, who was scheduled to pitch. Donny had already hit and felt he had shagged enough fly balls. As Donny was walking with the group, he wasn't watching the batted ball plummet from the clear sky toward him. Before it hit the outfield grass, the hardball struck the small bones on top of Donny's pitching hand. His right hand began to swell. We threw some ice in a plastic bag, covered his hand before he climbed on the bus, and hoped for the best.

Donny was able to pitch, but he squeezed and opened his right hand after every batter he faced. He gutted it out and pitched well enough to get us to the late innings, so we didn't need to bring in Ben on short rest until near the end of the game. We hit the ball hard and scored some runs, but Nonnewaug's pitcher had an effective "atom" ball. Whatever pitch he threw, we hit the ball hard, but right at them (Nonnewaug's fielders) for outs. Baseball can be cruel that way. Hard line-drive outs never show up in your batting average and can sometimes make you a goat, but bloop singles or swinging bunts can sometimes make you a hero. As the 1930s Yankee pitcher Lefty Gomez is believed to have coined, "I'd rather be lucky than good."

Things went from unlucky to unbearable. Pete doubled but ended up getting picked off second base on the old hidden ball trick. John Anroman decided to avoid the sun by sitting on a rickety old backless bench under a maple tree in deep center field during our change of pitchers. He kicked his feet up like an executive. D screamed at him louder than the steam whistle bird on the *Flintstones*. Assistant Coach Luneau got into a shouting match with our shortstop, Joey Martin, for pouting after Joe hit a Howitzer to right field that tailed exactly where the outfielder was positioned for an out. We almost needed Mills Lane to separate them. But despite the chaos, we were still in the game.

In the bottom of the sixth inning with a tie game, the bases loaded, and a three-two pitch, Ben threw a straight fastball right down the middle. Our catcher, Pat McMahon, never moved his mitt. As the batter stood frozen in his stance, Ben started to run off the field, but the home plate ump called ball four.

The hometown call caused the umpires to lose control of the game. It turned ugly. We were angry, our fans were angry, and we ended up losing. In Derby, that's a recipe for certain disaster. When the close contest ended, the shouting and finger-pointing at the puffed-up man in blue didn't, and it was a long way for him to his car. If we weren't playing at Nonnewaug's field with umpires from Nonnewaug's league, I believe we would have gone on to the quarterfinals.

Our fans got into it with Nonnewaug's fans, who should have simply shut up and been thankful for the gift they had gotten from the hometown ump. Eventually, our players got into it with their players. Lucky for Nonnewaug's kids, we were able to encircle our team and corral them onto our bus without a riot starting. Nonnewaug's field was about a half mile away from where our bus could park. Our kids were itching their noses, and they would have kicked the crap out of the Nonnewaug players, as most of our team members were also football players. They didn't need much of a reason to commence a slugfest. Nonnewaug didn't even have a football team.

On the bus ride back, I sat across from D and beside a pile of zippered canvas ball bags. The bus shifted into another gear and jolted forward and back. "I believe I could make my schedule work next year for the whole season again," I said, raising my voice over the steady roar of a school bus in second gear.

D flicked the ashes from his cigarette out the adjacent window. "I don't know, Riles," he replied. "I'm tired. It was a tough season for me. I have to think about what I'm going to do."

"The year off gave me a chance to ask myself why I coached in the first place," I explained. "I like the challenge of trying to get us in the tournament every year, but, more important, I also realized I coached for the comradery of the coaches. I missed that."

At that moment, Pete maneuvered his way purposefully toward the front of the bus and sat behind D, leaning over the top of the seat like a kid watching his favorite afternoon TV show. "You coming back next year, Riles?" he asked with a dimpled, youthful smile.

"I'll come back if D comes back. If not, I'm out."

D dragged the smoke deep into his lungs and exhaled like a man without a worry. "If you come back, Riles, I'll come back."

Pete smiled as if he just crossed home plate, turned, and began to make his way to the back of the rocking bus. "Yesssss," he said under his breath as he pumped his right arm and grabbed the top of a seat with his left to keep from tumbling. We were losing six starting position players, but D was still grinning. "We still got Donny and Ben back. They got thirteen wins this season."

"Yeah, but pitching isn't everything," I pointed out. "We still got a lot of holes to fill."

"Riles, if pitching is, as they say, 75 percent of the game, we should be OK."

I looked at the water dripping down the side of the orange Gatorade bucket in the aisle between us. I twisted the bucket's dirty, white lid to stop the flow. I wondered why we hadn't dumped the water out at Nonnewaug's field before we had gotten on the bus, then remembered why it hadn't been our first priority. "Who makes up those stats anyway, pitchers?" I asked.

"I don't know, Riles, but there has to be a reason they say that."

13

Team Meeting 1992

After the Thanksgiving Day football game of 1991 had ended and I had promised Pete I would see him in the spring, I walked past the black-and-white scoreboard above me. I glanced at the final score: Visitors 27, Derby 14. I knew the electronic board would be turned off long before the booster club's concession stand closed, the goal post padding and goal line markers were packed away, and the clubhouse was empty. Turning off the scoreboard used to be one of the last tasks completed before the field closed down, so that cars driving by could still catch a glimpse of the final score as they traveled up Chatfield Street—but not today.

While I walked up toward the gate on the north side of the field, I heard the sound of dry leaves being kicked by the fans around me, hastening to beat the gridlock out of the parking lots that followed most Derby football games. Many of the fans I passed talked about how bad Derby was. "Six turnovers," grumbled an elderly fan, as if his holiday were ruined.

"Three interceptions," bemoaned another, shaking his head.

"If Bartone couldn't take a snap from the shotgun without fumbling, why didn't they give the other kid a chance?" asked another as he jostled his keys. Nobody mentioned that Shelton was clearly the dominant team. Nobody mentioned the effort of the undersized, outmanned, and overmatched Derby gridiron warriors, despite the loss. To them it didn't matter; they didn't get it done, and the Streak was over.

After I squeezed through the gate, I walked across the all-dirt softball infield to the sidewalk beyond the first baseline. The sidewalk cut through a steep, wooded hill that led to the upper parking lots adjacent to the high school. I grabbed the black metal handrail that divided the walkway and started my ascent. The horns of Shelton cars began the celebration, accompanied by the echoed sounds of stadium horns.

I continued up the walkway and, after stopping momentarily to catch my breath, told myself not to look back. But I couldn't resist a glance through the barren row of maple trees at the white two-story clubhouse across the football field. I wondered how badly Gino, Donny, and Ben would take the loss. When I reached my car in the upper parking lot, I proceeded into a line of cars already backed up a quarter mile. As I sat waiting for the line to move, I wondered what Big Lou would have said to them and thought about giving D a call.

During that winter, D and I met up during and after the holidays. D lamented the end of the Streak and the total frustration of the eleven-week football season. D rocked faster in his favorite upholstered living room chair whenever we discussed our annual fear that the baseball players who also played on the basketball team would turn into undisciplined losers. We knew Joey G., Pete Chrzanowski, and the freshman kid Joe Lizza played basketball.

Several times with tongue in cheek, I mentioned to D we should give coaching the basketball team a crack. About every three years, the varsity basketball job became vacant. Each new, idealistic coach took about three seasons to get sick of watching the other teams double their point output, the other teams put their scrubs in before halftime, or the visitor's side of the scoreboard rollover. In three years, the coach would finally realize the prospect of changing things was dim and resign, hoping only to get a one-liner in the *Evening Sentinel.*

Since the basketball team only averaged one or two wins a year, I often asked D how we could do any worse. I posited to him my theory that, if we were coaching the basketball team, we could persuade everyone on the baseball team to sign up. We could run drills in practice that also enhanced a player's baseball skills. I envisioned throwing in a few plays similar to hit-and-run plays or steals, and every time there was a loose ball we could train the boys to go after it as if they were sliding headfirst into second base. If the basketball team was going to lose in front of fans who left by halftime anyway, perhaps no one other than the players would even notice we were practicing baseball during the basketball games and practices. All we would have to do was blow a whistle.

When the basketball season ended, it was no surprise they had wound up with a losing record again, finishing 1–19. There was no uproar to remove the coach, no letters to the editor, and not a single parent complained that their son wasn't given enough playing time. Nobody cared. I knew the way they had lost would make it much more difficult to instill a winning attitude into the former basketball players on our team. Unless the baseball team amassed a winning record, this year's senior class would graduate with the dubious distinction of not having any major sport with a winning record. At the least, the baseball team would have to make the postseason state tournament to salvage something.

Every year in the first week of March, D scheduled his initial team meeting after school in Room 121, his corner classroom. At the meeting, he ripped a single sheet of lined white paper from a cheap one-subject spiral notebook for the freshmen coming out to print their name, address, phone number, and position played. If he passed out a sign-up sheet for the returning players, it would have looked like a major league all-star ballot when it was returned. As the timid rookies watched in silence, D spoke to the returning players about pitchers and catchers' week as well as the schedule of scrimmages.

My brother-in-law, the junior varsity baseball coach, Jocko Veillette, leaned against the blackboard with Tules. His full-time job was as a route man for Stella D'ora. Jocko was a right fielder on my Senior Babe Ruth team back in 1977 but had never gone out for the baseball team at Derby High. Jocko's passion in high school had been football. He had been the "monster back" when he had played for Coach DeFilippo. He had also played Division II college football for a couple of seasons for the University of New Haven and was the headhunter on their kick-off team. The head hunter is the guy who runs with reckless abandon toward any wedge-blocking scheme the returning team on a kickoff might set up and smashes his way though it.

Jocko had a rapport with the football players on our team; he spoke their language. Jocko was also famous for his—as we called them—"Jockoisms," or nonsensical statements. Prior to the season, Jocko had been the freshman basketball coach. In one of his halftime speeches, Jocko had tried to lambaste his hapless harriers but had yelled, "You're playing like your butts are up your asses." Word of that one had rippled throughout the gym. They didn't break the mold after they made Yogi Berra, it just morphed into Jocko.

Ben entered the bright classroom without plaster around his wrist; I thought that was at least a good sign. I learned Donny had had his arm blessed by the reverend at his church, so I knew he had taken his preparation for the season seriously. Pete, Ben, and Donny sat in the front row with Joey G. and Gino DiMauro behind them.

Last year, on the prom day practice, I had whacked ground balls to Gino's left, right, and straight at him until his legs had turned into rubber. He hadn't complained. D had used that practice day each year to work with the kids who weren't going to the prom. In most years, it was the bulk of the JV team. During the prom practice last year, I had dubbed Gino the Pizza Box kid. He wasn't fleet of foot and didn't look like he was going to win any Presidential Physical Fitness

Awards, but I liked his spunk. I asked Gino once during batting practice whether he had ever hit a home run in his life. He said he had, but then he had woken up.

In the second row at the meeting was Joe Lizza, the king-sized freshman who Pete had told me about. His 6'2" 250-pound frame looked cramped in the desk he sat in. I never saw a freshman baseball player at Derby that I couldn't walk side by side through a doorway with before. Whenever Joe talked, his neck became bulled. No wonder he was nicknamed "Horse." I learned from D that Joe's uncle was Ernie DiStasi, a former Ansonia catcher who had played minor-league baseball for the Mets after they had drafted him in the tenth round in 1971. Joe's mother, Rose Lizza, worked at Derby High.

George Hay, a two-way football end and first baseman and Carlos Ortiz, a football lineman who also played first base on the JV team when Jocko didn't put his 250-pound frame into left field, lounged in the last row before the gray cinderblock wall. Junior Mike Massie, a football defensive back and a JV pitcher/outfielder last year who was always asking his girlfriend, "What did I do?" also sat in the far row. Adjacent to Mike was Junior Ken Cronk, an outfielder/pitcher on the JV team who significantly raised our team's average SAT score. Juniors Rich Calvert and Greg Malyska, who were both on the wrestling team, sat next to each other in the third row. Sitting beside them was Junior Angelo DiRubba, Nicky's younger brother, who was a JV outfielder as well as a linebacker on the football team.

Also sitting in the back, looking as if they needed bigger seats, were Juniors Rob Zielinski and Brent "Tiny" Cavallaro, both two-way lineman on the football team. Sophomores Keith Trimarki, Shawn Bittman, and Jeff Robinson, all of whom were on the football team, filled in the middle seats. David Anroman, a junior tailback on the football team and the younger brother of John Anroman, rested on top of the floor-mounted air conditioner in the far left corner of the room next to Tules. When I coached Johnny on the Babe Ruth all-star team, David had been a member of the Little League all-star team. In the far-right hand side of the back of the room sat the timid freshmen who were scribbling their names, addresses, and phone numbers on the official sign-up sheet.

"Everybody shut up," barked Ben over his shoulder with a feigned look of anger. "Go ahead, D."

"Thanks, Benjy," said D with a grin that disappeared faster than an umpire after a game. "I shouldn't have to tell you last year was a disappointment. We should've beaten Nonnewaug and gone on to the quarters. Nonnewaug lost by one run in the quarters to Trinity Catholic, who ended up winning the whole thing. I shouldn't have to remind you about the disappointment of the football season either. For the seniors, this season is your last chance to redeem yourselves from the loser label. Everyone thinks you are losers—the town, the teachers, your fellow students…even Charlie thinks you're losers. Riles, you got anything to say?"

I paused as if I had something monumental to say. "I'm just glad to be here," I said. Pete laughed, since at the prior initial team meetings I had attended that's all I had said.

After the players filed out of D's classroom, the student desks pointed in more directions than a broken compass. D said he wanted to continue with a private meeting of the coaches. D unraveled his spring green tie and motioned us to follow him to the teachers' lounge, which was adjacent the school's cafeteria. He wanted to talk about the upcoming season away from the players still mulling around in the hallways. I knew from past experience that going to the teachers' lounge gave D a chance to smoke without finding a written warning the next day in his teacher's mailbox atop his prior ones. When we entered the rectangular lounge, it was empty.

A faint odor of ammonia told me the janitors had come and gone. D, Tules, and Jocko pulled some molded plastic chairs from under a folding table, causing the metal legs to screech across the shiny linoleum floor. I approached the Coca-Cola machine on the room's opposite end.

"Anyone want one?"

"No thanks, Riles," came a reply.

My wrinkled dollar bill was rejected faster than a lopsided baseball. "Ugh," I said as I shook my head. "I hate when this happens." As I put the bill into the thin metal slot again, D brought up Ben again.

"We just have to find out from the get-go whether Ben can play," pointed out D as he lit up a cigarette. "The football season was all screwed up since nobody knew whether Ben was coming back."

The red and silver Coke inside the machine banged and crashed its way to the bottom. I pulled the cold can out, popped the tab, and returned to the table. "Why didn't they just assume he was out for the season?" I asked.

"Maybe they should have, but it wasn't that easy," D replied. "You see, since the backup wasn't as good as Ben, they kept hoping against hope Ben would return before the season was over."

"Well, we gotta know if he's playing or not playing," added Tules as he leaned back in his chair. For a moment, I wondered how strong his chair was.

"Exactly," Jocko interjected.

D took a long drag from his cigarette. "The football coaches didn't think Ben wanted to return as fast as they thought maybe he should have," D said. "Ralph was thinking about the fact that Ben also played baseball and didn't want to hurt his chances of playing baseball either."

It was the first time I could recall any parent worrying a football injury could hamper their son's interest in playing baseball at Derby High. The controversy about Ben's delay in returning to football was hard for me to believe. Here we were, in the middle of March, talking about an injury Ben had been feeling the effects of since September.

"We just have to know whether he can pitch," I added. "If he can at least do that, maybe we can DH for him."

"Yeah, but can he even field a ball hit back to the mound or swing a bat?" Tules replied.

"How bad was he hurt, D?" Jocko asked.

"Pretty bad. He had extensive surgery; they put in pins and stuff. He just got the cast off."

"You know, D," I said as somebody pulled on the solid wood door but didn't enter, "maybe what we could do—when Ben gets his turn in the batting cage—is use those plastic pickle balls in the JUGS machine. That way we could ease Ben into hitting without any risk of hurting him, and he won't be afraid to get hit."

"This is crazy," D said as he tapped his cigarette on the edge of a coaster-sized silver paper ashtray. "We just have to find out once and for all what his limitations are. I'll ask Ralph if he can get Ben examined again. Let's see what Dr. Lewis says about what Ben can or can't do. Then we'll go from there."

After coming to a conclusion about Ben, the conversation switched to the other players and the possibilities we had of putting a team together. At that point, Ron Luneau, who I heard wouldn't be able to help D out this year, entered the lounge. "Hey, guys, I don't know if you realize this, but Ben, Donny, and Gino were standing outside the door trying to listen to everything you were saying." Jocko and I popped up and stepped outside the door. I saw them scurry away farther down the hallway with their backs to us and turn a corner. We didn't call out to them.

After the meeting, we exited the empty cafeteria into the school's main foyer. Ben was standing alone before the glass entrance doors. Gino and Donny were nowhere in sight. Ben told D he was waiting for a ride home. D seized the chance to talk to Ben and offered him one. Although I think Ben was reluctant to step into D's van (all the players knew D could never teach driver's ed), he disappeared down the front steps with him. I told Jocko, if Ben had enough guts to jump into a vehicle with D behind the wheel, I found it hard to believe he was milking any lingering injury to his wrist. The next day, D told me that during his drive with Ben he had recommended a final exam with his orthopedic surgeon, so Ben could determine what his limitations were and we could determine how to proceed with the season.

Ben did schedule an appointment that week with his orthopedic surgeon, Dr. William Lewis. Through the years, Dr. Lewis had treated injured football team members. If Dr. Lewis told Ben he couldn't do a certain physical activity, D felt it was the truth, since he believed Doc Lewis was not one to coddle an athlete's injury. D learned from Ben's dad that Dr. Lewis had stated that Ben's wrist was healed about as good as it was going to get and that Ben should slowly increase his activity. We hoped the diagnosis was enough to convince Ben it was OK to start swinging a bat again.

The Monday after pitchers and catchers' conditioning week was over, we were officially allowed to commence a full practice. As planned, whenever Ben took batting practice, we fed white plastic pickled balls into the JUGS machine instead of hardballs. His first time in the cage, Ben took fifteen tentative swings and got out. A couple pitches tailed inside and bounced off him. The next day he took twenty hacks. Each day he increased the number of swings. The plastic ball strategy worked. After the first week, Ben decided to swing at hardballs. Though he guarded his wrist with every inside pitch as if it would crack like a Twix bar if it were hit, the preseason scrimmages showed him it was possible for him to hit in competition.

If Ben could field, we would have a shortstop whenever Donny pitched. Last year, Ben had made the all-state team as a third baseman. The switch could cost him the chance of repeating on the team since, each year, shortstops outnumbered third basemen on coaches' all-state ballots. Ben unselfishly agreed to play shortstop whenever he didn't pitch.

Although the situation with Ben was solved, we still had to put a team together. We learned Joe Lizza was good enough to put behind the plate. His bat speed was good enough to hit varsity pitching, remarkable for any freshman. We decided to bat him fourth in the lineup, as we felt he might be able to sneak up on teams who pitched around Donny Shepard, our third hitter. Joe's arm wasn't as strong or as accurate as Pete's and he frequently complained of soreness with it, but it was adequate enough for us to allow Pete to anchor the outfield in center field.

Joey G. proved he could field routine ground balls and throw across the diamond to first. Gino DiMauro was able to body bang the ball down at second base, pick it up, and throw a hitter out at first. The only weird thing was that Gino preferred to do it with his plastic protective goggles on. Though a stiff wind could change his course, Mike Massie showed he could chase and catch fly balls in left field with Ryan Field's eight-foot chain-link fence behind him.

David Anroman's running back speed proved him the better fit for right field, as our field didn't have a fence in right. In the scrimmages, however, we learned putting David in right had its downside. His attention was everywhere but the game whenever any of his football buddies watched him play from the adjacent football stands. We solved the problem by having Jocko sit at the bottom of the right field stands whenever we spotted David's fellow football players. Like an automaton, before every pitch, Jocko cupped his hands around his mouth and shouted, "Romo, get ready."

George Hay didn't talk much. For some reason, he removed his hat whenever he had the chance. George was a decent power hitter and proved he could dig out bad throws at first base. He was a tall target, which made it easier for our infielders to throw to first.

When Sean Barker, the local *Evening Sentinel* reporter, contacted D to give his outlook on the season, D stated, "If pitching is 80 percent of the game like they say it is, I've got the two kids coming back who won all my games for me last year. I guess we're in pretty good shape."[3] The day after the article appeared in the paper, I asked D what made the percentage go up from seventy-five.

During our practices, prior to the season opener, a short, stocky old man with short, thick fingers wearing black-framed glasses showed up. His first name was Mickey. I never knew his last name. Mickey hung around the clubhouse and struck up a friendship with the kids. When Lou DeFilippo coached football at Derby, several retired gentlemen had watched every practice and attended every game. Lou had named them the "Sparrows." Mickey was more than a sparrow. He shagged foul balls for us without being asked and quietly put them back in the dirty canvas ball bag. Without hesitation, Mickey did anything else D asked him to do, like retrieve something from the clubhouse we might've forgotten or needed before carrying our equipment to the field.

The boys took a liking to Mickey, as he brought them treats every day. Before one practice, Mickey sat on the park bench adjacent the clubhouse doors and waited for the players and coaches to file out. As the players put their hats on under the afternoon sun, Mickey ripped open boxes of half-melted ice cream sandwiches that disappeared down the food chain, with only a couple left for the JV players to share.

My wife, Sue, wanted to go to as many games as she could. Although she had attended few past games, I finally convinced her she might enjoy them. Since I bought her a new Canon 35MM SLR camera, she decided she wanted to take action shots during each game, get them developed, and have me hand them out to the players. I liked the idea, since I could also use the photos as a coaching tool. The shots would show the players what they were doing wrong, reinforce what they were doing right, and give them mementos of their high school playing days. I knew Sue would soon become proficient in knowing when to click the high-speed pictures. She also planned on taking snapshots of team members who weren't in the game but were encouraging players on the field, keeping the scorebook, or doing something else to contribute, so they didn't feel left out.

14

The Season Begins

The afternoon of our opening day game against Kolbe Cathedral High School of Bridgeport, I arrived in the clubhouse with a crusty Italian submarine sandwich from a place in Shelton off old Route 8 called the Full Belly Deli. On the way to the field each day, I picked up a salami, lettuce, tomato, and Gulden's mustard-covered sandwich. D was already in the coaches' room dressed in his red and white uniform, which looked like he had slept in it the night before. We sat across from each other on gray metal folding chairs. He looked like a man in the middle of a hunger strike.

"You want a chunk of this?" I asked as I unrolled the manila sandwich wrapper that was twice the size of the footlong sandwich.

"Nah."

I lifted the sandwich in both hands but didn't take a bite. "Did you eat yet?"

"I can't," he said as he handed me a line-up card, the kind we got for free each year from Blanchette Sporting Goods in Shelton.

"What do you mean you can't?" I asked as I turned the card over on my chair. "What was for lunch today in school?"

"I don't know."

"You mean you had no lunch today at all?" He shook his bowed head from side to side. I ripped the grinder in two and put the half sandwich before him. "Have some of this," I said. I wiped the scattered crumbs and shredded lettuce off my pin-striped navy blue suit. "How the frick can you coach a game without eating any lunch?"

D took a bite, hitting a glob of the spicy brown mustard. A burning sensation shot through his sinuses and down his nose. "Whoa," he said as he lifted his head and breathed heavily through his widened nostrils. He took another bite.

"Good stuff, huh? Now you're ready to coach."

Kolbe Cathedral was one of our two nonleague games. Each year we tried to schedule our first two games against nonleague foes we felt we had a better than fair chance of beating. If we won those two games, it would begin a winning streak and give our kids confidence going into the eighteen-game league schedule. To qualify for the postseason state tournament, you had to have at least a .500 record. If we won those two games, we only had to go 8–10 against the competition in our league, but it was still no easy task.

Although we needed to beat our two nonleague opponents, we also had to make sure we didn't win by too great a margin. If we blew a team's doors in, they might not choose to schedule us the following year. This year was the first time we ever scheduled a game against Kolbe Cathedral. We scheduled the second nonleague game against Emmett O'Brien Regional Vocational Technical School. For many tech school athletes, sports took a backseat to finding a job, getting a car, or having a girlfriend to walk the halls with. O'B Tech, however, was a rival for us. The school was in neighboring Ansonia, and some of the players lived in Derby.

When we scheduled Kolbe, we knew their record last year wasn't good, but they had hired a new coach named Kurt Kepshire, who had previously pitched on the St. Louis Cardinals for the "White Rat," Whitey Herzog. D and I met at D's house the night before the game. We decided to throw Donny Shepard and, depending on Donny's pitch count and the score, give Ben a couple of innings, as our next game wasn't until the following week. We also discussed a strategy D had thought of. He wanted to somehow stroke Kepshire's ego with the hope he would let his guard down and not realize he was in for a dogfight until it was too late.

When Kolbe arrived at our field, D took three new pearl white Wilson 1010s, met with the strong-chinned Kepshire near home plate, and asked if he would sign them for him and our team. Kepshire readily agreed and started to tell D about his playing days with the Cardinals. When D returned to the dugout, he lamented we had to use new baseballs to accomplish the task; they could now only be used in practice. He chucked them into our canvas ball bag like somebody would toss dirty pairs of socks into a hamper.

I don't know whether D's strategy of stroking Kepshire's ego worked or not, but we ended up walloping Kolbe 14–0. Once we were safely ahead, we emptied the bench and tried to keep the score respectable so they might consider scheduling us next year. Donny and Ben combined for fourteen strikeouts. Our freshman catcher, Joe Lizza, broke into varsity baseball, crushing a three-run homer beyond our left field fence. George Hay also proved he was capable of hitting the ball hard. He lined a three-run double that dented the fence in the left center gap.

Our second scheduled game was against Emmett O'Brien, but it was rained out. Our Housatonic League schedule began against the Seymour Wildcats, one of our Valley rivals. The game was scheduled to take place at the Wildcats's home field, French Memorial Park in Seymour. I arrived at our clubhouse with two foot-long subs from the Full Belly Deli in a brown paper bag. I knew I would repeat the ritual before every game. The only way I was going to convince D to eat was to shove a sandwich in front of him and guilt him into taking a bite. Some players ended up eating the other half of mine and some of D's. The players couldn't believe anyone had named their store the Full Belly Deli. They vowed to check it out themselves to see whether I was joking.

As we were walking to the bus, D and I noticed Joe Lizza had gotten a buzz haircut that revealed the number 45 on the side of his head. Though having a unique haircut for football was nothing new in Derby—in years past players got Mohawks or shaved their entire heads—it was the first time I saw anyone sport one for baseball. D then helped Mickey step up on the bus. As far as he was concerned, Mickey was part of the staff.

While the Wildcats had a great pitcher named Rob Cafaro who could throw an 85 mph fastball, D and I also heard he was a temperamental pitcher. If we got him riled, he might act out or start walking hitters. If he did, we also knew his coach, our friend Bob Kelo, might remove him from the game. Kelo didn't tolerate any outbursts from his players or walks from his pitchers. Whether you were a star or not didn't matter to him. If you didn't play the game the way it should be played and throw strikes, you'd be on the bench. Our team rattled Cafaro's nerves and Coach Kelo removed him from the mound, but the strategy backfired on us. Cafaro's replacement, Jay Ambrosio, struck out eight in four innings of shutout relief.

At the end of the seventh inning, the score was tied 4–4. Ben put us in a position to win, having whiffed ten Seymour batters. With nobody out in the bottom of the first extra inning, Ben surrendered his first walk. A rare passed ball put the runner on second. The Wildcats all-state catcher, Billy Brooks, stepped to the plate, bounced, and spun his bat. Billy took a swing for the fence in right center, but the ball rolled in the infield grass. With his running back speed, Billy beat the throw to first. On the next pitch, he stole second unchallenged, leaving runners on second and third.

We brought Donny and Joey G. up until their spikes hit grass. Seymour's quiet third baseman, Jeff Little, stepped to the plate. He swung his bat back and forth until Ben kicked. "Squeeze!" came the delayed cry from D and me. With no outs, we hadn't expected Little to square.

Joey G. charged hard from third, but the ball popped up between third base and the pitcher's mound. It flew past Joey G., allowing the game-winning run to score. Joey had made a great effort to catch the ball in the air. If he had been able to snag it, we would have likely been able to get out of the inning on a triple play, since Seymour's runner on second base had also bolted on the pitch.

We couldn't afford to dwell on our tough loss to the Cats. Two days later, we faced our next league foe, the Lyman Hall Trojans of Wallingford at home. As I stood near our first base side dugout before the game at Ryan Field began, I noticed a familiar young man in a wheelchair parked in dead center field behind the four-foot chain-link fence. After I squinted through my glasses, I knew it was Michael Regan. The guy behind the chair wearing glasses and tending to Michael was Ray Ray Montini, the middle of four Montini brothers who had played football at Derby High. Ray Ray was Michael's friend and about his age.

At the age of eleven, Michael had tragically injured his neck when he had fallen from a slide—which, along with chain-link swings, wooden seesaws, and a horseless merry-go-round had been built adjacent to the clubhouse—landing on his head. The severe trauma to his neck had left Michael a quadriplegic. At the time of his devastating injury in November of 1980, Michael had been a little blond boy who lived in one of the three-story blocks of apartments on Hawkins Street's south side, near where Pokey, Willow, and Donny Shepard lived.

Before his tragedy, Michael had been a talented player on the Derby Pop Warner football team, on a path to someday be an integral part of the Derby High School football tradition. At the time of his injury, a Derby High football game had been in progress. I had been there. I had spotted the ambulance crew tending to someone near a pile of leaves in the unenclosed playground area off in the distance from where I was sitting but hadn't known what the commotion was about. The next day, I learned the full extent of the tragedy.

After his injury, Michael had continued to attend most Derby High football games. I always saw him in a corner of an end zone with Ray Ray beside him. Michael had befriended several of our players as well as D, who referred to him as Reegers. Michael had also watched our first home game from the same center field spot. I mentioned to D that if Reegers was going to attend our home games, why not let him sit in the dugout instead of beyond the center field fence. Without hesitance, D agreed. We sent somebody out to ask Mike if he would like a better view of the game from our dugout, but he declined.

If Reegers had watched the game from inside our dugout instead of deep center field, he would have seen me chewing away on a double wad of Bazooka; the game was tied going into the bottom half of the sixth. With one out, David

Anroman doubled. The Lyman Hall infielders and pitcher, Mark Acero, didn't respect Dave's speed. He shuffled off second far enough to tempt D to call for a steal. D looked at the ground before him, then flashed me the steal sign to relay to Dave from my third base coaching box. After Acero came set and lifted his front foot, Dave tore up the infield dirt and sped toward third. With arms stretched like a wishbone, Romo dove headfirst to the back side of the base. Romo wasn't a student of the game like Pete, Donny, or Ben, but he knew what it was like to run and dive. The player who profiled his face in our team picture was a natural at stealing. "Safe!" yelled the umpire as Romo popped up quicker than toast and dusted himself off.

Mike Massie then hit a short fly ball to center field. "Tag!" I screamed. "Tag!" Romo tagged up, but with the wrong foot. "Left foot, Romo!" I yelped. "Left foot!" Romo turned toward the fielder.

When the center fielder caught the ball, Romo pushed off the base and dashed for the plate. With Romo's speed, only a perfect throw could get him.

Romo slid like a shuffleboard puck toward the plate.

The catcher caught the ball up the third baseline. A cloud of dust appeared like a magic act.

The catcher swept his tag.

"Safe!" screamed the umpire as he waved his arms. Romo swaggered toward our dugout; Massie was credited with a sac fly and RBI. Donny Shepard didn't have his best stuff, but he had enough to get the side out in the seventh, making Romo's run the winning one in a 5–4 victory. While Romo and Massie teamed for our go-ahead run, the game also showed us Ben was still able to hit the ball well, despite his prior wrist injury. He ended up three-for-three.

Our fourth game was against Mark Sheehan High, Wallingford's other high school. Sheehan couldn't use their own field; their grounds crew discovered jagged glass each time they dragged the infield. Since Sheehan's field was unplayable, we traveled to Lyman Hall's field. D and I thought that might be an advantage for us. We knew the effect a lack of a home field could have on a high school team's psyche. Road warriors are hard to create. The twenty-game season hadn't even started yet, and a team could think nobody cared about them enough to make sure the field was ready for the season. It was not the same as pitching on your own mound, hitting off your own background, or sitting in your own dugout.

We were also glad we were playing at Lyman Hall's field since Sheehan's field is on the opposite, northwest side of Wallingford. Unless we make the state tournament, the forty-five minute bus ride to the home of the Titans on Hope Hill

Road is the longest ride we have every year. The route to Lyman Hall's field was an easier one for us riding a school bus. We traveled there by way of I-91. D and I knew from experience that the longer the bouncing school bus ride, the less likely we were to win. To alleviate the bus ride's impact on the game's outcome, you had to get to the field with enough time before the first pitch to shake off the effects of the journey, as well as take batting practice.

After we reached the gravel parking lot and walked down the small, tapered grass hill to our visitors' dugout, one of our players remembered to search for the time capsule last year's team had planted inside. Each year when we played at Lyman Hall, a member of our splinter squad would use his metal spikes to dig up a baseball buried in the first base dugout by the prior year's team. The players chuckled as they passed the mold-infested baseball along the bench and read the scribbled messages to this year's team. Before each game's end, the players would bury a new ink-covered ball in the same spot under our bench. I never wanted to see what they wrote on the ball each year. I hoped whatever was written on our cowhide connection with past players somehow helped motivate the team to win.

The field was wet and sloppy. The light beige color of Speedy Dry was prevalent near the baselines and around the infield's edges, where scratch lines hinted the Titans had broomed off the morning rain before our arrival. Although Donny worked himself into a bases-loaded jam in the first inning, he escaped it without surrendering a run. Sheehan never recovered from the lost opportunity. Donny shut Sheehan out, allowing only two hits and retiring the side in order in the bottom of the seventh.

We scored our seven runs by showing patience at the plate—a virtue in high school baseball—and running Sheehan's starting pitcher, Mike Boudreau, ragged. Even Joe Lizza stole second on a perfectly executed fake-squeeze-steal. Whenever we had a man on first and third with less than two outs, we called for the decoy play. When the pitcher kicked to deliver, our runner on third charges down the line, the batter squared as if to bunt for a suicide squeeze, and the runner on first raced for second. As soon as the catcher heard everyone scream, "Squeeeeeeeze!" in stereo, he concentrated on the third base runner and forgot about the man stealing. Even a slow runner could get to second on the play. Every time we employed the play it worked, even when our opposition suspected it.

We got the only run we needed in the first inning. Pete worked his way into a walk, stole second, and scored on Joey G.'s sharp single. In high school baseball, it's a huge advantage for a road team to jump out ahead in the top of the first. The lead gives your pitcher confidence, as he doesn't think he has to be perfect.

With Donny or Ben on the mound, our team believed if we scored at all we had a good chance to win.

Romo continued to surprise us. In the second inning, he walked, pilfered second, got sacked to third by Massie and scored on a hit by Gino, who also got another two RBI double in the game.

On the long but loud bus ride back, D and I reminisced about our last time together at Lyman Hall's field. After we lost the drawn-out, close game, some of our players had succumbed to the scent of boiled hot dogs and snuck off to buy some for the half hour trip back from a beach-umbrella-covered vendor behind the bus in the parking lot. We were furious our guys had even considered splurging on fat frankfurters with the works after a loss. That game was always remembered as the "Hot Dog Game," but on this day, we spawned a different memory.

Our next game was the makeup game against Emmett O'Brien. Last week's rain sandwiched the makeup contest against the Vo-Tech Conference Condors in between the Sheehan and Cheshire games. But the night after the Sheehan game, the April rain returned. Fortunately, the city's groundskeeper, Buster Jadach, who doubled as Derby High's successful wrestling coach, swept, turned over, and dragged the infield for hours in his tractor to mold the surface into playable condition. Emmett was one game we counted on to make the tournament. We wanted to play them to keep our record above .500 going into the more difficult games ahead.

We thought Emmett was a team we should beat but couldn't chance starting someone other than Ben or Donny on the hill. If we built a big enough lead, we planned to give the long-haired Mike Massie, our top JV pitcher, a chance to show whether he was capable of seeing Varsity mound action in a pinch.

The Condor's Chris Duda handed us two runs in the first inning. Joey G. singled. Ben and Donny got free passes, and Joe Lizza hit into a fielder's choice that was followed by an error. In the third inning, Lizza clobbered a monster three-run homer to deep left center that snapped a few brittle maple tree branches beyond the center field fence, putting us ahead 5–0. In the meantime, Ben struck out eight batters in four innings and Donny pitched a scoreless fifth. Mike Massie junk-balled both the sixth and seventh and preserved the shutout. We ended up winning 7–0 and gained our fourth win.

The next day, we trekked through the hills of Route 42 to play Cheshire. Like most years, the Rams were loaded with veteran talent. In the first three innings, they banged Donny around like a Slugfest pinball. Trailing 7–0, D and I stood, arms folded, before the silver chain-link fence that covered the front of our third base dugout. Tules paced before us, shaking his head. "D, we better get the players together and talk to them," I said. "They are getting too down over this."

As the players started walking off the field at the third inning's end, D hollered, "Everybody up, right here!" pointing to a spot before him with both hands. The players on the field jogged into a tight huddle around us. The younger players on the bench crept out of our silent dugout and stood outside the huddle, hoping to avoid the brunt of the lambasting D was about to give. "OK, fellas, what's it gonna be?" D said with a wrinkled forehead under the edge of his red hat. "You gonna quit? You want to go home, now?" Some players shook their heads while revealing the button on the tops of their caps. "We knew we might have games like this against teams like this. What? Did you think it was gonna be easy? When things go bad, we're gonna go into the tank? Now let's get our heads out of our asses and start toughening up. Let's start hitting the f—king ball and show this team we can play with them."

"Let's start playing this game the way you know you can play it, huh. How about it?" Tules interjected.

"Guys, what's our goal?" I asked as I looked as many players in the eye as I could.

"The state tournament, Coach," said Joe Lizza with a look of disgust.

"Exactly," I said, looking at Joe in the eyes. "So let's not lose sight of our goal. We aren't going to let anybody sidetrack us from what we want to accomplish. We're going to keep our focus where it belongs, no matter what happens in any one game."

As D, Tules, and I distanced ourselves from the huddle, Pete and Ben shouted words of encouragement to the other players. The players put their hands together in the middle. "One, two, three, *win!*" they yelled, and the huddle broke.

From that moment on, with help from Cheshire who tried to sit on their lead, momentum shifted. Ben relieved Donny in the fourth and shut the confident Rams out for the rest of the game. We rallied in the seventh. After George Hay and Romo both smacked RBI doubles, we closed the gap to 7–5 with the tying runs on base. Burt Leventhal, who was still Cheshire's coach, began to crap his pants and summoned his senior ace from center field, Jim Shanley, who finally squelched our comeback.

On the ride back, the bus shifted into low gear as it started to climb one of Route 42's several winding hills. I barely heard myself think as the diesel motor roared. D stood and pushed down on the latches on the top sides of the window next to him with his thumbs. After a few attempts, he finally got the stubborn window to slide and click into place. He thumbed the metal roller on the back of his Bic lighter until a fingernail-sized orange and blue flame appeared. He took a drag from his cigarette that left him unsatisfied. I took in a whiff of diesel exhaust as the bus shifted gears again.

"We were fortunate, D, the game ended the way it did," I said, raising my voice above the racket of the eight-cylinder engine.

"How so?"

"Well, at least we didn't get distracted from our goal. If we hadn't come back like we did and gotten buried, the team might not think we're any good. We would have trouble keeping them focused on the tournament."

"There are no moral victories, Riles."

"I know, I can't stand it either."

"Can't stand what?" D asked as he jammed a cigarette butt over the lowered window's top.

"Losing."

15

Battling for Ten Wins

As soon as our next game against Shelton was washed out, D's and my thoughts turned to the North Haven Indians. Their team didn't worry us, just their coach. With the most wins of any active high school baseball coach in Connecticut, it seemed like Bob DeMayo had been around forever. He had coached North Haven when I was a player and even as far back as when John's father had been Derby's coach.

A hard-nosed coach, DeMayo was a psychology teacher at North Haven High. He was a master strategist, but often overwhelmed his players with criticism to motivate them to perform. Sometimes I thought they performed just to shut him up. If prodding his players didn't work, he would try to intimidate the umpires. Unless an umpire insisted he stay in or near the dugout, which wasn't that often, DeMayo stood as close to the field as possible to try to influence what was happening.

Even though D and I felt we could counter his tactics, DeMayo also had great ballplayers. To beat North Haven, we needed to sustain hitting streaks during the extended delays DeMayo caused whenever his opponent threatened to score. If we got a man on first, he visited the mound. If we reached second base, he might bring in his best pitcher to throw the rest of the inning, then bring back the starter the next. If we scored, he would either go to the mound again or remove the pitcher, causing an even greater delay. Because North Haven was an L-size school, the second largest of the four high school divisions and comprised of schools with three hundred fifty to five hundred boys, Coach DeMayo had plenty of pitchers with which to play the pitcher merry-go-round. If your pitcher couldn't throw a strike, his hitters were disciplined enough to walk around the bases until they won.

Bob DeMayo was also North Haven's football coach. But he was not nearly as successful on the gridiron as he was on the diamond. As a football coach, he was despised by Derby fans. No coach at Ryan Field was ever booed as loud or with as much profanity as he was. As far as I could recall, Derby had never lost to a North Haven football team DeMayo coached. That streak wasn't lost on Charlie DiCenso either. One year, some North Haven football fans had wanted DeMayo out as the football coach. Charlie had come to his defense. D and I often wondered whether Charlie had defended him because he thought the attempt to remove him was wrong or that it would prevent North Haven from hiring a new coach who might beat Derby.

Although our game against North Haven was only one game in our quest to make the state tournament, it was far more significant for Coach DeMayo. If he beat us, he would break the state record for the most wins by a high school baseball coach in Connecticut. The record was currently held by the legendary coach, John "Whitey" Piurek, who coached at West Haven and Plainville, amassing 526 wins. Because DeMayo was so disliked by Derby fans, we didn't want him to break the record at Ryan Field.

Ben wanted the ball. He vowed the Indians would not win the game on our field. Adding to the game's atmosphere, a local television station positioned a camera on the last row of the first base stands. Our players knew if North Haven won, we'd be on the television sports news that evening as losers.

Ben ended up dominating North Haven's hitters, breaking a Derby record that will likely hold for many years. I never saw a Derby pitcher compete as hard as Ben did that afternoon. With adrenaline pumping for seven innings, Ben struck out a phenomenal eighteen batters in seven innings. Ben was so dominant over North Haven's hitters that he struck out five in a row and seven of eight batters in the middle innings. An error and a couple of timely hits, however, let the game slip away from us. After the game, the ageless Coach DeMayo in his maroon jersey and hat searched for Ben who stood dejected on the infield grass. He approached Ben and offered his hand, recognizing that Ben had left everything he had on the field.

As D and I walked off the field toward the clubhouse, we asked each other what we could have done differently. DeMayo outcoached us, and we wondered whether we didn't have the superior talent on the field that day. The game ended with Bob DeMayo surpassing a record that took another legend a lifetime of high school coaching to obtain. DeMayo attained his 527th win; he deserved the accolades from his team and the television coverage on the evening news sports segment. Yet the effort Ben Bartone had given, trying to prevent the record from being broken, had been lost in the television newscast.

After every game, it was our custom to address the players as a group before they left the locker room. After D spoke to the team, if Tules, Jocko, or I wanted to say anything, on most occasions we got the chance.

The coaches gathered in the coaches' room while the players silently filed into the locker room.

"What can we possibly say to these guys to keep them up?" I asked. "What can we possibly say to Ben?"

"Wow. I can't believe we just lost this game," Tules interjected.

D walked into the adjacent bathroom and flicked what was left from his filtered cigarette into the open toilet. After he came out, a small grin sneaked out the corner of his mouth. "I know what to say," D said while bobbing his head. "I'm going to take a page out of Lou's book. Follow me."

We trailed behind D into the locker room. D, George, Jocko, and I stood opposite the players who slumped on two red wooden benches. The sun still shined through the windows behind the team and above the red wooden lockers. The sound of cars traveling on Chatfield Street reached our ears, then silence blanketed the room. Everybody knew Ben was inconsolable. He sat alone on the far end of the second bench before the emergency exit door at the room's far corner adjacent the shower room. It wasn't his usual spot on the bench. Embarrassed to sit with the rest of the team, he bowed his head and pushed his red hat down over his eyebrows to hide his emotion. I ached to say the right thing to Ben that could somehow diminish the agony of this defeat. D spoke first.

"What Ben did today, fellas, was unbelievable. He deserved a better fate. Each one of you should learn something from his effort and from now on give Ben the support he gave you today. Every once in a great while a coach and his team are lucky to witness a monumental effort by an athlete. Today," D said, raising his voice, "is one of those days. I feel privileged to have witnessed Ben's effort today. Let's all stand and give Ben what he deserves." While Ben sat among his standing teammates, D led the coaches and players in giving Ben an ovation.

When it came my turn to talk, I drew a deep breath. I felt my eyes moisten, but I knew I couldn't rub them. I waited for the team's full attention.

I looked directly at Ben. "I just want to say how proud I am to be associated with you as well as the other members of this team. I'm standing here in the same locker room where every Derby Baseball player in the past, including myself, once stood, and I feel privileged. I am rededicating myself to put in the effort you displayed today. If life, like baseball, Ben, all boils down to effort, you have nothing to be ashamed of and a lot to look forward to. Whatever goal you have in life," I said, looking at the players, "just focus in on it and don't let anything or anybody get in the way of what you want to accomplish."

I removed a game ball from my jacket and tossed it to Ben, forcing him to look up to catch it. I crouched before him to look into his eyes underneath his red hat; the word *Raiders* was scripted across its crown in black. Still unable to make eye contact, I said, "While you're sad today, Ben…what difference will it make…if you…have the ball in your hand…on the mound…in a state championship game."

In the *New Haven Register* the next day, DeMayo was quoted, "If this was going to be a record win, this is the way I like to win them." He felt it was too bad for anyone to lose a game with eighteen strikeouts and added, "I think we're just lucky to get out of here with a win."[4] While the compliment was no consolation to Ben, D and I both felt fortunate to have been witnesses to one of the greatest, if not *the* greatest, effort and performance a Derby High school pitcher had ever made. We knew we could never forget it.

After the North Haven loss, we prepared to face our archrival Shelton at home. We needed to get our team focused on our tournament goal but worried we might not recover from our emotional loss to North Haven. Shelton's baseball tradition had begun back in the seventies. Shelton had knocked off the Naugatuck Greyhounds and their legendary coach, Ray LeGenza, in the semifinal of the state tournament at a sold-out standing-room-only Yale Field. The loss had halted Naugatuck's sixty-four-game winning streak and prevented them from breaking the national record for most wins in a row.

After snapping Naugatuck's streak, the Shelton team bus had received a police escort back to town. Shelton won the state championship that year, as well as the next two under Coach Joe Benanto, who won a total of eight Housatonic League championships before becoming Yale's coach from 1979 through 1991. Though Shelton's baseball team had experienced an enormous amount of success, for the most part their football team during the Lou DeFilippo era had been dominated by Derby, causing their fanatic fans on Turkey Day to shout, "Drop dead, Little Red," as if it had been rehearsed. As a result, whenever Shelton played Derby in baseball, the fans would arrive by the hundreds to hope Shelton kicked our asses.

After Coach Benanto left Shelton, one of his former assistants, Ed Marocco, had taken over. An ex-navy man, Ed had continued Shelton's baseball tradition. His players were fundamentally sound and wouldn't beat themselves. Ed taught his players to respect the game. They always ran on and off the field and played hard.

When I became a coach, I always wanted to beat Shelton for a personal reason. In 1973, one of Shelton's state championship years, I had been cocaptain of Derby's team. We had traveled to Riverview Park in Shelton for our opening game. In the top of the seventh, we had trailed by only a single run, as our runner on third took his two-out lead. But the game had ended on a ground out to third while I swung my Louisville Slugger in the on-deck circle. While our bus was leaving Riverview, a 6'5" twenty-something Shelton fan with long, straggly dirty-brown hair approached the side of the bus I sat on. "You'll never beat Shelton in baseball," he shouted as he flipped us the bird. I remember the feeling when I heard him say it, as if he was only taunting me. I had thought that when I became a coach, I could chalk the guy up as just some idiot who had taken a high school baseball game too seriously, but I couldn't.

Shelton was struggling with a 2–4 record. We felt we had the more talented team and were playing them in our house. Our players' chance for a small measure of revenge from this past football season finally arrived. They didn't want to let it slip away, especially if we could help prevent Shelton from making the state baseball tournament for the first time in our memory.

During our pregame infield, I fungoed a ground ball to Ben at short. It took a wicked hop into his face. Blood gushed from his nose across his crimson shirt. Like a hospital trauma team, we rushed him into the dugout, stuffed cotton in both his nostrils, and iced his nose. After a few anxious minutes, the bleeding stopped.

We didn't have a backup shortstop when Donny pitched. Our only option was to put Pete at short, move Romo to center field, and put another outfielder in right. D knew if we moved too many guys to new positions, we would likely lose. Ben knew our predicament and decided to continue playing, even though his swollen nose was packed with blood-soaked cotton, his shirt two shades of red.

Despite Ben's injury, he played errorless shortstop. The entire team hit Shelton's starter, Jeff Minder, hard. George Hay bombed a two-run triple to right center that rolled near the clubhouse. Even Mike Massie surprised us, launching a high fly that cleared the left field fence.

With a 9–3 lead in the seventh, D experimented and put Pete on the mound. Donny's pitch count was high, and we wanted to give him a break if the opportunity arose. We wanted to see if someone other than Massie might be able to give us some innings if we ever faced the quandary where both Ben and Donny became ineligible to pitch because of the infamous ten-inning or, to be more exact, thirty-out rule.

A couple of years ago, the CIAC had established a rule limiting the number of innings a pitcher could throw. The rule limited a pitcher to thirty outs in any three consecutive calendar days. The premise of the rule was that high school coaches could not be trusted to protect their pitchers' arms from overwork.

Although based in good intentions, the rule had its flaw. Whether a pitcher threw a thousand pitches in any one seven-inning game, it didn't matter. He just couldn't pitch to anyone after he had thrown ten innings until two calendar days had passed after the day he had pitched. The restriction had a greater impact on smaller schools. With fewer players coming out for the team, most Class S schools had fewer pitchers.

In the Housatonic league, we were the only Class S school. League games were played every Monday, Wednesday, and Friday. The rule meant that we could throw Donny in our Monday game, but, if he pitched seven innings, we could only throw him three innings in our Wednesday game if Ben needed help. But if Ben hurled all seven innings on Wednesday, we could pitch Donny again on Friday for seven innings and bring Ben in for three if Donny got in trouble. Or we could reverse the order of pitchers and confuse ourselves even more.

The rule made it one of the few times my legal experience gave me an advantage. Overusing a pitcher was not something we wanted to do anyway, but we had to hope our Wednesday pitcher went the distance to make it work.

If the weather didn't cooperate, we would be in trouble. We rested our arms for three days after the Shelton game's initially scheduled date was rained out. League rules required us to reschedule a rainout on the next available date. The postponement forced us to play three games in a row and four games in five days. We had to play North Haven on Monday, Shelton on Tuesday, East Haven on Wednesday, and then Branford on Friday. Everybody else in the league was also strapped, but that was little consolation for an S school.

The weather drove D nuts. If he couldn't see the stars the night before a game, he would clutch his black plastic remote with his thumb on the previous channel button and flip back to the Weather Channel in between innings of a Yankee game. Although I told him not to worry about the things he couldn't control, it didn't matter. He felt he also had to control the New England weather if we were going to make the tournament.

East Haven was another game we were counting on for our ten-win goal. With only a day's rest, Ben had to start Wednesday's game against the Yellowjackets. Even if Ben lasted the entire game against the Easties, Donny would still have to pitch Friday against Branford on just two-day's rest. D didn't want to think about what we would be required to do if neither of our two stellar pitchers had it on a certain day. To D, not having it on any given day was unacceptable.

In the top of the first—with a man on first—Ben grooved a fastball and tracked the ball as it flew over the left field fence. When he got the third out, Ben grabbed his right arm, held it close to his chest, and grimaced in pain. D questioned whether Ben was experiencing arm difficulty or was just suffering from the age old "Loser's limp." Loser's limp is a feigned injury claimed by an athlete to beg out of a game he is losing in. I guess D experienced the ailment a lot while coaching football; he was preconditioned to believe in the possibility of it surfacing in one of our games.

Loser's limp for a pitcher translates into the sore arm. To beg out a game when he can't find the plate or wished an L screen would pop up in front of him, a pitcher will sometimes feign an arm injury to mask a lack of intestinal fortitude to gut it out. I saw it a lot in Little League and Babe Ruth games. The injury's symptoms only last until the score turns for the better, at which point the pitcher finds a miracle cure better than any late-night infomercial and wants back into the game. It's a lot easier pitching when you are winning than when you are losing.

In the locker room before a game, we could sense when any of our players were having arm problems. The nose-awakening odor of Icy Hot, Atomic Balm, or some other liniment would sift its way up the vent above the locker room drawing board and into the coaches' room.

I had a hard time believing Ben didn't have a sore arm in light of his Monday performance against North Haven and especially since he was pitching on such short rest. We couldn't put Donny in so early in the game, as he had only three innings of eligibility, so we gave Pete another shot at relief. Pete proved why he was the center fielder. By the time we began the bottom of the fourth, we were behind 9-0 as we fell apart like a dropped pizza.

With the huge lead, East Haven's pitcher, Ken Mead, tried not to walk anyone. But when he threw a fastball on the inside part of the plate to Lizza, Joe made the navy blue and yellow-shirted Mead pay with—what former Baltimore Orioles's manager, Earl Weaver, called the best offensive weapon in baseball—a three-run homer. When the ball sailed over the left center field fence, our bench awoke. George Hay followed with a solo bomb of his own, and the momentum turned.

Trailing 9-4, we brought in Donny to freeze East Haven's offense and continue our surge. Donny prevented further damage. Since Ben was our shortstop whenever Donny pitched, we reinserted Ben back at short and returned Pete to his normal spot. When we asked Ben whether he could play shortstop, he said he could; his ailing arm felt better.

We scored another run in the sixth when Romo crossed the plate on a rare hit by Gino. In the seventh, Ben doubled in Joey G., but it wasn't enough to overcome the huge deficit. We lost 9–6, leaving us only one game over .500 at 5–4.

Our bad luck didn't miss our second sacker, Gino. Gino's head snapped back after he got popped in the face with a nasty hop off our cement infield. The emergency room doctor needed seven stitches to close it. Now we knew why he wore the goggles.

On Friday's forty-minute bus ride on I-95 up the Connecticut shoreline to Branford, D and I reminisced about the last time we had ridden to the home of the Hornets together. Two years ago, when we stepped off the bus at Branford's field, David Anroman's older brother Johnny had approached me next to the right field line. "Who bats first, Riles?" he asked, his face serious.

I hadn't wanted to hurt his feelings. "They flip a coin at home plate before the game," I explained without laughing, "just like football." He thought D had lost the flip when our batter stepped into the box after the ump cried out, "Play ball!" When I told D the story, he pulled his metal-rimmed glasses down and eyeballed me from above the lenses. It reminded him of what we had to deal with in Derby to try to win baseball games.

Although I got along with David and John Anroman, Tules had a closer relationship with them. Tules tipped the scales at about 255 pounds. You didn't want to hear Tules's voice if you were alone in a back ally, unless he was on your side. He reached John Anroman on his own level, wherever that was. When John acted up once, Tules warned him he was headed in the same direction Tules had already gone earlier in his life. Tules told me that when he had been at his lowest, he had hung out in Father Panik Village in Bridgeport, waiting for trouble. Tules revealed to me he was a recovered drug user. He'd encountered some depraved individuals, not just those who thought they were tough, but those who would just as soon kill you if you looked at them too long.

I always believed Tules's stories. I had experience practicing law in Bridgeport's overburdened Golden Hill Street courthouse, where each morning accused criminals in Connecticut's most populated city were brought into the court's lockup, chained together like sausages.

At first, John Anroman wouldn't believe Tules. "While you might think you're tough," Tules cautioned Johnny, "there's always somebody else tougher than you." Once, Johnny had tried to make light of Tules's history and mocked his toughness. Tules threatened him in his Luca Brasi-like voice. "If you don't cut it out, I'm going to reach down into your throat and pull your lungs out." John got the message. From that moment on, he had never given Tules any trouble again. It had been Tules's way of telling Johnny he loved him. Now married with two young children, Tules was just trying to stop Johnny from beating his chest and becoming an asshole. Some kids just have to be frightened into growing up, and Johnny was one of them. It had been the beginning of a long friendship between Johnny Anroman and Tules.

Like his older brother John, David Anroman had also developed a close relationship with Tules. Like John, David had tested the limits of Tules's patience. David had angered Tules once after getting a base on balls. David tossed his Easton on the ground, snapped his fingers, and pointed to the bat—while looking at Tules, as if telling his big bad bat boy to pick it up. Tules scoffed Romo off, but he made him a promise. If Romo ever hammered a home run over a fence, he could drop his bat at home plate and Tules would pick it up for him.

As we traveled on I-95 past Exit 52 in East Haven, Gino stepped to the front of the bus. He eased himself onto the front edge of the seat behind D; a powder blue bat bag flattened the rest of the cushion. He patted the small bandage on his left cheek that covered his stitches to make sure it was secure. He folded his hands over the top of D's cushioned seat, revealing a red Mizuno sweatband on his left forearm.

D eyed Gino creeping up the aisle in the long, rectangular mirror above the driver. D leaned back. "What's up, Gino?"

"I was wondering, D—I don't know if I can play second base with these stitches."

"Why not?" D asked. He raised his eyebrows and shifted his eyes to catch mine across the aisle.

"I might get hit in the face again by a ground ball," he explained. The bus lurched forward, and Gino dabbed his cheek to make sure the bandage was still in place. Five rows back, Pete leaned forward and rested his chin on his folded arms atop the seat cushion before him.

"Are you telling me," D said as he searched for the brown Scoremaster scorebook, "you don't want to play?" D flipped it open and grabbed his lucky red pen inside.

"That's not what I was thinking," Gino replied as he watched D follow the names on the ink-scribbled page until he found Gino's name at the bottom of the line up.

"I don't know, Gino. I would probably have to put Pete at second, shift Romo to center, put either Calvert or Cronk in right field, and DH DiRubba."

"Oh, I thought I would just be the DH instead," Gino said, looking at the ribbed rubber floor. Behind us, Pete chuckled and ducked his head under his arms.

In a patronizing tone, D replied, "Well, what's to say you don't get hit by a pitch? Nah, if you can't go, Gino, I'll have to put Pete there."

Gino rose and started back down the thin aisle with a face as long as a waiting list for low-rent senior housing. He dropped beside Ben and tilted his head. While Gino picked at the black tape on his bat's handle, he listened intently to every word Ben was feeding him.

D clicked his pen, put it back in the spiral bound book, and closed it. "Gino isn't even batting his weight and he wants me to put him in as a DH?" Pete lifted his head, shook it, then leaned back in his seat. D continued, "You know, it's OK. If Gino doesn't play second, we'll at least find out if we're better off playing Pete at second and getting somebody else's bat in the lineup."

As the bus exited I-95 at Exit 54 before a crowded McDonald's, Gino worked his way up to the front of the bus again, grasping the top of each seat he passed. "I thought about it, D. I'll just add another bandage and play."

"Are you sure, Gino? I wouldn't want the injury to get infected or anything."

"I'm sure," he replied. His neck became bulled and his voice deepened. "I'll just put another bandage over the one I got and gut it out."

After Gino earned his Oscar and threaded his way back to his seat, D leaned over the aisle and gestured to me to come closer. "Do you think he ever heard the story of Wally Pipp?" [5]

"Maybe not," I replied. "But I'm sure Ben has."

Despite Gino's injury, he ended up spinning three double plays with Ben. The incentive Tules had provided Romo was enough. After Joe Lizza doubled and George Hay got a base on balls, Romo tattooed a three-run homer over the flimsy snow fence in left field. When he jumped on the five-sided slab of rubber with both spikes, he eyed Tules and pointed several times to his Easton on the ground before the plate. Grinning ear to ear, Tules strutted to home plate from his first base coach's box, double high-fived Romo at the plate, and picked up the bat.

David's hitting became contagious. Joey G. smacked two singles. Hay hit a bullet to deep center, but a wind gust and the lack of a center field fence in Branford denied him a four bagger. Branford did get two hits in the fourth, but Donny struck out the side to end the threat. When the final out was recorded in the spiral scorebook, Donny had humbled the Hornets with nine k's on just two-day's rest; we scored six runs. We were now 6–4, only four wins away from making the tournament.

Having faced every league opponent once, the league schedule repeated itself. Seymour was now 9–1 and playing some of the best baseball in the league. Ben's fastball was popping, but the Wildcat hitters were patient. They jumped to a lead in the top of the first on a couple of rare walks. A bad hop past Gino and an error and we were quickly behind 2–0. In the bottom half of the first, we tied it up. Ben lined an RBI triple to the right center gap, and Donny singled to right. But in the fifth, Ben surrendered a two-run homer to Billy Brooks. After the Wildcats scored another run in the seventh, making it 5–2, we couldn't touch Seymour's fireballer, Rob Cafaro, who went the distance this time and allowed only one hit and one walk after the second inning.

After the game, D and I were concerned we weren't getting any better. We knew if we weren't getting better, we were getting worse, as our opponents were likely improving with each game. Joey G.'s batting average was dropping fast. Ben's record stood at 1–4, despite the fact that he pitched his ass off fanning nine Wildcat batters. With Donny's record at 5–1, we worried Ben's confidence could crash. We were lining up Donny against the teams we thought we had a better chance at beating, hoping Ben could battle the tougher teams, but the strategy had left Ben with a poor record. If we were going to make the tournament and have any chance of success in it, we needed Ben to believe he was better than his atrocious record.

With Joey G. slumping, we decided to put Ben in the second spot and lower Joey G. to eighth. In the eighth spot, Joey G. would see more fastballs. More importantly, we knew Ben would more likely come up in a crucial situation in the two spot. Our order was now Pete C., leading off with Ben, Donny, Joe Lizza, and George Hay following him. Romo hit sixth, Massie seventh, Joey G. eighth, and Gino ninth.

We tested our new lineup in the next game against Lyman Hall on the road. In the top of the first, both Ben and Donny reached base, and George Hay belted a two RBI double to the left center gap that rolled down the graded outfield to the ten-foot chain-link fence. In the fourth, Lyman Hall's pitcher, Mike Leonard, nailed Pete with a fastball. He refused to rub the spot. Pete didn't want the Trojan thrower to know that rest of the afternoon would be spent nursing an ice-bagged left arm. Ben and Donny walked, loading the bases for Joe Lizza.

Lizza stepped to the plate. Lyman Hall's coach looked at first base, but it was occupied. After the left-handed Leonard tried to junk ball Joe, he turned and watched the ball sail into the path-laden woods beyond the fence for a grand slam. Donny went the distance again and scattered just four hits in our 6–2 victory. The new lineup worked, and we were now only three wins away from our goal.

Donny was now 6–1, and Ben was up against supersized Amity High, population 1500 plus. Ben didn't complain, took the ball, and went the distance again, striking out nine batters with no walks. We took a 4–0 lead in the second inning off Amity's pitcher, Tom Minnix, with George Hay continuing his hot hitting behind Lizza. But batter by batter, inning by inning, the Spartans inched back and ultimately won it in the bottom of the seventh. They left us on the field when one of our outfielders missed a cutoff man. The ball rolled untouched across the low-cut infield grass as the winning run scored. The ball came to a stop, and Ben walked off the field—the best 1–5 pitcher in the state. With the 5–4 loss, our record dropped to 7–6.

The day after the Amity game was Mother's Day. We decided to avoid any controversy over practicing on that Friday by only scheduling early morning BP in the gym. With practice starting before the automated bell went off in the empty school, the players or the coaches couldn't miss any planned family gatherings.

After the players wiped the sand from their eyes, they began hitting in the netted cage hanging from the taut silver wires extending between the side walls of the gym. Ten minutes after we started, Ken Marcucio entered the gym and approached John as he sat in a school chair behind the net, coaching the hitter inside. A small paper coffee cup was next to John on the hardwood gym floor. Ken stood behind him and stared at the spots of light brown coffee on the floor beside the cup. "John, I received a wake-up call this morning. The board of education has ordered you can't practice. You have to stop."

"What?" exclaimed John as he stood up. "What do you mean the board of ed says we can't practice?" he asked. "Who called you?"

"I shouldn't say. Apparently, they're upset you're practicing on Mother's Day."

"I'm fighting to make the tournament, and the board of ed is telling me I can't practice?" The players stopped whacking baseballs and stared silently at D and Kenny. Gino's eyes shifted to the floor.

"I'm sorry, John," Ken said. "I'm just the messenger."

I yanked the plug on the JUGS machine. The twin tires spun more and more slowly until they stopped. We rolled up the fifty-foot orange extension cords, collapsed the net, and turned off the overhead lights. After we followed the disgruntled players out, D shut the gray side door to the school and tugged on the metal handle to make sure it was locked. "Who do you think did it?" I asked.

"Could be Gino's grandfather," D replied. "He's the only one on the board related to a player."

"Do you think the board would've ever told Lou DeFilippo he couldn't practice?"

"What do you think, Riles?"

Our next game against Sheehan made us wonder whether the Wallingford coaches ever spoke to each other. With the game tied at 1–1 in the bottom of the fifth and one man on, Pete reached first with a catcher's interference call. Catcher's interference occurs when the catcher decides to stick his glove hand into the hitting zone too early. Whenever it happens, coaches, parents, and fans gasp and cringe. A mitt often flies off the catcher's hand to the sound of a thud. You can only hope the catcher didn't lose his hand along with his glove.

To our surprise, Sheehan intentionally walked Donny to pitch to Lizza with the bases full. As soon as I saw the umpire point to first base and Donny toss his bat toward our bench and remove his red, black, and white Mizuno batting gloves, I held back my glee so as not to jinx what I knew would follow. Sheehan might as well have packed their bags and loaded them onto the bus.

Lizza walked to the batter's box to face Sheehan's hard-throwing lefty, Kyle Piper. Joey banged his bat on the rubber plate and rocked his hips. He proceeded to make Sheehan pay for their failure (to read our highlights in the *Register* sports section). He nailed another grand slam. As the red-stitched ball sped over the left field fence, it was still rising. Our eyes widened as the shrinking ball soared over a second fence that surrounded the Ryan Field complex and fell in the soft soil of the vegetable garden of Hank "Rondo" Rondini, a guidance counselor at Derby High. A second Wallingford coach had set Joe up for a grand slam only a few days after the first one. Joe's powerball provided us all the offense we needed, as Donny only surrendered two runs, raising his record to 7–1.

Now we only had to win two of our remaining six games to make the tournament. They were, however, against Amity, who had already beaten us; Shelton, who wanted revenge and to keep their tournament streak alive; Cheshire, whose record had only got better since they had last beaten us; North Haven; East Haven, who had already beaten us; and Branford.

The second Amity game at home turned out as bad as the first one. Ben pitched well again, but we couldn't string enough hits together off Amity's starter, Heath Cunningham. We trailed 6–1 in the seventh before we decided to hit. After Pete lined a single, Ben walked. Shep and Joe Lizza hit RBI singles, but the bottom of the order, as D would say, "couldn't hit a bull in the ass with a shovel," and we lost 6–3. Ben was now a dismal 1–6.

As the game ended, I spotted Ray Ray 450 feet out in right center field pushing Reegers's wheelchair toward the clubhouse driveway. D slumped on the bench and stared at the open scorebook on his lap as he searched for overgenerous hits he would instantly change to errors. "Reegers was out there again today, D," I said.

"He's been out there every game, hasn't he?" D spotted a dark ball in the corner of the dugout and retrieved it.

"Did anybody ask him again if he wanted to watch the game from our dugout?"

"We ask him every game," D replied, probably wondering who would want to sit in our dugout the way we played. "He's got an open invitation."

"Does Reegers know the game?" I asked, curious. I knew he was a Yankee fan, but not much else.

"You'd be surprised."

16

Pete and Joey G's Triumph

Ben and Donny had right arms longer than their left, but spring showers forced us to face Shelton on our third game in a row. To have a chance to win, the tired tandem had to split the game and we had to outslug the Gaels. After the Amity loss, Pete vowed to step up. Pete played well prior to the Shelton game, but he had not yet come into his own as the player both D and I knew he could be.

The game was played at Riverview Park, a field with a rich baseball history. Adjacent to a steep cliff directly across from the Derby Dam on the Housatonic River, east of the Yale boathouse on Route 34 in Derby—the park never changed. In the 1970s, Shelton's three consecutive state championship teams buried many opponents there. In a bygone era, our game and other Valley rival baseball games as well as state tournament games were broadcast live from Riverview on WADS. As you drove to the game, you could listen to Brad Harris or Lenn Zonder, then stand beside him behind the rusted backstop.

The field was adjacent to Route 110, a state highway and the busiest street in Shelton. The backstop was so near the street that foul balls bounced, ricocheted, and rolled between moving and parked cars. For many years, the field was the Shelton American Legion team's home park. During the evening and weekend summer games, a middle-aged man with a black hat and a cigar box filled with quarters handed a quarter to anyone who returned a foul ball. By game's end, the box was empty. The practice was stopped when kids started darting into the street and fighting for the two bits. The field had dugouts with painted orange cinderblocks for sides and shallow black wooden roofs. Whoever designed them never envisioned a team comprised of more than nine players. If you weren't careful stepping into or out them, you'd leave with a splitting headache.

Like Fenway Park, Riverview Park had its own green monster in left field. In left center, there was a war memorial building. To the building's left were several rows of three-story-high pine trees. Although befuddled left fielders chased balls that bounced into, under, and through the trees, Shelton never considered removing any. Each one had been planted in memory of a war veteran.

Before the game began, I noticed Reegers next to a park bench near our dugout. Arms folded, Ray Ray sat on the bench, his navy blue Yankees hat above his shaded eyes.

In the top of the first, Pete stepped to the plate to face Shelton's Ryan Clift. With Pete's short body frame, he silenced the Shelton crowd before they spread their blankets on the grass covered hill between the left field foul line and the street. He unloaded a home run over the right center field fence, the deepest part of Riverview Park. The ball shot through the gut of a tired maple tree and left it two branches fewer. At that moment, Pete's preparation in playing at Derby High for the last four springs, as well as playing in three hot summers, converged with the opportunity he had been presented.

Pete trotted around the bases without fanfare. He looked like a man who expected to hit the four-base bomb and just took care of his baseball business. Pete's father, Ray, however, was so excited that he retrieved the ball and kept it for Pete. Sue snapped a picture of Ray raising the ball in his white Derby hat, dark shades, and a wide grin under his light brown mustache. The historical facts of the poke had already been written between the ball's red seams.

Pete bunted, sprinted, and slid his way into scoring four more times as he collected five hits in five plate appearances. After Pete jump-started the momentum in the first, Lizza and Shepard also crossed the plate in the inning on back-to-back singles by Romo and Mike Massie. Pete's home run was not the only long ball he hit, as he walloped a stand-up triple in the fourth. His bunt was a perfect drag bunt down the third baseline chalk. Shelton wilted in the sixth inning, allowing six runs to come across while uncharacteristically making three errors.

Like a tag team, Donny started the game, and Ben relieved him. At one point before he was removed, Donny had retired eight Shelton batters in a row. When Ben picked up the new white ball before the mound in the fourth, the Gaels thought they had a reprieve; Ben blew the ball by six hitters and walked no one. Since Donny only pitched three innings, Ben got the official win and upped his record to 2–6. After the handshake line, Coach Marocco sought out Pete C., congratulated him, and handed him a game ball. We only had to win one of our next four games to reach the tourney, but we knew nothing was ever guaranteed in high school baseball.

The next day, I arrived at the clubhouse before D. The day's *Sentinel* was already on the coaches' bathroom floor, open to the sports section. "I'm glad for Ben," it quoted D. "I think he found himself today, and hopefully he will get on track. Shepard did a nice job. He held them early. I was worried about their arms. They're the only two I throw, and, with four games this week, I thought they might be weary."[6]

Before practice, we learned Tules couldn't switch his work time with any coworker at United Illuminating's Devon plant and was unable to make tomorrow's Cheshire game. Unfortunately, his options ran out as he had switched with other workers too often this year because of the rainouts we had experienced. He was dejected about having to punch a clock instead of straddling in his first base coach's box, trying to make sure a ballplayer didn't get picked off. He told the team of his unavoidable job obligation.

The players looked as disappointed as they felt but let Tules know they understood he had a family to feed. Tules asked us to have somebody call him with the score as soon as the game ended. We wrote his work number on the wall next to the pay phone, right below Roseland's, the local pizza place's, number.

After the team filed out of the clubhouse for practice, Joey G. approached me. He was worried about his continued hitting drought. It had been hard to coach Joey's hitting. Whenever we tried to tweak his swing, he would just look off into the distance. He always wanted to do things his own way. His batting average had to drop faster than a foul pop behind home plate before he asked us for help.

"Coach."

"Yeah, Joe," I replied. I padded my back pockets to make sure I had enough square Bazooka to last the practice.

"Can you help me with my hitting?" he asked, looking at the ground as if he was trying to find something he lost. Away from his friends, Joey looked like a lonely player in what can sometimes be a lonely game.

"I can show you some things after practice, but I'd be a crummy coach if I'm not brutally honest with you. That's the only way I can help."

"Say what you gotta say, Riles," he said as he gazed toward the empty infield, "I suck anyway."

"You've got to employ what I'm saying, or you'll continue to strike out, pop up, or hit weak ground balls."

"I'll do whatever you say."

I spoke to D about my plan to try to help Joey. "Give it your best shot," he said with an understanding smile that hinted he knew something I didn't. He knew Joey was the stubborn son of a legal secretary. D taught Joey G. in one of his classes; he had insight into Joey's temperament I didn't have.

During practice, some players suggested to D he consider resting Donny and Ben and allow someone else to pitch against Cheshire. Donny agreed with them.

Tules overheard the talk as he walked near our dugout. He stopped and stepped back. "I can't believe what I'm hearing," he barked, his voice reminding me of Big Lou's. "Now when your goal is right there you want to phone in the game? What's the matter, you guys don't think you can beat Cheshire?" His eyes focused on D's. "Don't tell me you're thinking about not pitching Donny," he said as he rolled his head and grimaced as if the thought sickened him.

"We'll decide the matter after practice," D replied.

After the last drill was over, the players began to pick up the gear and walk to the clubhouse. Joey G. separated the third base bag from its underground anchor mount as the other players reached the outfield grass beyond second base. "Follow me down the left field line, Joe," I said. "Get the balls and the bat bag."

Joe cried out to another player to carry the metal-pegged base into the clubhouse. Reluctantly, the player agreed. Joe returned to the dugout, picked up the bat bag by its strap, and tossed it over his right shoulder. With his left hand, he lifted the weather-beaten white canvas ball bag and hastened back.

"Why the left field line?" Joe asked.

"So nobody else can hear what I say to you," I replied. "We can use the left field fence for what I am going to have you do."

"Why don't you want anyone else to hear what you have to say to me?"

"You'll find out, Joe. You'll find out." I glanced over my shoulder. D mimed the words "good luck."

"What are we gonna do with the bats and balls?"

I hesitated to answer. I thought, *Why can't this kid just do what I say*? "Use them," I said. "No more questions. Remember the deal. You just listen and do what I tell you to do, all right?"

"OK, Riles. I'll listen to whatever you say. I can't hit for shit, and I gotta do something."

We stopped before the fence across from the left field foul line. "Get your bat out of the bag," I said. Joe found his thirty-four-inch aluminum bat. "Pick it up with just your left hand and extend it out."

"Why the left hand?" Joe asked.

"Because that's your bottom hand," I explained. "Now extend it out and hold it there." Joe extended the hollow bat with his left arm. Less than thirty seconds later, the barrel sagged toward the ground as the muscles in Joe's arm vibrated. "Notice something, Joe?" I asked. "Now put it down, pick up a thirty-three-inch bat from the bag and do the same thing." Joe slid one out the bag and extended his arm. "Notice anything different?"

"Yeah, this one's easier to hold out there."

"Exactly. You're not strong enough to swing a thirty-four like Lizza or Donny. Use a thirty-three, and you'll have more bat speed and a better swing."

"I'll try, Riles, but I don't know."

"That's all I ask. Now let's do some soft toss with the thirty-three. We also have to get rid of that lousy uppercut swing of yours. If it doesn't work, you can go back to what you were doing."

"I don't want to go back to what I was doing," he said. He swiped the bat at the grass. "I suck."

"That's another thing. Stop saying you suck. You're your own worst enemy sometimes."

A successful hitter swings the correct size bat for his own strength. A lot of players watch what the better hitters swing and think they must swing the same size and brand bat to succeed. The soft toss drills I had Joey perform were nothing new, but Joey could now do the drills properly with the lighter bat. While talking about a drill is simple and performing most drills isn't physically demanding, unless I could also convince Joey to buy into what I was saying, it wouldn't work in a game.

Most high school players want to do everything their own way. Joey G. was no different. No matter what you teach a player, if they don't practice it, it won't work. In the heat of a close game, a tense player will revert to his old bad habits unless a new and better way has been so buried into him that the new way you are trying to teach becomes his old way of doing things.

We stood near the chain-link fence as Joey whacked my inside, outside, high, and low soft tosses over and over into different knee-high links until the bottom began to curl. We continued until most of the other players left the clubhouse, gawking down the left field line and chuckling as if Joey's mom was giving him a haircut using a cereal bowl on his front sidewalk.

"You made a good start," I said as Joey and I walked toward the quiet clubhouse. "But if you want to succeed, you've got to commit to change."

"Thanks, Riles, I will."

After an exhausted Joey and I climbed the clubhouse steps together, I entered the coaches' room. D raised the subject of who should pitch tomorrow's game against Cheshire with Tules, Jocko, and me. Jocko and I agreed with Tules's feeling. D decided there would be no rest for the weary, not when we were this close to our goal. Donny would pitch against Cheshire again at home, and Ben would pitch again against North Haven under the lights at Sachem Field. As the discussion ended, Brian Marcucio, who was home from UConn for a few days, climbed the clubhouse steps to say hello. In case we needed someone to coach first base until Jocko completed the JV practice, D threw the startled ex-player a uniform and welcomed him to the coaching staff.

Entering the game, the Cheshire Rams were 10–4 and ranked fifth in the *Hartford Courant's* weekly poll.[7] Like most game days, we hustled and got on our field by 2:15 PM. The infielders scooped ground balls and snapped throws around the diamond while the outfielders hit in the fifteen-foot steel batting cage at the Little League complex above our field. When the outfielders finished hitting, we switched, and D hit ground balls and fly balls to the outfielders with JV players as cutoff men.

We tried for years without success to get a batting cage set up near our field. Before each game and during every practice, the players had to stride up a path behind the third base dugout, climb a steep path, cross Nutmeg Avenue, then bound up a fifteen-foot rutted hill to get to the steel cage to hit. The players worked tirelessly before each game at the cage. Whenever somebody fed the JUGS machine inside the metal cage, they had to wear a batting helmet. With each ball fed into the powder blue electric machine, we would hear the *fffffoop* sound of a yellow dimple ball as it was spit out the white tires, speeding toward the hitter. If the batter made contact, it would be followed by the loud clang of the hard plastic ball banging and ricocheting off the cage's steel fence posts. If a batter missed the ball, your ears would tell you.

The cage hitter not only got swings off the machine but also faced a live one. We used three-dollar practice balls, or blems, for live BP, as the life of a cowhide baseball in the metal cage was short-lived. When my right arm started to shake in between hitters, Pete jumped in and threw to any remaining batters.

Batters outside the cage hit balls off high and low batting tees and an ATEC soft toss machine until they got their turn to flip up the clasp, open the metal door, and step inside the cage. Adjacent to the cage, we set up a bunting station. We used a one-tire JUGS pitching machine designed for Little Leaguers and girl's softball and four orange cones to mark off where the batter should drop the bunt. By the time a batter descended down the hazardous path from the cage to the field below, he had hit off a machine, rotated at hitting stations, and faced live pitching.

Whenever Pete or I pitched live, we would throw five-four-three-two-one to each hitter. For the leadoff, second, seventh, eighth, and ninth batters in the lineup, we threw five fastballs, four curves, three fastballs, two curves, and a fastball. For the third, fourth, fifth, and sixth hitters, we reversed it. We designed the sequence so our middle of the order batters saw more curveballs, matching what they saw in most at bats. I never ended a player's BP on a swing and a miss. After each player had hit, I jumped into my Honda, exited the school parking lot, zipped down Chatfield Street, and hoped the gate was open or I could pull into an open space on the street near the clubhouse.

Before most games, I was exhausted by the time I reached the field. Our league rules stated that the visiting team got the field from 2:45 PM to 3:15 PM to do whatever they wanted. The home team got it back at 3:15 PM. After I arrived at the dugout, downed some lime Gatorade, and the visiting team vacated the field, I hit our pregame infield and outfield. After George Hay fielded the last ground ball and fired a sky ball above home plate for Lizza to catch, I rested on the bench as D, Ben, Donny, and Pete went over the ground rules with the umps and our opponent's coach and captains.

When Cheshire arrived, they skipped batting practice. Like most years, they were late. With their talent, they could afford to miss BP. After their pregame infield and outfield, Coach Leventhal surrendered the field to us to complete ours. After Donny completed his warm-up, he ducked his head and stepped into the dugout. His arm felt loose even on short rest. Donny knew what was at stake but was also looking for a measure of revenge from his first outing in Cheshire, when he had stunk up the place.

Cheshire decided to throw their ace pitcher, Jim Shanley. Shanley was the seventh inning relief pitcher the first time we'd played them, and had shut down our rally and earned the save. Today, he was the starter. Leventhal wasn't about to give us a break after we proved we could hit his other pitchers.

One of our reserve senior players, Carlos Ortiz, or Los as he was known among his teammates, sought D's permission to be excused from the game. He had previously committed himself to attending another high school's prom. Los didn't want to miss the game, but also didn't want to break his commitment to the girl involved. The request didn't sit well with D, but the day before the game, he reached a compromise with Los. I didn't know what the compromise was until I was walking toward our dugout and saw Los—his goatee now trimmed—standing beside it cheering us on in a tuxedo, cummerbund, and bow tie. From where Reegers sat in center field, it looked like a giant fat penguin wearing glossy black shoes stood beside our dugout. Leventhal must have thought we were nuts. I would have agreed with him.

When the game began, our bench roared like it was the bottom of the seventh. I wondered whether we could sustain that emotion level for seven innings. The game was scoreless until the bottom of the third, when Joey G. reached first on a rare infield error by Cheshire. Gino dropped a "between the cones" sacrifice bunt, advancing Joey G. to second.

Pete rocked back and forth in the batter's box. He swung his bat like a thirty-three-inch ax again and again as he waited. Pete leaned back as Shanley kicked and slung a fastball speeding toward him. Determined, Pete lined a single through the middle, putting us ahead 1–0.

In the top of the fifth, the Rams tied the game on a line drive home run just over Pete's reach at the four-foot center field fence, but that didn't stop our bench from their nonstop cheering.

In the sixth inning, Cheshire threatened again. The bases were loaded with no outs. As Donny rolled up his short sleeves, I remembered the time he had pitched for me in a game against Cheshire's American Legion team at Cheshire High's field. He had gotten himself into the identical jam. I had shouted to him from our dugout that I wanted to see him get out of it, allowing no runs. A forty-something-aged fan sitting on the Cheshire side—acting like he paid a week's salary for a box seat which granted him a license to taunt our players—yapped, "Yeah, I want to see him try and get out of it too." The pro ballplayers aren't the only ones who have to put up with fans who act like jerks. Although Donny rolled up his sleeves and tried his hardest, he allowed a run to come across the plate. The Cheshire Legion fan laughed loud enough for Donny to hear. When the inning ended, Donny entered the dugout and flung his beat-up glove on the bench. I told Donny he played American Legion baseball to face pressure like that so when the high school season rolled around, he would be prepared to succeed in a similar situation.

Donny bore down on the next Ram batter and got ahead in the count. Tules clapped his hands then cupped them around his mouth and challenged Donny to put the batter in the book. From the stretch, Donny kicked and fired a two-seam fastball. The spinning speedball tailed in on the batter's gloved hands and popped in Joey's mitt. The umpire raised his right fist and shouted, "Strike three!"

Donny fired a four-seam fastball to the next hitter. The ball popped up in the infield. The umpires pointed up in the air and shouted, "Infield fly!" The runners retreated to their bases.

"One more time, Donny!" we yelled. "One more!"

"Show me what you got, kid!" cried Tules. "Show me!" The next hitter stepped into the batter's box. Pitching from the windup, Donny heard the Cheshire fan from last summer still laughing in his head, but Donny was now bigger and faster than his July disaster. He looked toward the plate and saw nothing but Joey's mitt. He kicked and whipped his arm as if it were the last fastball he would ever throw. The batter swung, and Donny pointed straight up as the ball was lifted high above the infield again. The runner on third stepped on home plate; however, the run didn't count. The ball was gloved, ending the threat.

As he walked off the mound and stepped over the foul line, Donny pumped his right arm, looked at me, and pointed. When he reached the dugout, he said, "This one is for that guy in Cheshire who said I couldn't do it." I wished the same guy who had taunted Donny in the summer had been in the stands again. Little did he realize the effect he had had on a high school kid.

After Donny escaped the top of the seventh without giving up a run, I knew we had the "Hammer." The Hammer is baseball lingo for the last-at-bat in a game. Why they called it that, I wasn't certain, but I knew I would rather possess the Hammer than let Cheshire have it. Unfortunately, the bottom of our order was up.

Our players stood on the edge of the dugout with their rally caps on. Shanley overpowered Romo and Massie with fastballs for the first two outs and got two quick strikes on Joey G. The right-hander took the snapped throw back from the catcher. In less than a second, he was back on the rubber. He took the single-digit sign from the catcher and nodded. He rocked back, kicked, and fired a fastball toward the plate, thinking the game would go into extra innings.

But Joey G. connected. *Ping.* The ball headed high toward the left field fence. Cheshire's left fielder sped back.

From where I stood in the third base coach's box, it looked like the ball would bounce off the fence for a double. The ball hung in the air longer than I expected. Then it happened. The ball went over. Ecstatic, I jumped with my right fist in the air.

Joey slowed to a trot after he reached first base. He finally realized the ball had gone over the fence but still hadn't realized what he had accomplished.

The rest of the team went berserk. The players charged home plate as if we won the seventh game of the World Series. Anroman leaped onto another teammate's back for a piggyback ride. The players pushed and shoved each other for position behind the plate as Joey slowed around second base. He didn't want the moment to end. I raised my right hand, and Joey smacked it with his gloved right hand as he rounded third. D was on the edge of the plate, screaming at the players to stay back and let Joey touch home.

When Joey G., wearing number 13, finally stepped on home plate—ending the game and launching us into the state tournament—our team mobbed him. Players hugged each other. D shook Ben's face while looking him in the eyes and screaming, "Yeaaaaaaah, Benjy!"

Pete embraced me. "We're going to the show, Riles! We're going to the show!"

While I stood on the edge of the joyous pile at home plate, I eyed D on the opposite side. While the celebration continued, D noticed a pair of black plastic goggles on the ground. He sneaked up to the protective specs and stomped them like he was putting out a stubborn cigarette. Gino never noticed. When the team finally let Joey G. stammer away from home plate, his scratched-up red helmet covered his eyebrows. He tilted his head back and found his way to our dugout.

We were lost in the celebration, but, when Cheshire's left fielder had sprinted back toward the fence, he had crashed face-first into the chain-link fence as the ball flew over it. While I rushed toward home plate to join the pile, Coach Leventhal hurried toward left field. In the excitement, I hadn't noticed Cheshire's player lying on the ground. I ran to left field to see how bad the outfielder was injured and ask if Coach Leventhal needed us to call an ambulance or give his player any first aid. A bloody imprint of a tic-tac-toe board marred the player's cheek.

After his teammates helped the hatless Cheshire player to his feet and attended to his face, the teams lined up at home plate for the customary postgame handshake. When D and I greeted Coach Leventhal, he gave us what we called the "Fish." That's when the opposing coach extends his hand to shake yours and just puts limp fingers between yours. It's as if your adversary slipped a dead fish in your hand. We expected the lifeless congratulation, as Burt Leventhal had done the same thing the year Pokey's team beat them with Frankie Pecheco on the mound. Whenever Leventhal beat us, however—as he more often did—he would give us a firm handshake, look us in the eye, and say, "Good game." This time, we got to say, "Good game."

After Cheshire's bus left, our team remained on the infield as parents and friends congratulated us. Donny thanked me for keeping him pumped the whole game. Sean Barker, the *Evening Sentinel* reporter, scribbled on his small pad as he interviewed D near our dugout. After getting D's comments, he sought out Joey G. and Donny. He interviewed them on top of the mound.

While Lizza held Joey G. atop his shoulders, Sean asked Joey G. about his game-ending blast. After Horse let Joey down, Joey G. approached me, thanked me for helping him with his hitting, and offered his hand. Gino searched for his goggles like he had lost a hundred-dollar bill. He found them mashed into the cinder track outside the home plate area. They looked like a tandem drum roller had crushed them, but Gino thought someone in the pile at home plate had accidentally stepped on them. He picked them up as if they were a wounded baby bird and carried them to the clubhouse.

Sue approached me and handed me a small piece of wrinkled white paper she found on the grass area near our dugout. I recognized the sharp printing. It read, "Fist, steal; One flash, hit-and–run; two flashes, bunt." The piece of paper made me realize why D had been kneeling and looking at the ground while I was trying to keep eye contact from my third base coach's box. He used a cheat sheet to remember the three possible hand signals between us. Fortunately, there was no academic baseball rule against it.

As soon as we opened the metal clubhouse door, the players fought for the payphone receiver on the wall. Moments later, Tules answered the call. At the bottom of the stairs leading up to the second floor locker room, Pete screamed into the phone. "Tuuuuuuules!" came the background cry as other players tried to wrestle the receiver away from Pete.

After the players spoke, Tules told me he was ecstatic about the win. He called the clubhouse earlier and was surprised to learn we were ahead 1–0. After that, he hadn't been able to concentrate on anything but the game's outcome. I described the wide smiles on the faces of the players and told him how much they wanted him present for the on-the-field celebration and how they couldn't wait to call him.

After I spoke to Tules, I climbed the stairs to the jubilant locker room. Joey G. handed me a game ball signed by himself and the rest of the team. Joey had written the word *thanks* on it, next to his signature and number 13. I told Joey it was his willingness to learn and change that earned him the reward. After I accepted the memento, I noticed Romo's football number, 48—not his baseball number, 22—appeared in blue after his signature.

D addressed the team with two game balls in his hands. "OK, fellas, we got our first goal. Celebrate it today, as it's always a good win whenever you beat Cheshire. I'm extremely proud of you guys, since they were kicking your butts down in Cheshire until we started to make a comeback."

I tilted my head toward Jocko behind me. "Go downstairs and order some pizzas from Roseland," I said, just above a whisper. "Find out what Brian wants on one."

"No problem," he replied. Jocko whispered to Brian Marcucio, then slipped out the door unnoticed.

D continued, "Donny, that was gutsy the way you got out of that inning with the bases loaded and no outs. This one's for you, kid." He flipped him a ball. The team clapped as Donny balanced the scuffed ball on the shelf in his locker beside several others.

D raised the second ball. "Joey G., what can I say?" Joey smiled and high-fived Pete. "You finally decided we do know what we're talking about, and it paid off for you." D flipped him the second ball, and the team clapped again.

"Tomorrow," D said, "we'll begin seeking our second goal to win as many of our last three games as we can. Hopefully, we can get a home game in the first round of the tournament, so we don't have to travel up to Oshkosh to play."

"In the first two rounds," I added, "the games are played at the field of the higher-seeded team with umps from their league until you get to the quarters. We shouldn't have to tell you what that would mean."

"Yeah," interjected Ben, "we get screwed like we did last year."

"Once we accomplished our second goal," D continued, "we'll turn our sights to accomplish our final goal, one game at a time."

"When are we getting our new hats?" Ben asked, referring to a promise Ken Marcucio made to the players if they reached the tournament.

"I'll find out. Hopefully, you'll have them on your heads before the tournament."

Despite the wide-eyed smiles on Ben, Donny, and Gino's faces in the locker room that day, I still wondered whether making the state baseball tournament was enough for them, as well as the other football players, to make amends for allowing the Streak to end. Though among our team it would, I knew for a town that cared about football first, it most likely wouldn't make much difference.

The next day, the *Sentinel* quoted D: "The seniors in Derby have been shunned a bit. After a disappointing football and basketball season, it was great to see them come out here and make the state tournament."[8] Joey G. was reported as saying, "It felt good, but I wasn't sure if it was gone when I saw the left fielder running to the fence. That's the first one. I never played Little League." For Joey G., his first-round tripper was one he would never forget.

17

Winning Two while Missing Home Plate

We shivered in our red jackets as we did most spring nights when we played North Haven under the lights at Sachem Field. Without dugouts, the wind pounded our backs as we huddled like penguins on our wooden benches next to first base. Several prepared parents brought blankets and seat cushions, as they viewed the game from six rows of cold aluminum stands behind our bench.

Since North Haven played their home games at night, it was a distinct advantage for them. North Haven's night games tended to be filled with partisan North Haven High School students, as well as parents who attended the games after work. Their numbers extended from behind North Haven's third baseline bench to the two-door building housing the Diamond Club concession stand adjacent to the left field foul pole.

On occasion, some North Haven students who played football hung out along the right field line. They took pleasure in pestering our players and tried to pick fights. Although we complained to North Haven's school officials, it didn't stop.

Like the first North Haven game, Ben mowed down their hitters, striking out ten batters. He allowed only four hits in six innings, but North Haven's pitcher, Rob Marsoli, shut us out, scattering only four hits in his seven innings. Only Ben, Donny, and Mike Massie hit safely that frigid night at Sachem Field as we lost 3–0. Although Ben left most of North Haven's hitters with a lower batting average and on-base percentage, it was no consolation to him; his record was now a dismal 2–7. With another disappointing loss, D and I wondered how much more Ben could endure before he lost faith in his ability to win.

After the handshake line finished, the players sat on the bench to remove their spikes before they got onto our idling bus. Coach DeMayo, North Haven's legendary coach, approached our bench and addressed our players. "Go all the way, Derby. You can do it. You have the heart and the talent to get it done." At that moment, my feelings for DeMayo changed. I didn't think he was such a bad guy after all.

Two days later, we journeyed over the Q Bridge on I-95 to East Haven's field. With a senior housing center across the street from its backstop, the fenceless field was part of a complex the size of a city block, surrounded by a two-lane road. Beyond center field was a small diamond used for softball or Little League. An electric scoreboard down the left field line beamed each game's score.

Sometimes East Haven fans would park behind the backstop. The sun would reflect off their chrome bumpers and force our infielders to shun the rays that bounced off them. But when East Haven took the field, like a trick from a David Copperfield show, the cars would mysteriously disappear. Despite the occasional reflective obstacles, I never minded East Haven's field, since I could sit in a dugout when it rained and, when I needed to, use the facilities in the public works building across the street.

Since we had already clinched the tournament, D decided to start Los at the designated hitter spot. Los was anxious to prove he could contribute. Donny started the game on the mound, but after two innings we were chasing two runs. In our half of the fourth, we fought back. The Easties's pitcher, Chris Marchitto, walked Donny. George Hay singled, and Joey G. slapped a two-out single, scoring both runners. We put two more runs on the board in the fifth and took a 4–3 lead when Ben drove in Pete and scored himself on an error. But the Yellow Jackets came right back and scored two more runs in the bottom of the fifth to retake the lead, 5–4.

In the top of the sixth, Gino and Los both walked. Richie Calvert pinch ran for Gino. Kenny Cronk, a thin-faced scholarly looking junior who didn't see much action, went in to run for Los. Pete squared and sacrifice bunted them over to second and third to line up the tying and winning runs. Ben then blazed a clutch single to center. Both Richie C. and fleet-footed Kenny Cronk passed the plate standing up and high-fived Donny in the on-deck circle as the rainbow relay came in from the outfield. The Easties didn't even try to get them out. But when play stopped, we ended up with only one run.

The home plate umpire called Cronk out, ruling he hadn't touched home plate with either of his white spikes, negating our go-ahead run. Under high school rules that year, there was no appeal when a runner missed a base. If the umpire saw it happen at the end of the play, he simply called the player out. From the third base coach's box, Kenny looked like he had tripped over the plate, which would mean he at least touched it. The home plate umpire, however, had seen it otherwise.

Squeezing his red hat in his right hand like a sponge, D argued to the man in blue, Rudy Raffone, that the catcher had been standing there looking at the runners cross and hadn't made a peep when our second runner missed home. Rudy looked at D, shrugged his protector-puffed shoulders, bent over like a fishhook, and brushed off home plate with his pocket-sized whiskbroom. "What do you want me to do?" Raffone asked. "I was looking right at the plate, and the kid missed it." D pled to no avail that if Kenny hadn't touched the plate, what had he tripped on?

As Cronk stood motionless before the scraped-up red helmets strewn near the end of the dugout, D kept demanding Cronk explain to him how somebody could miss home plate. Since there was no play on him at the time, even if the slightest doubt had crept into Kenny's mind, he could have gone back to step on it again.

Not to let him escape without blame, D turned to Donny as he approached the plate and also blamed the senior tri-captain. If Kenny hadn't touched the irregular pentagon—or even if there was uncertainty of it—Donny should've seen it and insisted Kenny go back and tag it again.

When the bottom of the sixth began, Cronk sat in the far corner of the dugout, chewing his nails and examining the tiny white stitches inside his hat. D and I stood near the on-deck circle.

"How the hell can anyone miss home plate?" D asked loud enough for everyone on the bench to hear.

"I touched it," Cronk replied, his voice trailing off. He tucked his head between his shoulders, barely revealing his brown hair.

"D, maybe you should let up a bit on Cronk," I said. "He says he touched it. Maybe he did. From where I was standing, it looked like he tripped over something as he crossed it."

"He probably tripped over his own feet," D said angrily. "Even so," he added, lowering his voice, "Rudy didn't have to make that call. East Haven's catcher didn't say anything."

"It's over," I said. I picked up a bat and secured it next to the others in the rack attached to the side of our dugout. "We still have to try to win this game."

D moved closer to me. Trying to hold back his anger, he whispered, "I realize that, Riles, but answer me this. How does a kid f—king miss home plate?"

"I don't know," I replied as I tilted my head, turned my palms up, and flopped them at my side. I looked at Los on the quiet bench. Los stuffed some Bazooka in his mouth, read his fortune, and put his Blues Brothers sunglasses back on. He gripped his bat's black rubber handle with his strong hands, leaned forward, and tapped the cement floor. With his pink bubble about to burst, Los contemplated his future. He must have known that if D never trusted Kenny enough to pinch run him again, his own ability to get any further playing time would be severely hampered.

Ben took the mound in the bottom of the sixth. The Easties didn't touch him. After neither team scored in the seventh, the game went into extra innings. In the top of the eighth, Pete launched a rocket over the center fielder's head. The ball rolled forever on the freshly cut grass. When Pete reached third, I waved him on toward an inside-the-park home run. Exhausted, Pete stomped on the rubber plate with his metal spikes.

In the bottom half of the eighth, Ben put up another zero and saved the game, as well as Kenny Cronk's ass. Since we went ahead in the game while Ben was pitching, he notched the technical win and improved his record to 3–7. On the half-hour bus ride back, despite our W, D kept staring straight ahead repeating, "How does a kid freakin' miss home plate?" The ride back made me wish I had driven my car to the game or riden shotgun with Tules, who flew his two-seat Corvette to every game.

The next day we faced Branford, our final foe of the regular season, at home. It was Ben's turn to start. We asked whether he wanted to pitch even though he had thrown three innings the day before. We knew under the thirty-out rule he could pitch the whole game if it only went seven innings, but we wanted to be sure his arm wasn't tired.

Ben wanted the ball. It was his last chance to improve his poor win-loss record before the state tournament. The tournament was not for another ten days. If Donny started our first tournament game, Ben's rest would be even longer.

We got to Branford's tall pitcher, Kevin Hickey, before his arm got loose. With two outs in the bottom of the first, Donny was nicked by a curveball. Lizza singled, and Hay walked to load the bases. Two pitches to the backstop later, we were ahead two gifts to none. Although the score was still within Branford's reach at 4–0 after five innings, we blew them out with six more runs in the sixth. By games end, we tallied only six hits, but with all the walks, wild pitches, and hit batsmen, the Hornets were never in the game, and we won it easily 10–0. Despite pitching two days in a row, Ben went the distance, struck out seven, and retired the last twelve Branford batters in order. We ended the regular season at 12–8 but hoped it wasn't the last game the seniors would ever play at Ryan Field.

18

Losing Two Coin Flips

The day after the Branford game, Ken Marcucio drove to the CIAC's office off Route 10 in Cheshire. He learned who our opponent was the moment the pairings were announced and picked up our tournament packet. An hour into our practice, we spotted a maroon, four-door Buick sedan roll through the gate and knew it was Mr. Marcucio's. Ken drove up the driveway, turned in front of the clubhouse, and stopped, but he didn't get out his car. D and I greeted him while our anxious players remained on the field with Tules and Jocko.

"Who'd we get?" D asked, his cigarette burning in his cupped right hand behind him. Ken handed him the standard manila envelope through his driver's side window. D took the envelope with his fungo-blackened left hand.

"Coventry," Ken replied, wearing an unblemished hat with "Derby Red Raiders" embroidered in white across its crown—the bill of the red cap still flat as if taken from a tightly packed box.

"Who the hell is Coventry?"

"It's where Doc Chesler is originally from," he said, referring to our superintendent of schools.

"Did we get a home game?"

"No."

D envisioned the disappointed senior players' faces. Their Ryan Field career was over. "Why not?" D asked as he flicked his cigarette. Gray ashes floated to the tarred driveway behind him.

"We lost two coin flips between three teams with a 12–8 record. I think we ended up ranked seventeenth."

"Same as my uniform number," I interjected.

"Where the f—k is Coventry?" D asked. The ashes on the end of his cigarette were longer than the filter.

"It's a town somewhere east of Hartford, not far from UConn," Ken explained as he spotted smoke rising above the back of D's head. "Barring traffic, it's about a fifty-minute bus ride away."

"Great," D said as he shook his head.

"I'll see how early I can get you out."

"Maybe we should just rent hotel rooms and sleep there the night before," D said. He backed up a step and grinned.

"The tournament rules are also in there, along with each team's roster," Ken advised as he started his car's engine. As Ken drove away, D handed me the packet. I studied the brackets.

"D, I don't want to be the giver of bad news," I said, "but these pairings say if we beat Coventry, we get Portland, the number one ranked team, who has a bye."

"Do you know what leagues Coventry and Portland are in?"

"No, but I'll check the *Hartford Courant* sports sections I have in my locker. The standings of most of the leagues appear in the Sunday edition."

I hastened upstairs and rifled through my pile of newspapers. I learned Coventry was in the Cross County Conference. Their nickname was the Patriots. The "CCC," as it was known, did not have anywhere near the number of larger schools we played. Portland was the winner of the Charter Oak Conference, which contained no L (over 350 male enrollment) or LL (over 500 male enrollment) schools. I returned downstairs and told D what I learned.

"Maybe it's our destiny," I said. "Maybe we were meant to have to play everywhere and win."

"Maybe so, but we can't let on to the team we're at a disadvantage having to travel. I would've liked a home game."

"Me too."

As D and I strode back to the field and neared the dugout, the players approached us, along with Tules and Jocko. I passed the manila packet to Tules. He removed the pairings and examined them as if he were looking at his son's first report card.

"Good news, fellas," D said.

"Who we playing?" Ben asked.

"Coventry," D replied. He picked up the fungo bat with the dirty athletic tape wrapped around the barrel's dented sweet spot.

"Who the f—k is Coventry?" Gino asked, standing there in his red shorts, holding a bat against his chest.

"Who gives a shit who we play, Gino?" Ben interjected. "It doesn't matter." He shuffled dirt back and forth with his red Nike spikes.

"Yeah, who gives a shit who we play," added Romo as he tossed a darkened practice ball to Hay. Romo put his glove under his left arm pit, spit out his dead gum, and blew out his left nostril on the track.

"We playing here?" asked a concerned Pete as he stared at the packet between Tules's fingers.

"No. We lost two coin flips and get to play on the road," D said.

"You lost two coin flips, D?" asked David jokingly.

D must have wondered himself how we had gotten so unlucky. "No, the CIAC does it themselves," he explained.

"It would've been nice to get a home game, but it doesn't matter," said Pete.

"Where is Coventry?" Joe Lizza asked.

"Let's just finish practice, and we'll talk about it later, OK, fellas," D said. He hobbled stiffly toward home plate, swung his waist back and forth with his fungo in both hands, and grimaced. D no longer desired to think about our opponent. "Let's go," he barked. "We've got work to do."

After practice, we met with the players in the locker room to mentally prepare them for the tournament. The two benches were divided between players who were football players in baseball pants and the die-hard baseball players whose second sport might've been football. On the left bench were the die-hard baseball players: Pete, Ben, Donny, Joey G., Joe Lizza, and Mike Massie. On the right one was Gino, Romo, George Hay, Greg Maliska, Carlos Ortiz, and Angelo DiRubba. Across the aisle, to the right of where the coaches stood, were the rest of the players.

Each coach addressed the team about what he thought it took to win a state championship. D spoke about winning the games one at a time and not thinking about the next game until you won the one you were playing in. It was a line from the movie *Hoosiers*, which D had watched a thousand times and finally gotten the chance to use. It was similar to Jimmy Valvano's NCAA tournament philosophy of "survive and advance."

"The pros have a luxury we don't," I asserted. "The World Series is seven games, but in our tournament lose one game and you're out. You can't win a state title unless you can beat nine of either D, Tules, Jocko, or me. While boys can make this tournament, only men can win it." I pulled a purple ticket stub from my pocket and raised it in the air. "This is a ticket I saved from last year's Class S state championship game," I revealed. "I don't want to have to pay to watch this one."

Tules talked at length about how much he cared for each of the players. Their glassy eyes told him they felt the same about him. "Each team in this tournament starts with the same record," he added. "We got just as much chance as anybody else to win this thing."

D then asked Jocko if he had anything to say. The silence in the room and the grin on D's face made me sense Jocko—as he did all year—was about to give us some pearl of comic relief.

Before a JV baseball game earlier in the season, Jocko had read off the lineup to his huddled team. Tules eavesdropped as he leaned on the edge of the dugout. Jocko cleared his throat and began: "Leading off and batting first," but before Jocko could get the next word out of his mouth, Tules staggered like a dizzy bat contest loser at a minor-league ball game. Two players held Tules up as he laughed at the obvious redundancy.

After the season started, inclement weather once forced us to practice in the gym. The JV practiced after the varsity, and D and I watched as Jocko demonstrated to the JV players how to slide headfirst. He wasn't about to make his ballplayers do anything he wouldn't do himself.

Jocko lined up at the half-court line in front of his players and rocked as if he waiting for a starter pistol to go off. With his baseball cap covering his ears, he dashed toward the far wall, taking short, loud breaths.

Jocko leaped headfirst onto the floor and slid along the shiny maple surface like a hockey puck.

His frightened players were silent; they held their breath.

Jocko crashed into the cinderblock wall underneath the red protective padding. He felt his thirty-one-year-old body creak as he struggled to his feet. He brushed the dust off his red sweatshirt and coerced a smile—as if pain wasn't an option.

While his players fought over who was next in line, we suggested to Jocko that he might want to consider having his players start at the wall and run toward half-court before they slide.

Jocko had his own unique way of getting a point across to his players, but he was a loyal and hardworking coach. Jocko was never one to avoid the grunt work of coaching high school baseball. Whenever D asked him to do something, Jocko simply quipped, "No problem." He arrived at practice each afternoon in his Stella D'ora box truck, directly after making his deliveries. Jocko's players smiled whenever they saw his truck enter the clubhouse driveway, either because they knew the type of effort he made to get to the field on time or because they hoped he had some outdated breakfast treats or broken cookies they could feast on before the packages went in the dumpster behind the center field fence.

Jocko paused to gather his thoughts. The players to the left grinned as the players to the right wondered why. Acting as if he were Vince Lombardi, Jocko said, "In order to win, you have to sacrifice your body."

I was dumbfounded. D and Tules looked like their cheeks were inflating with their lips sewn shut, but the die-hard baseball players on the left bench weren't able to contain their laughter. Their bench teetered, and spikes skidded on the floor until they regained their composure and balance on the bench. To my amazement, however, no one on the right bench laughed at all. Instead, they nodded up and down like bobblehead dolls. David Anroman pounded his dry leather glove. "Yeah, you're right, Jocko," Dave blurted. "We gotta sacrifice our bodies, yeah, sacrifice our bodies." I didn't have the heart to ask Jocko how he proposed baseball players do that unless the opportunity to dive at a ball came up in a game or somebody intentionally got hit by a pitch.

When D, Tules, Jocko, and I retreated to the privacy of the coaches' room, D asked, "Jocko, what the f—k were you talking about?" Tules bounced his shoulders, and I staggered back into a locker as we burst into laughter. Jocko's statement was unorthodox, but at least he got the football players to stop looking like they were auditioning for roles as extras in the *Night of the Living Dead*. I hoped his pearl of wisdom might at least get the guys it reached to go to bed earlier. We already had players sleeping in the Eastern and Pacific time zones. Freshman Joe Lizza went to bed at 9:00 PM; Romo nodded off at about 1:00 AM after Leno or Letterman. Hopefully, Jocko's statement wouldn't end up getting one of our players hurt; we didn't have a deep bench.

After we stopped ribbing Jocko, D asked us what we thought about the pitching rotation. After the discussion, D decided to pitch Donny against Coventry and, if we won, Ben against top-ranked Portland.

19

Rounds One and Two

Our players walked out of school before 1:15 PM without getting a detention. Coventry was about an hour and a half away, but the school wasn't going to spring for an air-conditioned coach bus. Instead, we ended up stuck in a traffic jam on I-84 in a school bus with the windows down. I thought D might panic, but he didn't.

When the yellow bus grinded to a stop on the highway, we stretched out in the aisles to save time after we reached Coventry. D and I brainstormed how we could accomplish batting practice within the time we would have the field. We decided that, while the infielders loosened up, I would throw batting practice to the outfielders. When I threw to the infielders, the outfielders would loosen up. When I finished, I would hit the pregame infield and outfield.

When we arrived at Coventry High School, the team scrambled off the bus like a SWAT team. The infielders swarmed the diamond while I ducked under the batting cage net beyond the left field foul line and threw to the outfielders. Coventry's field was without outfield fences, but there was no cornfield at the end, only an asphalt parking lot five hundred feet from home plate in left field and a soccer field beyond right field. Our forest green wooden dugout barely held our team. A thin green striped metal pole encased in an exposed concrete footing stood in the middle and supported the roof, but at least we had a dugout.

With Ray Ray behind him, Reegers endured the trek from the parking lot to the first base side of the field. He decided to take the game in from behind our end of the backstop.

Pete led off the game against Coventry's Rob Buteau with a line drive to the gap in left center. He bellied the turn, flew past Tules at first base, and sped toward second. He slid and popped up on the base as the ball hit the cutoff man on the infield edge. D sensed Pete wanted to take third. He called for the steal. We caught the high-kicking Buteau by surprise as Pete pilfered third with a bent-leg slide. After Donny walked with one out, Joe Lizza smacked an RBI single to left, scoring Pete and advancing Donny to second.

Coventry then tried to employ a trick play I had seen employed by the University of Miami. Buteau stepped off the rubber and faked a throw to first.

The first baseman dove as if the ball got past him. The right fielder darted toward the line as if he was going after the ball.

I screamed from the third base coaching box, "The pitcher still has the ball!"

At first, Tules didn't know what was happening until he looked down the right field line and didn't see a ball. Thankfully, Joe, who was at first base, was not fooled and stayed put.

George Hay stepped to the plate. As if posing for a baseball card, he took two strikes without taking the bat off his shoulder. D decided to employ one of his own unorthodox moves: a two strike hit-and-run. I relayed the sign to George. His eyes widened. With Donny running on the pitch, Hay swung his bat and singled to left, giving us a 2–0 lead. Few if any high school baseball coaches would think about, let alone try, a hit-and-run with two strikes. But D always believed that once you gave a high school hitter the hit-and-run sign, he tried harder to make contact. Since Buteau had been around the plate and George had watched the first two strikes go by as if he had seen the take sign, D had just been trying to force George to take the bat off his shoulders.

Donny retired the first nine batters before surrendering a walk. He set the next nine down in order and almost put Mickey to sleep in our dugout. Coventry never threatened to score. By game's end, Donny had struck out nine, walked just one, and surrendered only one hit, a ground ball seeing-eye single in the sixth that barely reached the outfield grass. We won only 2–0, but we survived and advanced.

The next day before practice, I sifted through the newspapers in my locker. I dug out the sports section of the *Hartford Courant* I had picked up the previous Sunday. A photographer had captured a picture of the Portland team celebrating their Charter Oak Conference championship victory on the mound at Palmer Field in Middletown. The byline under the picture revealed one of the players in the photo was Portland's winning pitcher, Grant Copeland. While I was in the coaches' room with D, some of the players were climbing the stairs on their way to the locker room. As Pete walked by, I called him into the room. Ben, Donny, Joey G., and some of the other players followed him in. The room was too small for the whole team, so some of them waited outside the door.

"What do you notice about the Portland pitcher that's significant to you?" I asked.

After a glance at the picture, one of players said, "The pitcher isn't wearing stirrup socks."

"No, it's because he's a short kid," another said.

"It's the letter P on his hat," someone else suggested as a joke.

"He has an unusual first name: Grant."

D briefly studied the picture and looked up at me with a grin on his face. "The pitcher is a lefty."

Again, D and I were on the same page. We knew if Copeland was the pitcher Portland threw in their league championship game, it must mean he was their best pitcher. We hadn't faced many lefty pitchers all year. We adjusted the JUGS machine to throw lefty fastballs and curves and left-hander Kenny Cronk threw live batting practice. If we had the chance to take batting practice in Portland, Kenny would throw it as long as his arm would let him. Cronk was eager to hurl BP to help D forget his East Haven fiasco.

We also decided that if we reached Portland High before 2:15 PM, we would try to take over Portland's field and make it our own. We wanted our players comfortable and confident on Portland's diamond to erase the Highlander's home-field advantage. Ken Marcucio arranged it so that the players would get out of school early enough that a traffic delay would not impact our pregame preparation again.

The ride to Portland on school bus number 16, the same as Ben's uniform number, took us up Route 8 to Route 84, then to Route 66. Portland is adjacent the eastern side of Middletown. To get to the town of a little over nine thousand inhabitants, we had to travel past Palmer Field in Middletown. Palmer Field was the site where all the state championship games would be played this year.

When the bus rolled past the field of high school dreams, the players on the right side of the bus jumped over to the left to get a better look. One of them blurted, "There it is, boys. That's where we'll play if we win three more." The stadium surrounded its manicured infield. A metal roof atop the press box stretched out over the bleachers behind home plate, black netting draped from its edge to the backstop below. Multiple metal light posts surrounded the field. All the majestic field was missing was two survivors playing for a championship.

When we arrived at Portland High School, the home of the Highlanders, school was still in session. The city crew was raking and tamping the pitcher's mound and dragging the infield. The smell of fresh-cut grass told me the infield and outfield had just been trimmed. The home team dugout on the third base side of the field was atop a small hill, not surprising given their team's name. Anyone watching the game in the third base dugout would be looking down over the field. If the two sets of six-row portable aluminum stands were filled, the hill below them continued along the left field line and provided a soft place to view the action. A batting cage made of metal poles and black netting stood behind the Highlanders's afternoon home.

Our first base dugout, like the home team's, was constructed of brown cinderblocks. The structure had a wooden roof, a chain-link fence before it, and a forest behind it. Without a Porta-Potty in sight, I preferred the first base dugout. The only bathroom plumbing was at the school, a sixty-second sprint away. Nothing's worse than a field without bathroom facilities. A close second is a field without dugouts. More importantly, the first base side woods gave D a place to smoke during the game where no one would see him. The right field fence was a mere 252 feet away from home plate at the foul pole, but then it jutted out to a deeper distance. On the visitors' side of the field there were no stands and barely enough room for a couple lawn chairs.

As the city crew finished up, we took over Portland's field as if the city had just handed us a deed to it. D hit fungos to the infielders. I hit to the outfielders. Cronk pitched to the batters inside the netted cage who filtered in from the field. When the Highlanders and their coaches—in their maroon and white uniforms—left their gym locker room, they heard the constant banging of aluminum bats coming from their field. As they got closer, they must have wondered whether they were playing at home or on the road. By the time they reached their dugout, every one of our batters had hit off our diminutive lefty. Portland didn't take any batting practice in their cage. I suspected they might have already hit in their gymnasium.

I located Portland's left-handed pitcher, Grant Copeland, among his teammates with his maroon team jacket on. Our players were wearing short-sleeve undershirts under the afternoon sun. The jacket struck me as overkill, but it also told me he was a serious pitcher. He was shorter than I expected but reminded me of Aaron Sill.

After we hustled off our adopted field, the Portland team jogged on to start their pregame practice. Before their players got into position, I saw the blur of a large figure appear in the distance, the same way Clint Eastwood did in *High Plains Drifter*, only without the horse. As the figure approached the edge of the outfield, the blurred image became more focused. It was Tules. As usual, Tules drove directly to the field in his Corvette. It would have been a longer walk for him to go around the field and the backstop to get to our bench, so Tules started walking right through the field and Portland's outfield practice.

The massive man—wearing his red jacket and white baseball pants with red, white, and black stripes down the sides—ambled toward us. His stubble-filled face and the white letters "Derby Red Raiders" on his red hat became clearer as he got closer. He looked like Bluto in a baseball uniform as he strutted in spikes right through Portland's infield practice. The Portland players stopped what they were doing and let him pace across their practice without saying a word to him. From our dugout came the cry, "Tuuuuuuuuuules!"

Another player hollered, "You big dog, you!" Tules cracked a wide smile.

A few minutes before the first pitch of the game, Reegers showed up with Ray Ray behind his wheelchair. Undaunted, Ray Ray pushed the wheelchair across the terrain toward the backstop. Reegers finally took D up on his offer to sit inside our dugout. He stayed on the side of the dugout away from home plate with a small Yorkshire terrier leashed to his wheelchair. The world seemed in order as soon as he showed up.

When Ben began to warm up near the right field chalk line, he thought he was too close to the catcher. He questioned whether the marked-off pitching distance was accurate. I had measured the distance but decided to recheck it with him. We unrolled the cloth measuring tape and marked off the sixty feet six inches. The result was the same, but Ben still thought it was short. I took it as a good sign: Ben believed he was throwing shorter than actual distance. If he thought the plate was too far, I would've worried.

While Ben loosened up, I scanned the Portland side but couldn't find Copeland. Unless he was warming up in an opening behind the dense trees, it was highly unusual he hadn't started throwing. If he had already broken a sweat and thrown in the gym or somewhere else, he was allowing over a half hour to pass between his warm-up and his first pitch.

The umpires met with the coaches and captains at home plate to go over the ground rules. After D returned to the dugout, he told me he was bullshitting with the home plate umpire and learned he was a teacher of disabled students. D couldn't resist the opening. He revealed to the ump that his wife, Nancy, did the same. D thought he had at least something in common with him.

The game began with both teams putting up zeroes in the first two innings. Ben appeared to have his stuff but was throwing far fewer strikes than normal. On occasion, Joe would freeze his Mizuno mitt after the ump—wearing his bulked-up sky blue shirt and pressed gray pants—called a ball. I feared we were getting the shaft from the umps that covered Portland's league. I moved near the edge of the backstop to get a better look. From my new angle, it looked like the ump was calling a fair game. I thought Ben was merely experiencing early-inning jitters. Ben disagreed.

In the top of the third, Pete launched a stand-up triple to the left center field gap. As he took an aggressive lead down the third baseline, Ben laced a line drive single. Pete darted toward the plate with a white leather batting glove clutched in each hand. He stepped on the middle of the plate while the mustached umpire held his cushioned metal mask and stared at the plate to make sure Pete touched it. After Pete crossed the plate, he exhorted the players in the dugout to get pumped.

In the second inning, D learned there would be no accommodation for the special ed teacher's spouse. The umpire wasn't going to tolerate his smoking. He caught D and warned him not to do it again. To D, the tobacco tongue-lashing didn't mean stop smoking (as he couldn't), it merely meant he better hide behind the dugout next time he got the urge. D had a habit of lighting a cigarette and leaving it burning on the ground before him until he needed a drag. It wasn't that difficult for an umpire to see he was smoking. The evidence was smoldering right before him.

In the bottom of the third, Portland matched our run with a triple and single of their own. But we retook the lead in the fourth. George Hay topped a slow roller into an infield single. Romo's ground ball to short was misplayed, and Mike Massie executed a perfect drag bunt to load the bases with no outs. Angelo DiRubba went in to pinch run for Hay and scored on a 6-4-3 double play ball hit by Joey G. Anroman scored when Gino reached first on another Portland infield error, giving us a 3-1 lead.

In the meantime, Gino DiMauro was becoming the defensive MVP of the game. Without his goggles, Gino turned every ball hit anywhere near him into an out. On one of them, he dove, knocked the ball down with his outstretched glove, popped up faster than an automatic sprinkler head, and threw the runner out. On another, he stepped in front of a low-line drive, took a bouncing shot off his left leg, spun around, picked the ball up, and fired it to Hay's outstretched Mizuno mitt for the out. With each Gino gem, I imagined hearing ESPN highlight music. Each time Gino sprinted off the field at the end of an inning in which he had dazzled us with a great play, Los greeted him with a chest-to-chest collision with each of their hands held high.

In the fourth inning, the umpire nabbed D smoking again. He told D that if he caught him again, he would eject him. If D was Earl Weaver, he could have lit up a Raleigh in the locker room to dugout hallway and not get caught, but no such hiding place existed here.

Before we took the field in the bottom of the fifth, D shifted his eyes, then stepped behind our dugout, but not to use the forest facilities. Despite the umpire's final warning, he tapped his cellophane wrapped pack of cigarettes until one slid out and lit it with a blue Bic lighter. Pete followed him behind the dugout like a secret service agent charged with protecting the president. Anger lit his eyes. "D, what are we gonna do without you?" he asked. "You can't smoke, you'll get tossed."

"So what if I do? Riles will just coach the game."

More players went behind the dugout to beg D to stop; some started to panic. I peeked around the side of the dugout to see if the ump noticed our absence. As the team took the field, I reminded D of the CIAC rule that if a coach got tossed from any game, similar to a player, he would be ineligible to participate in the next game.

D stepped into the dugout with the lit cigarette in his curled-up hand. His options were running out. D examined the dugout, looking for a place to hide the evidence. He stepped over some deflated equipment bags to where Reegers was sitting in his wheelchair, wearing a turquoise shirt, shorts, and white sneakers. The small dog looked up at D. "Nice dog, Reegers."

"Thanks, D." D then held the smoldering cigarette underneath Reegers's small mustache. "Here, just keep this in your mouth," he said.

I thought my ears had deceived me but knew my eyes hadn't. "D!" I yelled from the middle of the dugout. "You can't do that! You might kill him!" All the eyes in the dugout widened in disbelief. D had just asked a quadriplegic to put a lit cigarette in his mouth.

Reegers laughed. The bench roared. D chuckled and turned around to search for another haven to hide the cigarette. Although I thought D had only been joking, a small part of me wondered whether he hadn't been.

The dugout events eased the tension caused by the game. Each inning, Ben fell into trouble with walks but somehow escaped it. We got an insurance run in the fifth. Ben changed his routine and slipped on a pair of red and white Mizuno batting gloves for good luck and reached first. Donny, who had struggled his last several times up and who had donned black Franklin batting gloves to try to change his luck, bunted Ben over to second. Joe Lizza roped another hit without changing a thing and pushed Ben across to increase our lead to 4–1. The outfield throw to the plate sailed over the cutoff man's outstretched glove, and Lizza scooted to second base. D entered Cronk to run for Lizza, giving Ken a chance to redeem himself from the East Haven debacle. Though Ken didn't get a second chance to prove he could step on home plate, at least he didn't get picked off. Partial redemption is better than no redemption.

When we finally reached the bottom of the seventh, Ben was in trouble again. Most of his pitches were high. He tried to compensate by shortening his stride and bending over like a pocket knife. Somehow, he managed to be around the plate. Portland got only one hit, but two walks loaded the bases with two outs.

D and I knelt on one knee between the dugout and on-deck area. "Ben's not pitching right," I said. "He's shortening his stride to compensate. He's throwing darts instead of pitching."

"I know," replied D, "but Donny pitched only two days ago and went all seven innings." Donny peered toward us. He sensed our debate and patted his chest with his right hand. He wanted the ball.

"Remember what happened against Wheeler when we brought in Pettinella to get the final out? If you had left Sill in, we might've lost." Portland's bench and fans exhorted their hitter. They sensed Ben's roll was down to the cardboard tube.

"We always said if we were going to go down, we might as well go down with our best pitcher," said D. He lamented that he might have to choose. "But answer me this. Even though Donny has the better record, is he the better pitcher?"

I had an answer for him. "I never thought so, but the only real question is who's our best pitcher today." Donny padded his chest again as Ben faced the hitter from the rubber. "You've got to consider bringing in Donny to get the final out."

Tules was leaning on the edge of the dugout wall listening like a divorce detective and overheard our conversation. He fixed his eyes on D, still kneeling on the ground. "Don't tell me you're thinking about taking Ben out," he snapped. "Are you?" D didn't answer.

Like a boxer trying to get up during a ten count, D started to stand. He knew he had to do it, but somebody was telling him to stay down. He fixed his red shirt under his elastic belt, but, if he was going to walk out to the mound and take Ben out, it was too late. Ben struck out the final batter with the bases loaded. I let out a long breath as I looked up at the light blue sky. Tules had made the right call. Ben pumped his arms, curled his glove in his left hand, and screamed toward our ecstatic bench as the players swarmed him.

We retraced our route back from Portland. After we crossed under the two 660-foot arch spans of the Charles J. Arrigoni metal truss bridge over the Connecticut River into Middletown, we approached Palmer Field again. The players scrambled to the right side of the bus to get another glimpse at the field used for each of the four state championship games.

After we returned to the clubhouse, I entered the coaches' room behind the other coaches and chuckled. "You see, D, you always think it wouldn't matter to the team if you got tossed," I said. "Did you see how the team freaked out when they thought you were going to be chucked?"

"Yeah, I did." D flicked his cigarette above the metal trash can, trying to dismiss the consequences of his habit. "I couldn't believe it. But if I did get the heave-ho, you, Tules, and Jocko would just take over."

"It's not the same," I added. "It does matter. It's like when an army in battle tries to take out the enemy's leader. It matters to our players, so it does matter if you get ejected."

"I guess it does, Riles. I guess it does."

Despite D's acknowledgment that his own presence mattered more to our success than he thought, I still didn't think it would stop him from smoking.

20

Triumph at Fort Courage

D picked up the receiver from the scratched-up clubhouse payphone and called the tournament director for the CIAC. After he reported our Portland victory, he learned our quarterfinal opponent was ninth-ranked Wheeler High. Wheeler defeated the Tourtellotte of Thompson Tigers in the opposite bracket. Our draw brought back memories of our narrow victory in 1998 over Caveman II in North Stonington.

We knew the Lions were the champions of the Quinnebaug Valley League, made up of mostly S schools. Based on their competition, I thought their record of 15–6 was probably deceiving. Even so, we couldn't afford to underestimate them in a single-elimination tournament.

Although we didn't know much about Wheeler, we knew we needed to find a Caveman to take BP against. We wondered whether the coach we faced in 1988 had resigned after that year as he said he would, despite his 15–5 record going into our game.

The next day in the coaches' room before practice, I looked over D's shoulder as he rattled an *Evening Sentinel* and reached the sports section. Portland's coach was quoted as stating our win was an upset only on paper since we played in a tough league. He also stated, "That area grows strong athletes with a lot of talent and a ball of fire in their eyes." The reporter, Sean Barker, heaped praise on Gino. Ben "gets the win in the book, but on the field it was Gino DiMauro." Gino "made four fearless stops, sacrificing his body with dives in the hole, flipping the ball to second for force outs."[9] D slapped his thigh and started to laugh and cough. We stared at each other in amazement. Could Jocko have had the right idea after all?

The tournament rules required our quarterfinal game be played on a neutral field approximately midway between us and Wheeler with a neutral set of umpires. The CIAC selected Daniel Hand High School's field. Hand High was in Madison, a shoreline town off I-95, about forty minutes away. The game's date was Saturday, June 6, my wife's birthday.

After practice, I drove twenty minutes past the Q Bridge on I-95 in New Haven to check out Hand's field. I wanted to see whether there was a cage or anywhere else to take pregame BP, as that determined how much equipment we needed to squeeze onto the bus. I found Daniel Hand High, parked, and searched for the field. Every few steps, I turned to see whether anyone thought I was nuts. I walked around the side of the school and found the diamond.

My eyes were immediately drawn to the outfield. The outfield fence was entirely stockade wood. In left field, the twenty-foot fence had only a small sign on it describing the Shoreline League championships Hand had won in years past.

From center field to the right field foul pole, the fence was six feet high. Center field was filled with advertisements by everyone from the local Rotary Club to a painting contractor. I walked disappointedly past the weather-exposed single bench on the first base side of the field until I saw a netted batting cage with an L screen adjacent to the back of the school. We would put it to use if we arrived before Wheeler.

Friday night it poured throughout Connecticut. Early Saturday, the CIAC postponed our game to Monday. Sunday night, I stopped over at D's house. When I arrived, D was lying on his living room rug, watching *Hoosiers* again. He loved that movie, especially the scene where the coach of a small Indiana high school basketball team, played by Gene Hackman, is about to get canned by the townspeople at an evening meeting in a local church. Hackman's character tells the audience about to vote his fate that he coached the team to the best of his ability. "I apologize for nothing," he said. Whenever Hackman said that line, D would voice it in sync with him. After the movie ended, D switched to the Weather Channel and waited for the game day forecast: possible thunderstorms.

When we left the clubhouse for the journey up I-95, it wasn't raining. When we reached Madison, however, the clouds overhead rapidly turned charcoal black. Soon, it would not be a good idea to hold an aluminum bat straight up in the air while wearing metal cleats. After we stepped off the bus, we commenced batting practice in Hand's cage. A canvas-covered pitching machine rested inside. The metal pitcher wasn't operational, so I started to throw to every player.

After I threw to a few hitters, the Lions arrived. I spotted Wheeler's coach, but, from inside the net, I couldn't be sure whether he was the same coach from 1988. As Wheeler's players—wearing white pin-striped uniforms, a maroon W on their shirts and hats, maroon numbers, and stretch socks—were dropping their equipment near their wooden bench, the clouds opened up. A flash of lightning caught my attention. I began to count the seconds until I heard the thunder. Before I got to one-Mississippi, the sky rumbled, and it began to downpour. Ever since my playing days, I scramble for cover whenever lightning flashes at a baseball game. I played in a game once that wasn't stopped, even though severe lightning lit up a dark sky above me.

Fortunately, with the school nearby, both teams took shelter under an entranceway on the side of the school to wait out the storm. Every few minutes, I ventured toward the parking lot to see whether Sue had arrived. Less than half an hour later, the clouds moved on. With five minutes of raking, the field was in playable condition. Sue arrived gripping a purple umbrella with her black camera bag over her shoulder. The storm had caused a traffic jam on I-95. Reegers showed up with Ray Ray and sat behind our bench. The world was back in order.

When I saw the Wheeler pitcher, Jamie Bruce, warming up behind their bench, I thought he was hitable. He wasn't hunched over and didn't have bushy hair or a beard. Despite our luck, the Lions were without a Caveman on the mound, we still were unable to score in any of the first four innings. In the first three, we ended up leaving six runners on base, five of whom were in scoring position. We were leaving our weaker opponent in the game instead of putting them away—always a bad sign.

Part of the reason Wheeler was still in the game was my fault. In an early inning, Ben had been on second base with nobody out. He had shuffled off the bag, and Shep had lined a single up the middle that appeared to be hit too hard for Ben to score. I raised my hands to hold him at third, but, when the center fielder bobbled the ball, I whirled my left arm and sent him home. I'd thought he could score but I was wrong. Even though the play at the plate was close, once Ben slowed with his back to the ball, sending him home was like trying to launch an F-14 from an aircraft carrier's flight deck after its tail hook has caught the arrestor wire. I should have held him up. A cardinal rule in baseball is you don't want to have the first out at home or the last out at third.

After Ben was tagged out at the plate, I knew what to expect. "Riles, there's no outs!" D yelled. I couldn't hear anymore, but lip-read, "Why?...There were no outs?" The criticism had been difficult for me to endure. All I could do was pace the confines of my limed barrier. If we lost by one run, it would be my fault.

Coaching third base in high school baseball is a thankless job. Whenever you wave a player home and he is safe by an inch, nobody ever says what a great call you made. But when a runner is out at the plate, you're second-guessed by everybody. If fans or parents shout at you, you don't want to turn around and acknowledge them.

At the end of that inning, Ben had jogged toward his shortstop position. "I'm sorry, Ben," I said as he passed me. "I should have held you up."

"Don't worry, Riles," Ben replied. "I'll pick you up." Part of me felt relieved; more of me felt grateful. Win or lose, I wanted to remember the moment forever. When the top half of the next inning came, I jogged behind home plate, past Wheeler's bench, and stopped inside the third base coach's box. I stretched my right leg out, then my left, and jumped. "Start it off for us, kid!" I yelled, cupping my hands, "Let's go now!"

In the fifth inning, Pete led off with a walk. On the next pitch, he stole second faster than the time it takes for a car behind you to beep when a traffic light changes. Ben was up next, and I remembered what he had told me. He ripped a fastball right past the startled Bruce, over second base, and into center field. I didn't make the same mistake twice and held Pete up at third. D wasn't happy; he thought Pete should have scored. As soon as I held him, I knew I would be subjected to criticism again. But I knew Pete wouldn't have scored. If I had sent him, I would have regretted it.

Shep then walked to bring up Joe Lizza with no outs. The Wheeler coach asked for a time-out. He walked to the mound slower than a tired turtle to talk to his pitcher and to try to break our momentum. I thought he might have heard about Joey and wanted to tell Bruce to paint the black part of the plate. The break gave D a chance to talk to Joey.

"I think he's gonna throw me a first pitch fastball to try and get ahead," said Joe as D put his arm around his left shoulder.

"I don't think so," D responded. "If the coach went out to the mound, it's because he wanted him to be careful with you. He hasn't walked that many guys, so my guess is he is gonna lead you off with a curve. If he does, don't let him sneak it by you. If it hangs, crush it."

Bruce hung a first pitch curveball to Joe. Joe's eyes widened, and he thundered the tightly wound leather ball into the woods on the other side of the fence in left center. The Wheeler pitcher's luck had finally run out. In one swing of Joe Lizza's bat, we were ahead 4–0, and I was redeemed. Joe's third grand slam of the season tied a state record and was only one shy of a national record. Upset, Bruce tried to fire a four-seam fastball past Romo, who tattooed the ball between the center and right fielders. The ball bounced until it reached the fence.

Romo flew past Tules. He stepped on the corner of second base and picked me up, exhorting him to keep going.

As Romo passed second, it looked like he expected somebody to try to tackle him. The ball was in flight toward the lined-up shortstop.

The shortstop turned to throw it. "Down! Down! Down!" I screamed as I pointed to the ground with both hands. Romo lowered himself headfirst toward the ground and slid into third a split second before the third baseman swept the tag. With the infield up, Romo scored when Mike Massie reached on an error, stretching the lead to 5–0.

In the sixth, Pete walked and stole second again. Ben stepped outside the barely visible batter's box, tapped his red cleats with his bat, and looked for the signs. I clapped and pointed to a spot up the third baseline. Whenever I pointed to a spot on the field, it was my hint to the batter that if he bunted the ball to the spot, I thought he could beat it out. Ben dropped his right hand down his bat's barrel, tapped the ball up the third baseline, and sped toward first. The third baseman anchored at the bag as Pete sprinted toward him. The surprised Bruce ran to the stopped ball, two feet from the baseline. He picked it up, planted his back foot, and fired it toward first, but Ben crossed the bag before the ball popped into the first baseman's outstretched mitt.

After Ben stole second unchallenged, Shep smoked a line drive to left field, scoring both Ben and Pete. Lizza was then plunked by a heavy pitch. Jocko jumped from our bench, ready to protect his players; he thought the HBP had been payback for Joe's grand slam. In the major leagues, it might have cleared both benches, but Joe just lobbed his bat toward our bench, jogged to first, removed his black-and-white Mizuno batting gloves, and handed them to Tules. Hay made them pay for nailing Lizza and singled, scoring Shep. The game was blown wide open when a throwing error plated both Lizza and Hay, giving us a commanding 10–0 lead.

The double-digit lead allowed D to give Los and Malyska a chance at bat. Shawn Bittman, a shy but tough kid who always wore his hat a little higher than it should be, also got a shot to step to the plate. Los and Richie C. stayed in the game. Los played first with his high-top black Nike spikes, and Richie C. jogged to right field. With the huge lead and Wheeler taking until Shep threw a strike, our tall right-hander, fired fastball after fastball, striking out the side. Shep finished with a total of ten strikeouts and walked nobody.

While the rest of the team sauntered back to our bus, I walked with Ben and thanked him for redeeming me. He just smiled. I told him if we had lost by one run and it had been my fault, I wouldn't have been able to ride the bus. D hobbled up behind me and, despite the 10–0 whitewashing of Wheeler, rehashed the play. I knew the teacher in him wasn't going to let go of the red correction pen. I tried to explain what was going through my head at the time, but it didn't matter. I heard about it all the way back to Derby.

When we reached the clubhouse, D picked up the payphone receiver again to call the CIAC's man in charge of scheduling, Ivan "Woody" Wood. We learned we wouldn't find out who we were playing until the next day, as our opponent (the winner of the Aquinas/Stafford quarterfinal game) had yet to be determined. Their previously postponed game, couldn't be scheduled for the same day we played Wheeler (Monday) since Aquinas's senior players had a date with a cap and gown. The CIAC decided to accommodate Aquinas and moved their game against Stafford to Tuesday. As a result, the semifinal game involving us would not be played until Wednesday.

As soon as we learned our game was moved to Wednesday, we realized the change would hurt us. Although it gave us an extra day to prepare for Aquinas or Stafford, if we won the semifinal game, we would be impacted by the ten-inning rule for pitchers. The championship game was scheduled for Friday night at 7:30 PM at Palmer Field. If Ben pitched all seven innings against our next opponent, he would only be eligible for three innings, or, to be more exact, nine outs against our final opponent. Additionally, the moving of the game devastated Tules. Although he would be there for our Tuesday practice, he wasn't able to avoid work Wednesday afternoon and couldn't be at the semifinal game to coach first base.

The team practiced Tuesday afternoon, not yet knowing who our next opponent was or where we would face them. In the evening, D and I sat near D's phone. When it rang, D picked it up on the first ring. Thirteenth-ranked St. Thomas Aquinas, who had previously beaten the Shepaug Valley of Washington Spartans and the Bacon Academy of Colchester Bobcats, had thumped Stafford 13–1. As a result, our semifinal game was scheduled approximately halfway between us at Cheshire High's field. The site selection satisfied us, since the Ram's field was a familiar battlefield.

We also learned Aquinas's seniors celebrated their class night banquet after the Stafford game. From our tournament package, we knew Aquinas had a significant number of seniors. Since D and I had experienced the effect a late-ending banquet could have on a team, we suspected the celebration hadn't been something Aquinas's veteran coach had preferred.

When D learned from Ken Marcucio that our players were going to be excused from school before 1:15 PM, we decided to try to leave for Cheshire's field by 1:30 PM. An early exit out of town would allow us plenty of time to purge the effects of the bumpy Route 42 bus ride from our players' systems and start hitting in Cheshire's cage before Aquinas could occupy it. If we arrived before Aquinas, we could lay claim to the first base dugout. The first base dugout had a better view of the entire field, and our fans would get the better stands adjacent to it. If Aquinas asked us to move—their prerogative as the higher-ranked team—it would only motivate our players more.

More importantly, if we sat in the first base dugout, D would be closer to Jocko, who was going to coach first base in place of Tules. Jocko coached third base for the JV team and had coached first base on the varsity level before. We knew he would keep the base runners on their toes, but having him closer to D allowed D to help him.

From a *Hartford Courant* clip I saved, we knew St. Thomas Aquinas lost in last year's final and yearned to return. Their 6'3" catcher had been voted the Gatorade Player of the Year in Connecticut. Aquinas competed in a league without any other Class S schools in it, so we didn't have the strength of schedule advantage over them as we had over Coventry, Portland, and Wheeler. We couldn't look at Aquinas's record as any barometer about how good they were. After discussing the game until I yawned more than I spoke, D wanted to watch his favorite parts of *Hoosiers* again.

21

Nobody Remembers the Runner-Up

He didn't tell us he was going. While we were running drills at Ryan Field, knowing nothing about our next opponent, Reegers decided to do something about it. He traveled an hour and a half with Ray Ray in his handicap van near the Massachusetts border to Stafford Springs and witnessed Aquinas's victory. He observed the acclaimed Aquinas catcher, T. R. Marcinczyk, tie a national record and break a state record by socking two consecutive grand slams in their 13–1 decimation of the Stafford Bulldogs. Reegers felt Aquinas's pitcher, who had only three eligible innings left against us, wasn't dominant. We hoped he was their best. During school, D had learned that Reegers would be at Cheshire's field and would tell us what he could about each hitter's strengths and weaknesses.

Before we left the locker room to board the bus, D addressed the team. The players heard most of the speech before, except the end. "I just want to thank you, fellas, for the season," he said. "No matter what happens today, I want you to know I love you guys, and, if you give 100 percent, you'll be winners in my book no matter what the final score reflects." Gino dropped his jaw. Suddenly, he couldn't concentrate. He looked like a kid who hadn't found the pink bubble gum in his pack of Topps baseball cards and didn't have any money to buy another. His face ashen, Gino turned and mumbled something to the players behind him.

As we were filing out the locker room, Gino twisted and squeezed past the other players behind me. "Riles, why is D talking like that?" he asked. Gino wasn't merely curious, he needed an immediate answer. "What does he mean if we lose?" Gino looked back at Pete. "We're not gonna lose, so why is he saying it?"

Pete shrugged his shoulders. "Maybe you should ask D, Gino."

"No," I said. "Don't do that, Gino." Our spikes clicked on the clubhouse steps. "D doesn't think we are going to lose," I added. "I promise. I'll explain what D meant when we get to Cheshire's field."

When our bus pulled up to the entranceway of Cheshire's athletic complex, no one was in sight. After we exited the bus looking like we just got off a roller coaster at Lake Compounce, Gino approached me again and asked me for the promised explanation of D's speech. I motioned to him to follow me as I moved aside from the rest of the team, but Pete and Mike Massie tagged along. They wanted in on the secret of the speech.

"Did you guys ever see the movie *Hoosiers?*" I asked. Pete smiled. I winked in his direction, and he hastened back to the bus to make sure the underclassmen hauled all the equipment off it.

"No," Gino replied with uneven grease lines under his thin eyes. My eyes met Mike's. He folded his arms over his glove and shook his head from side to side.

"There's a movie about a high school basketball team in a small Indiana town named Hickory that ended up playing in a state championship game. Their coach was played by Gene Hackman and—"

"Did they lose?" asked Gino.

"Wait," I said like a grammar school crossing guard. "There was a big game—I think it was the semifinals. The coach comes into the locker room before it starts and tells his team how much he appreciated their efforts. He then says if they tried their best, no matter what the score, they would still be winners in his book."

"But did they end up losing?" persisted Gino, clearing his dry throat.

"No," I replied as I imitated the clutch shot with my hands over my head. "They won the game on a last second shot."

"That's it?" Gino asked, no longer looking like a Chicago Cubs fan who had bought an advance ticket to the 1992 World Series.

"Then D doesn't really think we're gonna lose?" asked a wide-eyed Mike.

"No, of course not," I said, chuckling.

"Then why did he say it?" Mike asked.

"Because D is just being D, that's why," explained Gino, pumping his open right hand with each word like a politician.

"He just borrowed the line from the movie," I said with a smile. "It's called scholarship." Gino nudged some of the other players and let them in on the cinematic explanation. They were all nodding and smiling; D didn't think they were going to lose.

We made ourselves at home in the first base dugout. We emptied our helmet bag, lined up our bats, and hung our jackets. With plenty of time to spare before the game, the empty field and batting cage were ours. Cheshire's metal hitting cage had two separate nets inside hanging side by side. While D whacked ground balls on the already-dragged, lined, and wet-down infield, I threw fastballs and curves to each of the players. After Pete hit, he pitched to hitters who wanted extra BP under the net beside mine.

After we were half through hitting, St. Thomas Aquinas arrived. They spread out on Cheshire's field hockey field a couple hundred yards away. I saw a hitter swing, and a few seconds later heard the connection. After Aquinas's last batter hit, their confident team walked past us as we gathered the banged-up balls in the cage. Their players wore gold jerseys with their names on the back of them and olive green pants and numbers. As their metal cleats clicked on the tar walkway beneath them, several of our players asked me which one was the Gatorade Player of the Year. I spotted the name Marcinczyk above the number 13 on the back of the jersey of the tallest guy on the other team. For some reason, I thought the player headed to the University of Miami would have been bigger than 6'3".

The Aquinas players crossed the diamond to the third base dugout and unloaded their equipment. While we prepared to take our pregame infield and outfield practice, Reegers rolled into our crowded dugout with Ray Ray behind him. D asked Mike if he would sit near the corner of the dugout closest to home plate. D wanted to be able to consult with him during the game about how to pitch to Aquinas's batters, especially Marcinczyk. Before the game, several camera-toting reporters gathered around the Aquinas catcher. One of them asked to snap his picture. He obliged and kneeled on one knee with a bat in his hand. The pregame fanfare around T. R. Marcinczyk was not lost on D.

The stands began to fill on our side of the field. A white bedsheet with the words "Derby Baseball, You Gotta Believe" hung out over our stands. I could have read the spirited banner from the center field fence.

On the opposite side, Aquinas fans filled the single six-row bleacher section. Fans also stood and sat in lawn chairs before the thick row of pine trees on the third base side adjacent to fans who sat beneath the shadow of Cheshire's red scoreboard that was supported by two ten-foot-high steel beams.

I recognized Derby as well as Valley fans standing on the Aquinas side. Our side was standing room only. Sue arrived with her 35MM in tow and began clicking snapshots. My older brother Bob, a physician, was able to get away from the hospital he worked at and arrived with his wife Sheli. Bob felt any game he could catch that I coached with D would be worth at least double the CIAC ticket fee.

We ran onto the field for our infield and outfield practice. On the first round of infield ground balls, Joey G., Shep, and Gino misplayed them. The miscues made Joe Lizza as jittery as a fan in a bathroom line at Yankee Stadium in the bottom of the ninth and the game tied. I told Joe not to worry and assured him they would improve. I hit the second round much slower than normal. All the infielders started to look and feel like superstars. It was an old trick I learned at a coaches' clinic I had ventured to Rye Town, New York, each year to attend. I learned I could hit the ball softer whenever my infielders weren't starting off well and watch their confidence build. I saved a hard hit ball for the second time I worked double plays. The second double play would tell me their ability. I knew it was more important in a tournament game to build confidence. More importantly, I didn't want any more broken noses.

In the top of the first, our bench began talking the moment the umpire pointed to the right-handed Aquinas pitcher, Mike Grady, to play ball. Pete stepped into the box and promptly let Aquinas know they weren't playing Stafford anymore. He banged a fastball into the left center gap, never slowed at first and raced toward second. He slowed into the bag as the relay reached the surprised shortstop on the outfield grass. The fans in our stands—and crowding at the fence down the right field line—cheered.

Ben walked. D flashed his white glove twice, and I relayed to Donny the sacrifice bunt sign. Donny got a fastball and dropped a bunt in the infield grass toward third.

Aquinas gambled. They tried to get our lead runner, but Pete slid in before the outstretched arm of Aquinas's third baseman caught the ball. The failed force attempt left the bases loaded for Joe Lizza with nobody out. Aquinas played their middle infielders back, their corners up. Aquinas must have known something about Lizza as their pitcher kept the ball no more than a foot off the ground. Joe mashed the ball into the low grass. Three bounces later, the shortstop gloved it. He flipped it to the second baseman on the bag, who pivoted and fired to first before Joey was even halfway down the line: a routine 6–4–3 double play. As the ball moved around the infield, at least Pete scored and Ben advanced to third. George Hay took an outside pitch to right field for a single, scoring Ben, and before all our fans made the eighth of a mile walk from the parking lot to the field, we were ahead 2–0.

In the bottom of the first, Ben's two-seam fastball zipped into Joey's glove and his curve moved on two planes. After Ben retired the first two batters, T. R.

Marcinczyk stepped up to bat. D walked close to the first baseline. Sweeping his left arm sideways as he faced the field, he nearly lost his balance. "Good hitter!" he screamed. "Move back! Back up! This is the Gatorade Player of the Year!" He made the outburst with a seriousness worthy of a drama club teacher as I hid my face from the view of Aquinas's first base coach. I witnessed D employ this strategy before with success. He hoped to make the batter feel a certain bravado about himself and let up on his concentration or think he had to do more than merely get on base, lest he appear overrated. D knew a high school hitter—even a talented one—could get distracted by his planted psych-out seed, turning the hitter's at bat into an ordinary out.

The mental strategy reminded me of a game we'd played at North Haven's Sachem Field. When a certain North Haven hitter settled into the batter's box, D had shouted, "Time-out, time-out!" He took two steps toward home plate, pointed at the hitter with his white-gloved hand, and stated loud enough for both benches to hear, "This kid graduated already." Confused, the batter took his bat off his shoulder and started arguing to the umpire that he hadn't graduated and that our coach was nuts.

Coach DeMayo approached home plate to learn what the commotion was about. His player turned to him and, pointing with his thumb over his shoulder, told his coach we were trying to say he'd graduated. D apologized by maintaining the batter must have had an older brother that played, since many North Haven players had multiple brothers who came through their system. When the batter got back into his hitting stance, he thought the issue was over. "Don't you have an older brother?" D asked.

"No, I don't!"

The player began squeezing the black rubber handle of his bat tighter, and whipped it back and forth while waiting for the next pitch. When the changeup reached the plate, the hitter swung hard, and our pitcher pointed to the infield sky. As the ball spun in flight, the player flung his bat toward his bench. Running to first, he shook his head and muttered, "I didn't graduate yet, I didn't graduate yet." I wondered whether D had bantered with the player as a ploy or actually believed the kid graduated. D smirked as the kid jogged back to North Haven's bench and our scorekeeper wrote P-4 in our book.

I wondered what T. R. Marcinczyk was thinking, and if D's antics would have any effect on him. After Marcinczyk stepped into the batter's box, he turned his back pivot foot as if he were squashing a stubborn spider.

Ben glared at Marcinczyk with his glove in front of his chest, his right wrist resting against its heal. He kicked, pumped his arms, and fired a two-seam fastball. Marcinczyk's bat sliced the air like a light saber. He thought he had hit the ball until he heard it pop in Joe Lizza's glove behind him. "Strrrike one!" yelled the umpire. Surprised yet determined, Marcinzyk readied himself again.

After Ben got the second strike on his all-state adversary, Joe Lizza fired the ball back to him as fast as it came in.

Marcinczyk flexed his strong arms and readied again. But when he looked toward the mound, Ben was already back on the white rubber. With the untarnished ball in his raised glove, Ben saw nothing else but Joey Lizza's single finger. Ben's heart accelerated as his teammates behind him urged him on. He focused, kicked, and fired a fastball as his eyes lost sight of the plate and picked up the dirt before him.

The ball tailed inside. Marcinczyk sped up his swing, but not fast enough. "Strike three!" shouted the umpire as Ben looked up and pumped his right arm. The mighty Marcinczyk turned and jogged back into the third base dugout with a befuddled look on his face. D pivoted on his white coaches' shoes toward our dugout from his usual spot near the on-deck circle. "Oh my God, Ben," he jokingly gasped, loud enough for everyone on our bench to hear, "you just struck out the Gatorade Player of the Year." The bench roared in laughter; D was in his prime. Ben walked off the mound like he was Catfish Hunter, but I knew Marcinczyk was no slouch hitter. He looked like he did everything right at the plate except make contact with the ball.

In the bottom of the second, our team's emotions got the best of us. On a ground ball to Shep's left near the second base bag, he scooped it up on three bounces and launched it over the fence beyond first base. Our gloveless fans screamed and ducked as the errant ball whizzed over their heads. "Settle down, Shep, settle down," D barked. "Stay within yourself." That's another one of those baseball sayings that don't make much sense when you think about it, but the player thinks he knows what you're trying to say. It's just like telling a player to "be the man." After runners got on second and third, Aquinas bounced a base hit up the middle. Our first inning momentum vanished as Aquinas evened the score at 2–2.

In the top of third, Pete walked and Ben hit a frozen rope to left field that reached the fielder on one long hop. D thought two moves ahead and called for the bunt. Shep executed another sacrifice bunt. The memory of the prior bunt flashed through the Aquinas pitcher's head. He snagged the ball, spun, and threw to first.

With men on second and third and one out, Joe Lizza stepped in the box, expecting to be intentionally walked. Aquinas gambled and decided to pitch to

Joe, probably because Hay batting behind him had already gotten an RBI single his last time up. Joe made them pay and bashed a two-run double to the base of the left center field fence before the 360 feet sign. Ahead 4–2, Ben continued to gain confidence and shut down Aquinas.

The second time Marcinczyk stepped into the batter's box, first base was open with two outs. Despite his whiff the first time up, D was contemplating putting him on with an intentional walk and pitching to the next batter. Ben read the fretful look on D's face and was upset. He didn't want to give Aquinas anything and felt he could blow the ball by Marcinczyk again. He told D from the mound he wanted to pitch to Aquinas's leader. D relented.

Ben kicked and threw a fastball, chest high, not where he wanted to throw it. *PING.* Marcinczyk hit a high fly ball to deep left center. We held our breath. If we were in a dome, it might have bounced off the roof. Looking over his shoulder, Pete sprinted back until he caught up with the tiny ball and followed it through the blue sky as it dropped toward his raised glove. After Pete snagged the major-league fly, we exhaled. Pete turned and glanced at the four-foot fence only a few steps behind him. It was obvious to everybody, including Ben, that Marcinczyk was just a little under the ball. If a couple more words of the label on the barrel had come in contact with the ball, it would have been halfway up the pines beyond the left center field fence, and Aquinas would have taken the lead.

Through the middle innings, D kept asking Reegers about each hitter and the kinds of pitches he had seen them swing at when he had scouted them in Stafford. Without reference to any notes, Reegers told D what pitches the Aquinas hitters had and hadn't hit in the previous game. Before one hitter stepped to the plate, D approached me as I studied the game from the far side of the dugout. He asked me whether he should relay to Lizza the pitch Reegers thought should be thrown.

"God wouldn't let Reegers be wrong," I said.

The reliance on Reegers was invaluable, as he was right time after time. Jocko proved up for the role of acting first base coach. He yelled at, prodded, and coaxed our runners to stay awake on the bases.

In the top of the seventh, Gino, hitting in his usual nine spot, faced Aquinas's relief pitcher, Jim Rondini, who had entered the game in the fourth. Gino fouled off a few pitches and worked a walk. Pete decided to force Rondini to throw strikes and also walked, pushing Gino to second. Ben tried to move the runners over but couldn't, and Gino was forced out at third. With one away, D let Shep swing away. The right-handed Shepard sliced a tailing ball to right field, which was misplayed. Pete scored, and our lead increased to 5–2.

In the bottom of the seventh, Ben began to tire. Aquinas threatened with a man on second and third and one out. Marcinczyk then stepped to the plate. D faced another season make-or-break decision.

"Ben, step off," yelled D, his white-gloved hand cupped around his dry mouth. Ben lifted his spike off the rubber and walked behind the mound. Marcinczyk stepped out of the box and took a couple smooth swings at an imaginary ball speeding toward him. "Riles, Jocko, come here," D yelled. "What do you want to do, pitch to him or put him on?"

"If you pitch to him and he hits it out, the game's tied," I said. "If you put him on, you put the tying run on and bring the winning run up."

"Yeah, but if you walk him, you force Ben to throw strikes, as he can't walk anybody," replied D.

"But you set up a force at any base," added Jocko.

"He's their money player," I said. "We don't want the newspaper tomorrow to say Marcinczyk tied the game with one swing."

"Yeah, Riles, but conventional baseball wisdom says you don't put the tying run on," said D, as if the phrase was written in a baseball teacher's manual.

"Yeah, but what's conventional about us?" added Jocko.

"Remember his last at bat. He almost jacked," I said. The ump peered at us, his patience taxed to the limit. In a second, I thought he would cry out, "Let's play ball." We needed to decide quickly.

"We could play the infield back and still pitch to him," said D.

I glanced at Ben to see whether he gave any hint of what he wanted to do. Before Marcinczyk's last at bat, we considered putting him on and Ben had been upset. Ben pointed to first base. "D," I said, surprised. "Ben's signaling you. He wants to put him on."

"He does?" asked D. "Yeah, but we gotta make the decision. What do you think?"

"You can't pitch to him now," I argued, almost relieved, "not if Ben wants to put him on. We can't force him to pitch to somebody he doesn't want to pitch to. You've got no choice now."

"I agree," said D. "Put him on."

Even though Marcinczyk didn't want to, he had to trot to first without a chance at redemption. Whether he would ever step to the plate in a high school game again before he was picked in the major-league draft or went to the University of Miami was now out of his hands. Unlike the major leagues, in high school baseball you need not go through the motion of throwing four pitches with the catcher holding one of his hands out to accomplish an intentional walk. You can just tell the home plate umpire you desire to put the batter on first, and the hitter must drop his bat and walk there.

With the bases loaded, the cleanup batter, Aquinas's starting pitcher, Mike Grady, stepped in the box. Ben kept the ball low, and Grady topped a ground ball to Shep at short. Anticipating a game-ending double play, Shep bobbled it and stepped on second base a split second before Marcinczyk's sliding foot reached the square white bag. On the fielder's choice, the runner on third scored standing up. Aquinas was now chasing two runs and had a man on first and third. If Grady stole second, Aquinas would have the tying run in scoring position with the potential winning run at the plate.

I feared the decision to intentionally walk Marcinczyk backfired. I thought conventional baseball wisdom finally caught up with unconventional high school strategy. I was afraid the decision to allow a player to make it for us would haunt D and I forever.

Ben looked at Donny as if to tell him not to worry about his miscue. Ben already had eight strikeouts, but wanted one more. Ben reached back and fired his two-seam fastball until their were two strikes on the hitter, senior Ted Cichy. Cichy stepped out the box to refocus. Our fans were on their feet. Our bench crew cheered, banged, and shook the chain-link fence in front of the dugout. Cichy stepped back in.

Still from the stretch, Ben kicked and fired another two-seamer. The ball tailed in on Cichy's hands, but it was high in the zone. Cichy swung but couldn't catch up to it. As the ball popped into Lizza's mitt for strike three, Ben leaped straight up and launched his glove over his head as high as the Cheshire pines. The rest of our team mobbed Ben on the mound as our fans pumped their arms in the air and cheered. Caught up with the excitement, I rushed to the mound to greet Ben with my right fist in the air. In the pile before me, some of the players cried out, "We're going to the show! We're going to the show! We're going to the big dance!"

After the celebration on Cheshire's mound, Aquinas's coach asked D who was pitching the final game. After D pointed Donny out, the Aquinas coach walked over to him standing beside his teammates. "Don't be satisfied," he said. "We made it to the finals last year; we were satisfied and lost. Go out there and pitch the game of your life. You kids deserve it." After the newspaper reporters interviewed D and some of the players, we began the slow trek to our bus. I met Sue, my brother Bob, and Sheli. We strolled together with Ben and talked about the game and the strategies employed during it. I knew the players were going to have some great game and postgame Kodak moments; Sue had exhausted four rolls of film.

After our players boarded our jubilant bus, D grabbed the left side railing and climbed the steps with the brown spiral scorebook clutched in his right hand and stopped. I waited behind him. "Hey!" he hollered. "Calm down…We haven't won anything yet." As the banter continued, D's face began to redden. "Just remember this," he yelled, still staring at the players. "Nobody remembers the runner-up."

D might have stated a truism, but as soon as he voiced the warning, my eyes searched for Donny's. Donny stared straight ahead in silence as the players around him continued to celebrate. His mind was preoccupied; he felt alone. Donny knew he would be the starting pitcher in the championship game. The possibility of him losing it had already crept into his mind. D might as well have told him that if he lost on Friday night to forget about the free bus ride home and move out of town before the sun rises.

As a result of the win, the team broke the single season record for most wins ever by a Derby High baseball team. If Donny won his next outing, he would tie a single season record for most wins by a Derby pitcher. The next day, *The Evening Sentinel* quoted Ben: "The fans have been terrific. The people of Derby support the teams whether they win or lose. They love their kids and they love their sports." The article continued, "The smallest city in the state, known for annually producing high school football champions, has found itself becoming baseball fanatics as its Red Raiders draw standing-room-only crowds that cheer their team to victory. From the Varsity softball team to Little Leaguers to grandparents they proved it was more than a team win, but a city win."[10]

Despite the win and despite the newspaper and everyone else's glee about going to the big dance, I rode home that day wondering whether D was correct. What if we did lose? One way or the other, the seniors of this year's team would never be forgotten.

22

Benanto's Advice

We only had one day to prepare. I decided to ask somebody who had been through it before and succeeded how we should prepare the team. On my way to my Trumbull office, I stopped at Zaps, a small breakfast and lunch nook on Bridgeport Avenue in Shelton. Sometimes when I stopped there, I bumped into Joe Benanto, Shelton's legendary baseball coach. Joe often got the breakfast special there before opening his B & B Indoor Training Center up the street behind Blanchette Sporting Goods. During the season and our tournament run, we had discussed high school baseball.

I lucked out and found Joe seated in his usual sidewall spot. After he congratulated me on our last win, I asked him how he had prepared his players during the practice before and on the day of each of his state championship games. Although preparing a team for a baseball state championship game was a first for D and me, it wasn't for Joe. With the sureness of someone who had won eight Housatonic League championships and brought home an orange and black banner for Shelton's gym after all four state title games he had coached, he gave me his thoughts.

I worried we were playing under the lights. I asked Joe whether he would try to practice at a park with lights to acclimate the team to playing under them. Joe said he wouldn't even mention the subject to the team; the lights would equally affect both teams. He felt if we talked about the lights, our players would worry about them, and we might give some players an excuse to fail.

I heard Derby High might hold a pep assembly like they did the day before a rival football game. Joe said he had gone along with the fanfare that had taken place before his title games. He thought any event the school might have to boost school spirit and attendance at the game in support of the team would be OK.

When I asked him what he would cover at practice, he said he never practiced more than an hour and a half before a state championship game. He might fine-tune a couple things, but felt by this point in the season there wasn't much you hadn't covered before anyway. In his experience, the players were going to have enough problems dealing with their parents. They were going to put enough pressure on the kids, so it would be counterproductive to overwork them.

In the coaches' room that afternoon, I discussed Joe's thoughts with D. He agreed. The school had already rocked the auditorium with a morning pep assembly D hadn't told me about. I wondered whether it had been like the raucous football assemblies they'd had that year before the Ansonia and Shelton games. I wanted to believe D thought I wouldn't be able to attend because of my tight work schedule. I didn't make a big deal about the assembly when we met in the clubhouse. I knew if I raised the subject, he might dwell on it the entire afternoon.

After we started practice, I quickly learned Coach Benanto had known what he was talking about. Since Donny was scheduled to pitch, we told him to rest his right arm and take batting practice with the outfielders when they went up top in the cage. While D and I alternately fungoed rapid-fire fly balls and ground balls to the outfielders, Donny paced up and down the left field line like an anxious third base coach.

After D and I felt the outfielders had had enough, I drove to the cage and met with the outfielders and Donny to throw them live batting practice. When it was Donny's turn to enter the metal cage, he acted like a prisoner trying to escape solitary confinement. Whenever Donny didn't hit a pitch as well as he thought he should, he banged the steel walls of the cage with his bat like a maddened caveman. Luckily, the aluminum bat he was denting was not one anyone was going to use the next evening.

After Donny exited the cage, he walked alone around the barren field, which in times past had been the football team's practice field, and swung at the air with his banged-up bat as if swatting his anxiety. During intermittent moments of quiet thought, he swung at the edges of clumps of grass like a complacent retired golfer. But when his anxiety returned, he lofted his bat up in the air, picked it up, and swung it some more in frustration.

Once the outfielders finished BP, the infielder's climbed the hill to meet us as D, Tules, and Jocko drove to the cage. Five minutes later, D told Donny to go home. He didn't want Donny's anxiety to infect the rest of the team. I kept thinking that what might be repeating in Donny's head like a looped recording was D's statement: "Nobody remembers the runner-up".

After practice, we spoke to the team in the calm locker room. D advised the players about what time to arrive at the clubhouse the next day. I mentioned that I had watched American Legion Tournament games last summer at Palmer Field and knew there was only one batting cage (behind the left field fence). Since there was no guarantee we would get to hit in it before the game, we decided to take live batting practice in our cage before we boarded our bus. D ended our short talk saying, "Fellas, if we are gonna be in a state championship game, we might as well win it."

That evening I stopped by 15 Bluff Street again. We sat at D's kitchen table and discussed our approach to the game.

"I think we should be very aggressive in this game," D asserted as he slurped coffee from his favorite World's Greatest Dad mug.

"Why change anything, now?"

"In games like this players tend to be timid and wait for the other guy to do the job. If we force our guys to be aggressive by calling a lot of steals and hit-and-runs, they will concentrate harder on what they're doing," D said.

"Take the pressure off us and put it on Terryville," I replied.

"We're going to do it to them before they do it to us."

"I agree."

"Just to be sure, fist…steal, one flash…hit-and-run, two flashes…bunt," D said, referring to the signs he would relay to me with his white-gloved left hand.

"If we get the third base dugout, even if I have trouble seeing your left hand after it gets dark, it still should be easy. We could virtually talk to each other."

"Let's just hope we don't see a lefty."

As I sat at his kitchen table with the CIAC tournament package lying beneath the hanging round lamp, I harped on D to phone the coach of Terryville's prior opponent. For some reason, D was hesitant to do it. Finally, at the time WNYW Channel 11 would say, "Do you know where your children are?" I convinced him to grab the shiny white receiver from the wall and dial. I hoped that at that late hour the coach wouldn't tell him to go f—k himself, but I wanted to at least learn something about Terryville other than what I had read in the newspaper clippings I collected. After D apologized for calling the guy that late on a school night, he set his cigarette in the notch of his white plastic ashtray and picked up a small pad and pencil from his kitchen counter. With his yellow number-two pencil, D started scribbling everything he was listening to through the receiver like he was Columbo trying to solve a mystery.

We learned Terryville employed a multitude of trick plays. If they had an opposing base runner who they didn't think their catcher could throw out on a steal of second, they would run what is called a "pop-up play." After the pitch was thrown and the runner took off, the catcher would lean back and chuck the ball straight up into the air. The infielders would all yell, "I got it," and repeat the phrase as they whacked their gloves while the rest of the team would scream, "Baaaack!" The goal is to get a clueless runner to think the batter popped the ball up, causing the runner to try to return to first base, at which time the defense could try to get him out.

Some teams add in a sound effect. Somebody on the bench bangs two bats together when the ball is thrown high above the infield. The fact Terryville used the play told us their catcher likely did not possess an outstanding arm. If we could run on Marcinczyk, we could likely run on Terryville's catcher.

Whenever Terryville was faced with men on first and second, they liked to try to sneak in the first baseman behind the man on first and pick him off instead of the man on second. It was an ingenious move. With men on first and second, everyone expects you to try to pick off the lead runner.

On offense, they sometimes employed a delayed steal with men on first and third to try to catch the defense off guard and score the runner on third. We decided to tell Lizza, if Terryville tried a delayed steal, not to throw the ball down to second. With our pitchers, we would likely get the next batter out anyway.

Additionally, when Terryville had men on second and third with two outs, they might run what is commonly called a "fall down" play. After a pitch, the runner on second falls down and makes a scrambling attempt to crawl back to second. If the catcher takes the bait, he throws all the way to second, thinking he has a good chance to get the runner. When he does throw to second, the man on third trots home before the defense realizes they've been fooled into throwing through to second. Some teams consider running it whenever they don't expect the batter up to get a hit or when the batter is facing a pitcher's count, such as no balls and two strikes.

At the conversation's end, D thanked the coach for not hanging up on him when he answered the phone. After he untwisted the white cord and hung up the receiver on the kitchen wall, D admitted that even if he did wake the coach, it had still been worth calling him.

As I stood to leave, D begged me to watch his favorite parts of *Hoosiers* with him one final time in his living room. If it rained the next day, I knew I might have to watch the small Indiana town try to get rid of Hackman's character again. D clicked on the television, pushed the worn-out tape already resting in the VCR, and rocked in his favorite chair as I sat captive on an adjacent couch. After I watched it for a while with one eye closed, the scene came up where Coach Dale told one of his players—kneeling and praying in the locker room before one of the tournament games—it was time to go play, that God wanted him to play.

"On that note, D, I think God wants me to go home and sleep. I'll see you tomorrow."

23

Riding Bus Number Seven

Before the alarm clock buzzed, I thought about what would happen if we lost. I sped to the office with the air conditioner cranked on high. At work, I couldn't concentrate on anything but the game. At noon, I returned home to relax for a while, eat, change into my uniform, and go to the clubhouse early. I couldn't resist turning on the Weather Channel. The forecaster said the stars would be out tonight, but with temperatures more familiar to a hot-stove summer league coach.

I cranked open a can of Charlie Tuna, forked it on some white bread, then dropped onto my living room couch in my red and white uniform. After *Matlock,* I gazed at a radar image of the Northeast and wondered why I hadn't become a meteorologist. I tried to convince myself I only had to give the players my best. After that, the result was somehow in someone else's hands. But what if I blew a call at third and cost the team and city a state championship? What if I cost Ben, Donny, and Gino their chance at redemption?

It wouldn't be enough to bring home a runner-up plaque—not in Derby. Whenever D discussed his desire to win with the players, he told them the story of Barry McDermott. Barry had been a Derby High football player and a fierce competitor. A victim of childhood polio, Barry had one leg that looked like a broomstick compared to the other. Despite his handicap and lack of size, Barry persevered and was selected to the *New Haven Register's* all-state football team.

Barry had also played slow-pitch softball for a team that once came in second in an invitational tournament. After the final game, Barry and each of his teammates were awarded a metal baseball player standing with a bat on his shoulders connected to a wooden base with the words *Second Place* engraved on its face plate. After he received the small runner-up trophy, Barry walked to the nearest trash bin and flipped the trophy in it, as if he were tossing away a chewed-up ear of corn. To Barry, there was no reward for finishing second.

I promised myself that once I got through this game, I would never worry about coaching in any game again. The vampire butterflies in my stomach made me sympathetic with what Donny must have experienced yesterday and what he must be suffering through today. After all, he was only a seventeen-year-old kid. I remembered the *Honeymooners* episode where Ralph participated in a "name that tune" contest and didn't know the author of "Swanee River," though Norton had played it constantly during their practice sessions. I didn't want to end up like Ralph mumbling, "Homina, homina, homina," and naming Ed Norton as the creator. I couldn't let it happen. Though I couldn't play, my job was to help show the players the way.

I arrived at the clubhouse long before anyone else did and waited in the coaches' room. With the door open, I rested on one of our gray metal folding chairs and scanned the old sports pages in my locker. Some of the articles were from a few weeks ago, but their stories seemed like ancient history.

The clubhouse door creaked open as players entered. As they climbed the second set of stairs from the landing, the excitement in their voices sounded like it was the last day of school. Even Donny appeared to have somehow shaken off yesterday's jitters. D arrived and looked like he did during a school vacation week. He even ate lunch. I wondered why he wasn't nervous but wasn't going to ask him.

As the players filed into the locker room, one of them pushed the button on the black plastic boom box atop the first locker. They listened to the same tape-recorded rock music they had played before each game this season. Many times this season, D had rolled his eyes and thought about making the dust-covered boom box suffer the same fate as Gino's goggles. Today, the portable stereo system had no effect on him. He didn't want the players doing anything other than what they had done before each game.

After Tules and Jocko arrived, we trekked up to the cage to take our last batting practice as a team. For some reason, George Hay was running late. I couldn't fathom how a player could be late for a state championship game, but I knew D wasn't going to let it distract us at this stage. When George arrived, his hatless head revealed a haircut above his ears. I persuaded some of the players to agree—win or lose—to return to the cage the next day to take batting practice. I was going to miss throwing it to them.

After I threw the usual fifteen pitches to every player, the lack of shade in the cage got to me. Fortunately, Sue drove by to wish me and the team good luck again before she journeyed to the stadium with my dad and two brothers. I asked her to pick me up as many Gatorade, Snapple, or Arizona Ice Tea bottles as I could stuff into my red bat bag.

When she returned, I chugged a couple of the dark bottles and packed the rest in my bag, the same bag I had lugged to every game during the season and the tournament. D called it the "magic bag," as it reminded him of Felix the Cat's bag. The bag contained every conceivable thing I thought a high school baseball player might find a need for during a game: everything from Tylenol, Pepto Bismol, a glove repair kit, scissors, white tape, flip-up sunglasses, eye black, a left-hander's glove, a right-hander's glove, batting gloves, some chemical ice bags, and about twenty packs of Bazooka. I double-checked the bag for the pink Pepto bottle, as I worried I might need it more than a player this time.

After finishing BP, we returned to the locker room. As we entered, Ben told someone to shut the tape player off. D stood silently before the blank whiteboard until the boom box was squelched. Tules, Jocko, and I stood to D's right, across the open locker room door. Behind us was a second whiteboard on a brown paneled wall. Throughout the season, we had posted newspaper articles and some of the pictures Sue had taken, along with anything else the coaches and players felt would motivate us, on the second board. Above Tules's head, handwritten on the drawing board, was, "There is no I in team." Following those words was printed, "or in tournament or in state champs." At the bottom of the board a player had written, "Bring ya ass."

D removed his glasses and cleaned them with a wrinkled white handkerchief. He put them back on and pushed them against the brim of his nose. He held a piece of folded paper. Everyone's eyes focused on the document as if it was their report card. He unfolded it and told the team it was a telegram from Dave "Nud" DeRosa. Dave was the center fielder on Derby High's 1977 championship team, as well as the first baseman on my Senior Babe Ruth championship team. Dave now lived in California, where he could play baseball and softball year round. He wished the team good luck. After D finished reading the wire, he folded it and paused. Each player's eyes were glued to his face.

"OK, listen up, fellas," he said as his eyes scanned the entire bench. "We've discussed this among the coaches and decided we're gonna be very aggressive in this game. Every chance we get we are gonna run, hit-and-run, squeeze, or do whatever else it takes." On the edge of the bench, Ben rapped his glove, Pete let out a long breath, and Donny was tight-lipped, but Romo was as relaxed as a pitcher with a twenty-run lead and one out to go.

"Your jobs," D continued, "will be to concentrate on what we are asking you to do. Fellas, I've said this before, if we're gonna be in a state championship game, we might as well win it." The team clapped loud enough to be heard on Chatfield Street. D paused until they stopped.

"Last year, before the football team got on the bus to go to their state championship game, Coach DiCenso asked each player to write the name of the person they were dedicating their effort to on the board behind me. I'm not gonna ask you to do that, unless you want to. I think each of you should think about a person, other than yourself, who you want to dedicate your effort tonight to. I know I am. I'm dedicating my effort to my dad. I know he'll be watching." Stepping back against the board, D gestured toward me with an open hand. "Riles, you got anything to say?"

I stepped forward and made eye contact with each member of the team. "I know I've also said this before, but tonight, if we become men, we can beat this team. It's not going to make a difference who has the better team. What's going to matter is who has the better team tonight. We have to stay focused on what we're doing. Don't wait for the other guy to do the job. *You...*are the other guy. We can't get distracted by any of the plays we told you Terryville might try. We have to pick each other up and keep our poise no matter what happens during the game, no matter what the distraction. Remember, we are *all* in this together."

After we spoke, we exited the room to allow the players a moment alone. We dragged the rest of the gear from the downstairs equipment room. We inspected each bag to make sure we had everything we needed. The JV players lugged the equipment to the idling yellow school bus parked on Chatfield Street outside the gate. Even when you travel forty miles to a state championship game, you still get a school bus with only a small noisy metal fan next to the driver's window that looks like it was bought at a flea market.

As the players were boarding the bus, I stood near the open folding door. "Hey, Pete, come here," I said, stepping toward the front of the bus. I looked up at the face of the bus, its red lights alternately flashing at the top. Pete walked toward me, along with a few other players. "Take a look," I said. Pete and the other players walked in front of the bus and followed my eyes to the upper left portion of the face of the bus.

"Wow, Riles, that's unbelievable!" Pete exclaimed as he stared at the black number 7 printed there as large as the number on the back of his jersey. I knew it would have a special effect on him. I wondered whether someone had specially ordered that number bus, if the bus company had thought of it, or if it had simply been a coincidence.

Once everyone else was on board, I climbed to the top step of the bus and called out the equipment we needed to bring. The players double-checked the bags. Heaven forbid we should forget something now. As I turned to sit beside D in the bench seat behind the driver, I turned to the team. "Let's do it!" I shouted. The driver reached over and pulled the silver door lever toward him. The folding doors squeaked shut. The air brakes released, and the bus jerked as we started to crawl up Chatfield Street.

The bus was quiet as we headed north on Route 8. The familiar sound of a glove being pounded caused me to turn. I looked at Ben sitting three seats behind me on the driver's side of the bus. He was alone with his tan Rawlings baseball glove on, pounding it's pocket with his right fist. His eyes glossed over as he softened the leather. He fought off the urge to blink until I turned away.

I nudged D. "Take a look at Ben," I said. D looked over his right shoulder. I gestured to him to turn around the other way. "See how badly he wants to win this game."

D glanced behind his left shoulder. "As long as he isn't crying in the game, we'll be OK," he replied. As the bus rumbled up Route 8 and then east on Route 84, we talked about everything these young kids had faced, how far they had reached, and how much they had grown. Ben, the young sandlotter who I once saw striding down Chatfield Street with a fishing pole, his only worry to get home on time, was now about to play in a state championship game.

Our bus pulled into Palmer Field's asphalt parking lot. No other bus was around. Terryville hadn't arrived yet. A WVIT Channel 30 satellite uplink truck was parked near the main entrance. With a satellite dish connected to the top of its metal mast, it was the type of vehicle news stations rushed on site to cover a breaking news story.

When I reached the front gate carrying my red bat bag, I stepped past the chain-link entrance gate adjacent the windowed ticket pavilion into the park. I then stepped back outside and walked past the gate again to repeat the gratifying feeling. I told some of the perplexed players I now knew what it felt like to attend a state championship game and not have to pay. Once inside the park, I could already smell hotdogs cooking on the grill in the concession building to my left. On another night, I might have walked there first.

We passed through another chain-link gate to reach the playing area. Groundskeepers in shorts were putting the final touches on the infield. Two men were lining it, two were raking it, and another was circling it in a small gray tractor with a chain-link drag net in tow, smoothing the infield. The grass didn't look cut, but there wasn't a single weed. The surface was as level as a pool table at the Hilton Casino in Atlantic City. Although the mound consisted of brown dirt, the rest of the dirt area of the infield and the home plate area, as well as a path leading from each dugout to the home plate area, was granite gray. I learned from watching a rain-delayed game there once that the crushed stone surface drained better than regular infield dirt.

Since Terryville had a higher seeding than us, we were considered the visiting team. Terryville not only had the Hammer but the choice of dugout as well. They chose the first base dugout. For the first time in the tournament, we had the third base dugout. It didn't bother me, since it would be easier for D and me to communicate when we were at bat. Our dugout would also be in the shade, and Terryville's players would face the unblocked sun until it disappeared behind the tall trees beyond the left field fence around a quarter after eight.

We piled our equipment into our cinderblock dugout. The players were pleased. The spacious dugout was not only equipped with metal hooks for our jackets, but had a working water fountain attached to the side wall.

Since we arrived early, we decided to take some extra BP in the empty cage beyond the left field fence. Behind a worn-out hole-filled L screen inside a drooping black net, I threw again to every hitter. After the last batter, I went into the dugout and took one of the ice tea bottles from my red bag. In less than half a minute, I had twisted the metal cap back on and dropped the empty glass bottle into the gray plastic garbage can in the dugout.

The familiar repetitive beep of a school bus in reverse told me that Terryville had arrived. By the time they had departed their bus and entered the gate, we were already on the outfield grass loosening up our arms. Since we had an odd number of players, I decided to throw with Keith Trimarki, one of our JV players. I took three baseballs from the ball bag and stuffed them into my back pockets. Whenever anyone warmed up with Keith, they were forced to shag his throws when they spread to a long toss distance. After throwing BP again, I didn't have the energy to spare. Trimarki didn't have that accurate of an arm, but he was all heart. I was lucky I had brought the extra baseballs. I needed them all.

As I stood on the outfield grass just past third base, Terryville's coach strode past us. He was a short man about my age with a thick blond mustache, wearing a black hat with an orange T on its crown. His white uniform had an orange number 4 on the front and back of the jersey; orange stripes ran down the sides of the jersey and pants.

"Hello," I said.

The only thing I knew about Terryville's coach, other than his employment of trick plays, was that he had taken over a team in turmoil in April and turned them into state championship contenders. That fact worried me. It meant there might be a motivation driving his team's success—more than the fact that Terryville hadn't played for a state baseball championship in thirty-six years.

I knew I had seen Terryville's coach somewhere before, but I couldn't place him. I entered the dugout and asked D whether he knew his name.

"Their roster is in the booklet we were given with our tournament packet," he replied. I found the manila envelope containing the packet. I pulled out the rosters and flipped the pages until I reached Terryville's. The coach's name at the top of the roster was "Gregg Hunt." I knew I had heard the name before but couldn't recall where. I obsessed with trying to remember, until it hit me like an inside fastball. "Oh my God, it's him. My God, it's him."

D walked toward me. "Who's him, Riles?"

"Terryville's coach," I replied as I held the open pamphlet.

"What about him?"

"He's the one," I murmured.

"The one what?"

I opened a pack of Bazooka, peeked at the fortune, and started to chew. "The same guy I coached against fifteen years ago while I coached Senior Babe Ruth when we won the title back in 1977," I explained. I reminded D of the stories I had told him about the teams I ventured with to Bethlehem.

The significance of the coincidence was lost on D, but not on me. Hunt was a guy who was downright obsessed with the game of baseball as much as we were. He would coach a game anytime, anywhere, under any conditions, if someone else would agree to play him. The fact Terryville employed several trick plays now made sense to me. I wondered whether there was some greater significance to our playing *this* coach at *this* time. I thought, *Was Terryville the Cinderella team of destiny and not us?*

If I had picked up a *Waterbury Republican* that afternoon before driving to the clubhouse, I would have noticed a feature article in the sports section that spoke about Coach Hunt's and Terryville's remarkable journey to the finals. He had started this season as Thomaston's baseball coach. He had also coached basketball at Terryville, as well as the Bethlehem tri-state summer baseball team, and a Nutmeg State Games baseball team. In his baseball career, he coached everything from Little League to Twi-Met adult baseball. He left his position as Thomaston's baseball coach in the beginning of the spring; some said he'd had a dispute with parents that concerned an early morning Saturday practice.

The article went on to say that two weeks after he left Thomaston, he received a call from Terryville High asking him to coach their baseball team. While coaching Thomaston in 1984, he had advanced to the semifinals. Ahead by a couple of runs with two outs and nobody on, an error had cost them the finals. The next year he had reached the finals but lost to Putnam. It spoke about Hunt's work ethic and how his players were worked hard. His philosophy of coaching was "starting as if your players know nothing and not holding them responsible for anything you haven't taught them." He was further quoted as saying, "You can make all the mistakes you want, just don't repeat any."[11] It was no different from what I remembered about him—no different from my or D's passion for the game. Coach Hunt was going to make sure he and his team left everything on the field, win or lose.

Shortly before we took the field, Reegers arrived. We advised the event staff he was with our team. Ray Ray wheeled him into the side of the dugout closest to home plate. The fans began to fill both sides of the stadium and the metal-roof-covered stands behind home plate and below the press box. From inside our dugout, I heard the steady clomp of feet on the wooden walkway beneath each row of seats.

On our side, Derby's football cheerleaders sat together in the front row above our dugout, overlooking its brown shingled roof. They painted their faces with red sayings on them too small for me to read. Their red and white megaphones rested on the walkway before them. The enthusiastic girls draped banners over the railing and taped and tied red and white streamers and balloons throughout our side of the stands. Some of our fans carried in red plastic stadium horns, some brought in cow bells, and others held canned fog horns I had seen once in a while at football games.

An event staff member wearing gray shorts and grasping what looked like an army surplus walkie-talkie told us we couldn't put the "D.H.S. Baseball We Believe" banner near our dugout. A few minutes later, the red and white bed sheet appeared 330 feet away on the right field fence before a bleacher section in foul territory. The right field bleachers were where fans normally sat at football games played at Palmer. The staff did allow our cheerleaders to hang two smaller banners above our dugout, the first read "Just Do It," and the second was a sketch of a proud Indian chief's face surrounded by the words "Derby Red Raiders."

D approached Doug Martin, our portly manager and scorekeeper, in our dugout. Standing in his multicolored USA shirt and our team hat atop his head, Doug gaped at D without blinking.

"Doug, I promised the team I wouldn't smoke. I want you to hold my cigarettes and matches for me until the game's over."

"I don't know about this, Mr. D," said Doug, no longer desiring to make eye contact. "What if you ask me for them during the game?"

"I don't care if I beg, plead, or scream at you, don't give them to me. I don't want to break my promise."

Doug sensed the anxiety in D's voice and looked up. "You want me to keep them from you no matter what?"

"That's right, Doug, no matter what, OK?"

Doug took the two packs of Carlton Menthols and matches from D's hesitant hand and put them in the front left pocket of his black shorts. "OK, Mr. D."

I turned and breathed a sigh of relief that D hadn't given them to me. It would have been like somebody on the Titanic asking me to keep their life jacket from them no matter what happened on the voyage.

Half an hour before game time, our starting eight plus Los jogged on the field for our infield and outfield practice. I spit on my left ring finger, eased off my wedding ring, and slid it into my back pocket. I jogged onto the field between the plate and the mound with three new baseballs and my navy blue Easton fungo. Joe Lizza stood behind me on the infield wearing his red chest protector and shin guards. Donny walked down the left field line with Shawn Bittman to warm up in the bull pen. Before each game, D sat with our pitcher during his warm-up, and this game was no different.

I promised the team if I ever got to hit pregame infield and outfield in a state championship game that, on the first hit to left field, I would jack the ball over the fence. My routine was to hit to the outfielders first, so my attempt would have to be the first thing I did. I worried, not that I wouldn't hit the ball over the fence, but that I might miss the ball completely. Nobody in the stands would know I had tried to hit it out, but if I missed it completely, even a three-year-old would know.

I ripped a few blades of grass from the infield and tossed them into the air, and they drifted toward right field. I gripped my fungo bat in my right hand and felt the laces of the baseball in my left. I looked at the left field fence and shouted Massie's name in case I didn't hit it as far as I wanted. I tossed the ball up and took a hard undercut swing. The ball lifted high in the air and headed for the 325 sign in left field. Mike ran back, stopped with his back to me, and watched the ball clear the six-foot fence.

Though I surprised myself, I was more taken aback when a bunch of Derby fans above our dugout—who I didn't recognize—cheered. Someone even blew one of those red plastic horns. I overheard one fan say to another that we were ahead 1–0. I shook my head. A few of our fans were football fans who might not recognize the pregame practice, but they were still there to support Derby.

Pete's first toss back to the infield from left center field sailed over Ben and Gino's heads and rolled in the soft infield grass until it reached Joe Lizza. Pete was overanxious; his bad throw to second had been the first time he had done that all year. After the outfielders got their practice fly balls and ground balls, I hit infield practice. In less than ten minutes, we hustled off the field and I pushed and spun my ring back on my finger. Our fans cheered for us again as we entered our dugout.

While Terryville took their infield and outfield practice, I looked into the stands above. Sue arrived with my brothers, Fred and Bob, along with my father. Fred wore a suit and tie—he drove straight from our law office—and brought his video camera. I doubletaked as Fred donned a white baseball hat to shade his eyes. I spotted D's wife, Nancy, who walked in with Jessica and Jennifer and D's mom. A couple of rows behind them was Nick DiRubba, our former manager. A few rows across from him sat Derby's mayor (Gino's dad), with Gino's grandfather (Papa Gino).

"Pokey," our shortstop from D's and my first tournament team, stood alone behind the fence next to our dugout and the stadium steps. With everything Pokey had gone through with D and I, he deserved to stand on the field with us. As I thanked him for his support, I visualized Pokey with his multicolor inked cast on, yearning to enter the game.

Ed Wasikowski, the winning pitcher in Derby's 1977 state championship game, leaned on the round metal railing above the crowded steps near our dugout as if he wanted a uniform. "Waz" had pitched on my Senior Babe Ruth team, and I had rarely taken the ball from him before a game ended. Before each game he threw, he had manicured the mound like Mark the Bird Fidrych of the Detroit Tigers. "Hey, Waz," I called out. "Look across the field at Terryville's coach. You recognize him?"

Ed gazed and squinted through his glasses toward Terryville's dugout. "You're kidding me!" he exclaimed. He chuckled with me as we recalled the Bethlehem ballgames.

Standing with Ed were Dave Mikos and Rick Lucarelli, other players on the 1977 state championship team. Joey Pascuzzo, also a member of that state championship team and who ventured to Maine with my Senior Babe Ruth team as a fifteen-year-old, stood near the stands with his baby in a stroller. Gary Biesadecki, the first baseman on that same title team sat with his brother, Walt Jr., who had pitched on my 1973 team. Russ Scovin, a second baseman on the Senior Babe

Ruth team who had spent a night atop a splintered a picnic table twenty feet from a lake in Saco, Maine, and had later coached the Babe Ruth league Mets with me, sat with his wife, Lynn. Butch Bruciati, an Ansonia teacher who had assisted me for a couple Senior Babe Ruth seasons, along with his wife, Toni, and brother, Rich (a former senior Babe Ruth player) squeezed into the stands among Derby's faithful.

Derby's girl's softball coach, Joe DeMartino, and his players hung signs and streamers. Next to Joe sat wrestling coach Walter "Buster" Jadach and his wife, Carol. Assistant football coach John Oko—who D had once performed the Heimlich maneuver on and saved from a blob of Roseland Pizza mozzarella—sat with his wife, Mary, and five-year-old-son, John Jr. Football volunteer John "Moe" Monahan sat behind Pop Warner coach Jim Mascolo.

All the other Valley baseball coaches attended. Bob Kelo, whose Seymour Wildcats were scheduled to battle Tolland in the Class L title game tomorrow afternoon; Ed Marocco, Shelton's coach; Mike Vacca, Ansonia's coach; and Roy Vacca, Ansonia's American Legion coach and Mike's cousin all stopped at our dugout to wish us luck. Cheshire's Bert Leventhal, whose team was in the Saturday Class LL title game against Hamden, sat behind home plate, along with a few college coaches and a scout from the Major League Scouting Bureau.

After I put down my *Romper Room* Magic Mirror, I turned and watched Terryville's tall thin catcher, Jim Mischke, snag the last pregame infield pop up. Their team high-fived each other back to their dugout. Our captains, Ben, Donny and Pete C., strode to home plate with D to go over ground rules with the three umpires. After D and our captains shook hands with Terryville's captains and Coach Hunt, the four returned to stand before our dugout with the rest of the team. The stadium announcer read off the names of the players and coaches on both teams. He began with us, as we were considered the visiting team.

The National Anthem blared over the loudspeakers. With our hats off, we turned our backs to the crowd to face the flag atop the thirty-foot pole in left center field, more than four hundred feet away. The pole stood between two scoreboards standing on metal beams, one for baseball and one for football. The billboard-sized baseball scoreboard with its red Coca-Cola ad on top was lit up with orange zeros and a lone number 7 in the at-bat square. While the anthem played, several Derby fans behind me stood at attention and sang along. The flag flapped in the wind, and D and I knew it signaled the wind might be a factor above the lights.

24

The Game

When the "Star-Spangled Banner" ended, the team got into a tight huddle before the dugout. With their hands extended on top of D's white-gloved hand at the center, D told the players they had waited all their lives for this moment and to go out and play their balls off. A few seconds later, the team yelled in unison, "One, two, three, *win*!" and the players returned inside the dugout, except for Pete, our leadoff hitter, and Ben in the on-deck circle.

My heart started to beat faster as I jogged to the third base coach's box. I scanned the red stands on our side of the field, the orange and black on Terryville's side, and the mix in the stands behind home plate. The stadium was packed like a Derby-Shelton football game. The sounds of random conversations were no longer decipherable. Smoke was rising from the top of the concession stand. The scent of fresh popcorn reached the field. Close to 3,000 people were at the game, and more were still standing in line at the ticket booth, anxious to find a seat. Some fans were standing on the metal staircases leading up to the stands on both sides of the field. Others crammed shoulder to shoulder behind the fence along the left field line.

Our cheerleaders banged their megaphones on the wooden walkway before them in a rhythmic Indian chant. The first pitch of the game from Terryville's pitcher, Ben Kosikowski, to Pete was a curveball low. Our fans cheered as if they were warming up their vocal chords. Kosikowski then uncorked a fastball for a strike, causing the Terryville side to cheer. Three pitches later, the count was full. Kosikowski rocked back, kicked, and spun another curveball that bounced to the right of the plate and scooted to the backstop as Pete sprinted to first.

The count on Ben Bartone reached one ball and one strike. D flashed his white-gloved left hand once, indicating he wanted me to put on the hit-and-run. D had taken a lot of ribbing for that TP white glove the whole season by some of his friends. They often joked that D and Michael Jackson had something in common: both wore a glove on their hand that served no purpose. Little did they know that when D wore the leather glove during a night game, it was easier for me to discern how many flashes he gave me.

Ben adjusted his black Franklin batting gloves below his sweatbands and stepped in the box. I flashed a set of signs relaying the hit-and-run. On the pitch, Pete took off for second, but Ben fouled the ball off. The umpire grabbed a new ball from his black pouch and snapped it to Kosikowski. Before the next pitch, D switched the sign to a steal, as the count was now one ball and two strikes.

Kosikowski came set. He lifted his left foot, and Pete was off and running. Ben ripped the pitch past the outstretched glove of Terryville's shortstop, Dan Matulis. Without breaking stride, Pete kept on sprinting to third, and we now had men on the corners with no one out.

Donny tugged on his new red, black, and yellow Mizuno batting gloves and resealed the Velcro straps. He spread his red spikes in the batters box and bent his knees. I looked for the squeeze, hit-and-run, or the fake squeeze steal sign, but D was content to let Donny hit undistracted. With the count 2–2, Donny tried to go the other way with an inside pitch. He blooped a single to shallow right, scoring Pete C., who was met before the dugout by a host of our players high-fiving him. With the ball hit behind him, Ben never stopped until he was standing before me on the third base bag.

We now had runners on the corners again with our cleanup hitter, Joe Lizza, up. With the count 1–0, D flashed me the hit-and-run sign, and Joe muscled a base hit to center field, scoring Ben. Running on the outside pitch, Donny flew past second. Although I was thinking about holding him at second, Donny had already decided he was taking third. "Down! Down! Down!" I screamed as I pointed to the ground with both hands. Donny dove headfirst into third, kicking up a cloud of granite-colored dust and just beating the throw. I asked for time, and the umpire obliged. Donny stood and wiped the gray dust from his red shirt. We now led 2–0 and had runners on the corners again with no one out.

As the announcer blared George Hay's name as the next hitter over the loudspeaker, I looked at D kneeling on one knee near the gray on-deck circle. His face looked uncharacteristically confident, his left hand itching to give me another sign. He was in a zone and had no intention of leaving it. At that moment, I thought if I were ever in a foxhole—as Big Lou would say—I would want D next to me. If I couldn't make it out, he would carry me. I knew we wanted to be aggressive, but I never imagined the game would play out like this inning.

After the count was 0–1 on George Hay, D called for another hit-and-run. Though George focused hard and swung, he missed, but Joey still trotted into second as Terryville's catcher, Jim Mischke, held the ball. Hay, however, struck out, leaving men on second and third with one out.

Romo then grounded a low outside off-speed pitch to second base. Donny broke for the plate. Terryville's second baseman, Greg Fortier, decided to get the sure out at first, and we were up 3–0 with Joey Lizza on third and two outs. Mike Massie then hit a two hopper to Kosikowski, ending the top half of the inning.

Terryville led off with their regular season leading hitter, second baseman Greg Fortier. Fortier had also scored the winning run in Terryville's 1–0 quarterfinal win against Griswold and driven in the winning run in their 4–3 victory over Lyman Memorial-Lebanon in the semis. With a 2–2 count, he grounded a low outside pitch to Gino. Gino charged it with heavy spikes but fielded it clean and snapped it to Hay's outstretched black mitt for out number one. The second batter, shortstop Dan Matulis, swung at the first pitch and also bounced it out to Gino.

Terryville's first baseman, the left-hand hitting Chris Rogers, then roped a 1–1 fastball to center that reached Pete on three bounces. But Donny got the cleanup hitter, center fielder Keith Nypert, to sky the ball above the unlit lights behind home plate. In textbook fashion, Joe Lizza tossed his mask and gloved the ball as he backed toward home plate. It looked like we were on our way to an easy win, but it would be six more innings before we would even get another hit off Kosikowski, who retired fifteen of our next seventeen batters.

In the bottom of the second, Terryville threatened with a man on second and third and one out. Donny struck out designated hitter Rudy Crovo on an inside fastball. Left fielder Mike Rogers then hit a high chopper toward the mound. Donny leaped and snared the ball. He took a deep breath, stepped toward first, and tossed it to Hay to end the inning without any damage.

In the last half of the third, Fortier led off with a single and advanced to second.

After working the count to 3–2, Matulis walked.

Donny hit the next batter, Chris Rogers, loading the bases. I couldn't even recall the last time Donny had hit somebody.

Nypert topped a long one hopper to Gino. Gino gloved it, spun, and snapped the ball to Ben for the force at second. Ben glided across the bag and fired the ball to first, but Nypert stepped on the bag before Hay's outstretched mitt snagged Ben's throw. As Gino pivoted and tossed the ball to Ben, Fortier scored, and Terryville cut the lead to 3–1.

With one out, Kosikowski banged a hard ground ball to Gino. He couldn't field it on the short hop, and it bounced into his tightened chest. Gino regained his wind and kept the ball in front of him, but his throw to first was late; everybody was safe.

Donny struck out Mischke but walked the next batter, Rudy Crovo, to load the bases again.

From the stretch, Donny flung a dirt curveball to Paul LeClair that scooted past Joe and rolled toward the backstop. The ball didn't rebound off the firm cushion, and center fielder Keith Nypert sped toward home from third. He scored standing up, and the game was knotted at 3–3. Fortunately, Donny struck LeClair out looking and escaped with no further harm.

Everyone could see Donny was unraveling like a dropped role of toilet paper. Joe Lizza had already dropped to the ground to block Donny's pitches more times in this game than a linesman dropped a puck in a hockey game. The emotional pressure, which had begun the moment the Aquinas game ended, had caught up with Donny and broken his concentration. Donny had never come apart like that during any game this season, even when Cheshire spanked him the first time we played them this year. The euphoria of our first-inning barrage disintegrated like a sand castle on Milford beach at high tide; momentum clearly shifted to Terryville. When each inning ended, Ben repeated to me that Donny was not focusing.

In the bottom of the fifth, Donny rolled up his short red sleeves with each pitch, as even his shirt became uncomfortable. Chris Rogers swung his Easton and torpedoed a fastball up in the zone over Pete's head in straight center field. The ball rolled near the 410 sign before Pete caught up to it and long armed the throw back to the first of two piggybacked cutoff men in short center field. The monster blast frustrated and confused Donny. Expressionless, he scurried to back up third base and then turned to back up the plate as Rogers slowed into third with a stand-up triple. Donny had never had anyone hit the ball that deep off him. If the dented ball had been hit at Ryan Field, it would have rolled lopsided to the clubhouse door.

With one out, Donny's pitching adversary confidently stepped to the plate. The right-hand-hitting Kosikowski hooked a fly ball to Romo's right. Romo's momentum carried him away from the plate into right center field. The ball was hit well enough to allow Rogers to tag up and race home, giving Terryville a 4–3 lead. When the inning ended, our dugout was like a morgue at midnight. Donny entered and fired his glove overhand at the water cooler, popping its stainless steel shell off its guts. Some teammates and I snapped it back into place as Donny slumped on the bench.

In the top of the sixth, George Hay led off with a walk. Our chances to tie the game looked promising. The odds of a team scoring in a high school baseball game after a leadoff walk are far better than any Bazooka comic fortune coming true. D sent Angelo DiRubba into the game to pinch run for Hay, while D mulled over whether to call for a bunt. As DiRubba jogged to first base, he switched helmets with George. Hay jogged off the field without a helmet. Mischke rose from his crouch and walked toward the senior pitcher, who met him before the mound. When the ashen-faced DiRubba reached first, Tules instructed him while Angelo stretched his straight muscular legs, hands to toes. Kosikowski pondered Mischke's words as he fixed his right cleat against the rubber.

Angelo shuffled to a three-and-a-half-step lead. At the same time, the public address announcer broadcast Angelo's entry into the game. Nobody in our stands questioned the decision; they knew DiRubba was faster than Hay.

Angelo took another short step.

Kosikowski brought his hands together at his chest, tucked his head, and paused.

Angelo's leg muscles tightened.

In a flash, Kosikowski whirled and threw to first.

"Back!" Tules screamed.

Angelo dived back into first, but it was too late. He didn't sense the throw coming until the ball was already in mid flight toward the first baseman's mitt before the bag. Angelo didn't have a prayer. The ump raised his right hand high while clenching a fist, then pumped it toward the ground. "You're Out!" he yelled. Kosikowski pumped his right arm. The first baseman, Chris Rogers, snapped the ball across the diamond, ran to Kosikowski, and they slapped their gloves together above their heads.

Angelo trotted back toward our dugout without confronting what he knew was before him. He caught a glimpse of D's shoes as he passed him but never noticed D staring at his lowered head. Angelo entered the somber dugout without saying a word. He searched the dugout corners as if he desired to sneak out of the stadium through a trap door to a waiting taxi. What began as a good chance for us to tie the game turned into disaster. No sooner had the echo of Angelo's name—as number 18 pinch running for Hay—bounced back to our dugout than he was done for the night. He was easy prey for the veteran pitcher.

In football, a player can sometimes redeem himself as quickly as the next snap from center. But in high school baseball, a starter may reenter the game for his replacement only once, and I knew D was going to reenter Hay to play first again in the bottom of the inning. Angelo had no way of redeeming himself. He had to pray for somebody else to rescue him.

From my coach's box, I spotted Sue through the chain-link fence with her camera in her raised hands. My brother Fred stood beside her with his video camera, capturing a perspective of the game through a Terryville lens. I hoped they didn't have a close up of the pickoff recorded for posterity.

Angelo sat not far from Reegers with his back hunched and both arms covering his hatless head and thick black eyebrows. A two-way player on the football team, he asked himself why he played baseball in the first place. After all, on the varsity he was just a pinch runner. He looked up to see which one of his friends had cajoled him to play, but only for a second.

Our half of the sixth inning ended with us still trailing 4–3. After I walked into the quiet dugout, Angelo sat alone with his hands still over his head. Through his short muscular forearms, tears rolled over his round cheeks.

When Tules returned from his first base coach's box, D blamed him for the no out disaster. Tules argued that he had given Angelo a mini-clinic before he had taken his lead, but the explanation didn't satisfy D. I approached D in front of the dugout. I thought he should say something to Angelo, as it looked like Angelo wanted to kill himself. "He should kill himself, Riles," D blurted, his voice rising. Tules tilted his head in disbelief. D swatted the empty air with his white-gloved hand. "He just got picked off in a state championship game. We had no outs and a man on first. Where was he going?"

Tears were sliding over the eye black under some of our players' eyes. They knew, as I did, that we had to stop Terryville from scoring again in their half of the sixth and then try to tie the game with the bottom of the order coming up in the seventh. A better script couldn't have been written for Terryville: Take a lead into the last inning, then face our seventh, eighth, and ninth batters in the final inning with your best pitcher on the mound.

As our players started to drag themselves onto the field in the bottom of the sixth, a dry-eyed Romo wiped his small, thin black mustache with his forearm and turned to his teammates. "We still got one more at bat," he cried as he raced out to right field. Ironically, it took a football player to recognize what others couldn't see. David just didn't know that the Foxwood's odds were against us scoring a run before Terryville could get three outs, especially since we hadn't even gotten a hit off Kosikowski since the first inning. Despite the dugout depression, D, George, Jocko, and I kept exhorting the players and each other.

In the bottom of the sixth, things got worse. Crovo led off with a single. Coach Hunt went by the book and called for a sacrifice bunt to set up an insurance run. The next batter, LeClair, pivoted and bunted the ball toward Joey G. Joey charged the ball and picked it up but slipped to the ground on his butt. As an embarrassed Joey G. sat on the soft grass holding the ball, he wondered what else he could do wrong.

D and I knew Hunt was going to go for the jugular and call for another bunt. If we couldn't handle the bunt again, he would have the bases loaded and nobody out. If we handled the bunt, we could still be stuck with second and third and one out. A successful bunt would all but assure Terryville of at least one more run, unless we struck somebody out, induced a pop-up, or cut a runner down at the plate on a ground ball.

I agreed with D's feeling that Donny would have to be pulled in favor of Ben; Ben had more to prove than Donny did. Donny entered this game with a record of 10–1, and Ben came in at 5–7 even though, D and I knew Ben was Donny's equal. Ben appeared to be playing the game with focus. He anticipated what had to be done with each play and was the most confident man on the field, next to Romo, who didn't know any better but to think he was a stud. Ben had nine outs left under the pitching limitation rule, but he would have to pitch only three of them if we couldn't score a run in the seventh.

When Ben snapped up the white ball from D and fixed his cleat against the rubber, he looked like a determined warrior. Although the home plate umpire told Ben he had to remove the red Nike sweatband he wore on his glove hand, he didn't say anything about the thick black lines under his eyes. The first batter Ben faced, Chris Rogers, bunted the ball to Ben's right. Ben bolted after it, picked it up, and fired a bullet to Joey G.'s outstretched glove for the force out. Though the play was a bang-bang type of play, I thought the umpire called the runner out on principle. The runner didn't slide into the base; he toe-touched the bag standing up.

With a tight strike zone, Ben walked Fortier to load the bases. We signaled Donny and Gino to play at double play depth, and Joey G. and Hay to play up. Ben kept his fingers on top of the ball and Matulis topped a spinning curveball toward Gino, but it was a slow roller and Gino's only play was to first. Terryville got the insurance run Coach Hunt wanted and still had runners on second and third. Ben went after Chris Rogers with fastballs and got two quick strikes but plunked him on the leg with a breaking ball to load the bases again.

With the bases loaded and two outs, Ben kicked and fired a two-seamer. Fortier took his secondary lead off second base toward third. Nypert took the pitch. Fortier tripped and fell to the ground between second and third. A cloud of gray dust kicked into the air. "Where's he going?" someone in the crowd yelled. "It's a trick!" I screamed. "It's a trick!"

D's heart dropped into his stomach. "Don't throw it, Joey!" he cried. Fortier acted as if he was scrambling back to second; Lizza looked toward second but didn't bite at the bait. He lobbed the ball back to Ben, who stepped back on the rubber.

Ben fired another fastball, and Nypert hit a soft fly ball that drifted toward the right field line. I held my breath as David ran it down, stopped, and snagged it. The damage was limited to one run, but we entered the top half of the last inning trailing by two instead of one with the bottom of our order up.

Before the seventh inning started, the public address announcer voiced: "Ladies and gentlemen-*gentlemen,* at the conclusion-*clusion* of tonight's-*night's* game-*game,* please do not-*not* go-*go* onto the playing-*playing* field-*field.*" The unexpected cryptic-sounding statement felt like a jagged-edged dagger inside me. My mind started to go blank as he continued the echoing message to advise the crowd of a brief awards ceremony that would take place on the field at the game's end. I pressed my lips together as I fought to contain my emotion. If the statement affected me, I thought, how were our players supposed to try to make a comeback? *Whatever happened to the game isn't over until the fat lady sings?*

Moments after the announcer's statement, our team huddled one more time. With D in the middle, the coaches and players exhorted one another not to quit. While we were in a foxhole, every fan on the Derby side of the field stood and cheered to let us know they were in it with us. When the team returned to the bench, the players decided to put their rally caps on. Even our manager, Doug Martin, turned his cap inside out before putting it back on his head, revealing the jade bottom of the bill and the white strips in front and around its edge. After the huddle broke, Carlos Ortiz inched up behind D and said he wanted an "ab," which is short for an "at bat." Not doubting his courage, D said, "Carlos…it's not your time."

When Ben Kosikowski took the mound again, the first batter he faced was Mike Massie. With a two-one count, Mike slapped a bouncing ball to Fortier at second base and scrambled out of the batter's box. It should have been an easy out, but Fortier bobbled it enough to allow Massie to step onto first before Rogers could grasp the tardy throw.

Our leadoff man was on again, but since we were chasing two runs, we couldn't bunt Joey G. Joey was having a horrendous day, having already fanned twice on bad pitches, but we couldn't concede the out.

Joey hit a ground ball to short and sprinted toward first. He couldn't let it turn into a double play; he later told me that he thought he had already done enough things wrong.

Matulis fielded it clean as if he had counted the hops and threw to Fortier, waiting on the bag with outstretched hands. Joey G. pumped his legs as fast as he could.

Massie wanted to take out the second baseman to prevent a double play. He slid in hard at second and kicked up a cloud of gray dust, but it didn't affect Fortier, who stepped on the bag for the force and shifted his feet to throw to first. The left-handed Rogers stretched toward the throw from second.

Joey G. stepped on the middle of first base; the ball popped in the first baseman's mitt. Tules lifted his left leg and spread his hands wide.

"Safe!" yelled the umpire. Joey G., thank God, was safe.

Our ninth batter, Gino, swung his bat a few times and stepped into the batter's box. As he was swinging his bat back and forth preparing for the pitch, a black Franklin batting glove flopped out of the left back pocket of his white pants. I wondered why he didn't have the glove on one of his hands. Gino wisely took three balls in a row. He stepped out the box and banged his red high-top spikes with his bat.

On deck, Pete started to swing his bat back and forth faster and faster. He glimpsed at D, expecting him to flash Gino the take sign. Gino didn't need it. He knew that if he walked, we would have the tying runs on base with the top of the order up.

With the count 3–0, Kosikowski came set. Gino squared and waved his bat like a windshield wiper. Kosikowski threw a four-seam fastball right down the middle. Without any hesitation, the umpire turned to his right, pointed, and shouted, "Strike One!"

"*What!*" D screamed. He stomped toward the plate. Gino began to inch out of the batter's box when the umpire finally noticed D charging right up to home plate. D threw both hands in the air with his palms up. "That wasn't a strike!" he screamed.

The umpire removed his metal mask, which I didn't think was a smart move, and mouthed something back to D while pointing at him.

Knowing D's temperament, I hurried down the third baseline toward the plate.

The third base umpire passed me and pushed himself between D and the home plate ump.

Tules marched from his first base coaching box toward home plate with the first base umpire running ahead of him.

I grabbed D from behind to try to restrain him.

Jocko rushed from the dugout and got into the mix, along with Pete C., who was on deck. Shawn Bittman left the bench to help us pull D away from the umpire.

Ken Marcucio was glad he was stuck in the stands.

Gino just stood motionless with his twenty-eight ounce bat resting on his calm shoulders, wondering why D was complaining so much about a pitch right down the middle.

As the umpire lectured D with his cushioned mask in hand, D thrust his right shoulder toward the umpire and then jerked his left arm up, gesturing with his left hand as if he was going to backhand the umpire.

As our men in red shirts escorted D away, he barked, "I shouldn't have given you any ice! I should have let you die!" In an earlier inning, the umpire had gotten a full view of the Big Dipper when a pitched ball somehow ricocheted off the top of his head as he crouched behind Lizza. The dazed ump was dropped on his back for more than a ten count. We had given the ump an ice bag after he sat up.

The umpire kept shouting at D as if he were a misbehaving schoolboy, threatening to eject him from the game. I knew D should have already been tossed. We finally yanked D away, and he started back toward our dugout.

As D ambled toward our dugout, his red shirt hanging over the back of his pants, the Terryville fans booed loudly. But the Derby fans were giving him a raucous standing ovation, as if he had just eliminated the Connecticut State income tax.

As I walked away from the plate toward our dugout, I glanced over my left shoulder. Tules was still jawing with the home plate ump. Tules turned around and started to tread back to first with the first base umpire beside him. The home plate umpire voiced something to Tules as he pointed at the back of his XXL red jacket. Luckily, Tules hadn't seen him pointing.

Pete C.'s eyes flashed with sudden anger. He started hollering at D as he walked back to our dugout, chastising him for nearly getting ejected from the game. As D approached the dugout, he peeked at the standing crowd giving him the wild applause. At that moment, I wondered whether D had staged the event to shake things up, or if he'd felt the pitch was a ball. If he wanted to turn the atmosphere into a frenzy, he had succeeded.

When play finally resumed, Gino took the next pitch for a called strike two. The Terryville fans roared. Kosikowski had battled his way back to a full count.

"Come on, Gino!" one of our fans yelled.

"Make contact, Gino!" another cried. Gino fouled the next pitch to the backstop with an awkward swing—his back leg spun across home plate—but at least he was still alive.

On the next pitch, Gino swung and hit a sky ball to shallow right center field above the towering lights. Fortier drop stepped, ran out from second base, and pointed to the night sky. The ball had disappeared into the darkness and took forever to come down through the crisscrossing light beams.

The five-ounce ball reentered the stadium atmosphere. Terryville's right fielder, A. J. Sirianni, started to raise his glove. He and the center fielder, Keith Nypert, were close enough to catch the ball, but it appeared that neither had called for it. The base umpire hustled into the outfield and waved his arms over and over, signaling no catch as the ball dropped over Sirianni's head. What should have been out number two seemed like a base hit from Heaven. Our crowd roared, and multiple canned fog horns blared. We now had Joey G. at second and Gino on first with one out and the top of the order up.

Nypert tossed the ball in to the second baseman, Fortier. I cupped my hands around my mouth and yelled to Joey to stay on the bag. Kosikowski walked toward the infield dirt on Fortier's side of the field. Fortier tossed him the ball, but Kosikowski never stopped moving toward him. They met on the gray infield. Kosikowski then returned to the infield grass and stopped a few feet outside the dirt mound.

My face went flush. I pointed with both arms at the second base bag. "Stay on the bag!" I screamed as loud as I could. Joey G. never moved from the safety of the white square. He grinned and nodded; he already knew. "Not this year," I said under my breath. Their plot foiled, Fortier tossed the ball back to Kosikowski.

Pete took a deep breath and settled into his knee-bent stance next to the plate. He locked his focus on Kosikowski's black hat and swung his bat back and forth. The cheerleaders banged their megaphones on the floor boards in sync with a familiar rhythmic repetitive cry of "Let's Go Big Red." I had heard the same chant at countless football games as the offense headed toward the end zone.

Kosikowski threw two straight balls to Pete, and our fans kept up their raucous cheering and cow bell clanging. If Kosikowski walked Pete, we would have the bases loaded and one out. Barring a double play, both Ben and Donny would get a crack at knocking in the tying run from second. But Kosikowski, as he had done all game, got the count to 2–1. Not to be outdone, the Terryville fans stomped their feet, screamed, and waved their arms with closed fists, trying to match the enthusiasm of their adversaries across the stadium.

Mischke flashed the sign. Kosikowski nodded and came set, but didn't pitch. Instead, Terryville tried another trick play. Instead of attempting to pick Joey G. off second, however, they planned to pick off the tying run at first. Not a bad move, if our runner on first wasn't paying attention.

The first baseman, Rogers, started to sneak in behind Gino at first base.

Kosikowski turned to throw to first, but, since Rogers hadn't gotten to the bag yet, he didn't throw the ball. The first base umpire waved his hands to stop play. Then I heard that word from the first base ump that every base coach yearns to hear.

"Balk!"

The word echoed behind me as Derby fans screamed it in unison. Stunned, Kosikowski bent over with his black spikes spread. While facing the home plate umpire, he pointed his right index finger to an area of the mound next to the third base side of the rubber.

The third base umpire walked toward the mound. Terryville's third baseman, Paul LeClair, trailed him like a shadow and tried to get into his ear. "It's a balk! It's gotta be a balk! He didn't step off!" our fans screamed, as they tried to drown out the desperate cry of the Terryville side: "He stepped off the rubber!"

As the home plate umpire plodded toward the mound with mask in hand, Kosikowski was hopping and pointing to the ground. Like a sewing machine needle, the pitcher's finger bobbed up and down toward the area away from the pitching rubber where Kosikowski asserted he had planted his back foot. If he had stepped off the rubber before he turned toward first, it wouldn't have been a balk.

Before the home plate ump reached the area Kosikowski was pointing to, Coach Hunt jumped from the bench and beat him to the spot. He bent down and pointed to the same area. Despite the vehement protest, the home plate umpire was unmoved and refused to change the call. Getting no satisfaction from him, Hunt raised his hands up and down from his waist to his head with his palms up as he marched toward the first base umpire. While the frustrated coach approached, the first base ump began to walk to the first base side of the mound to confer with his two fellow umpires.

Hunt continued to plead that his pitcher had stepped off the rubber before he made the nonthrow to first. But no sooner had the umpires converged than they started to divide back to their positions, confident they'd made the correct call. Tules clapped and nodded behind the first base ump, and I knew the issue was dead. Kosikowski's move toward first without a throw remained a balk with both runners advancing one base. We now had two runners in scoring position with the top of the order up.

The moment after the umpires ruled it was a balk, I ran toward the dugout to talk to D about entering a pinch runner for Gino. D was reluctant to insert a runner in light of DiRubba's debacle but knew the tying run was on second and Gino was our slowest runner in the lineup. D turned toward the dugout. "Richie Calvert," he barked. The bench echoed Richie's name. Startled, Richie jumped from the bench. He jogged toward D and then toward second base, high-fiving Gino as he went by. After Gino left the field, he double high-fived Shawn Bittman before our dugout.

Kosikowski was still pacing near the mound. He couldn't believe the call but had to get past it and regain his poise.

Hunt tried to settle his pitcher as well as his team. With his arms extended and palms down, he implored his infielders to relax and just get the last two outs.

After Hunt returned to the dugout area, Kosikowski walked near the first baseline to try to obtain more instruction from his coach. Coach Hunt moved closer to the line without crossing it. He wanted to make sure his instructions weren't drowned out by the wave of shouts from the Terryville faithful still incensed over the balk call.

As Richie hustled to second base, I moved within a foot of Joey G., still standing on the third base bag. Joey G.'s slender frame and red-helmeted head cast a lollipop shadow into the infield. With his helmet on, Joey G. didn't notice the cool breeze that gave me a reprieve.

I didn't have much time. Like the short, mustached man on the FedEx commercial, I gave Joey G. instructions without taking a breath: "Joe, there's one out, we're down by two. Richie's run's more important. If there's a fly ball, think tag, but you have to score standing up to go. If you're out at the plate, game's over, we lose. If the ball bloops, go down the line so you can score if it drops in...If they play the infield back and it's grounded in the middle, go, but not if it's to the pitcher. Got it?"

"Got it, Riles."

"I've got to concentrate on Richie. He can't get picked."

"Go ahead. Watch Richie. I'm OK."

I tried to get D's attention to see whether he wanted the base runners to run on contact on a ground ball anywhere—as some coaches do with one out and men on second and third—or wanted me to make a split-second decision to send or hold the runner. The question was legitimate, but it was the first time I had asked it all year. I hustled toward D. The crowd noise forced me to scream the question. My voice went hoarse. D pointed to my third base coach's box. "You know what you are doing," he snapped. "What are you asking me for?"

I returned to Joey. "I asked D whether he wanted me to have you run on contact on a ground ball. He didn't answer. We're going to do just like I said before. I'll follow you down the line with each pitch as close as I can."

"Just make sure Richie doesn't get picked," he said while focusing on Kosikowski.

Pete stepped back into the batter's box. He swung his bat back and forth and rocked his hips. I cupped my hands again and shouted instructions to Richie. Still in the stretch, Kosikowski came set. He ignored Joey G. Matulis circled behind Richie and dashed for second. Kosikowski stepped off to check Richie's lead. "Baaaaaaack!" I yelled to Richie, my voice trailing off. "Get back on the base!"

"Darn it all, Richie!" D screamed. "Don't get picked!"

Richie didn't hear either of us. D removed his cap with his white-gloved hand. While he still held the squished bill of his cap, he wiped his sweaty brow with the back of his glove and put the cap back on.

Kosikowski came set again. He kicked and delivered.

Swing and a miss. "Strike two!" the umpire yelled as the Terryville side roared.

Pete asked for time. The ump raised his right palm toward Kosikowski. Pete stepped out of the batter's box and took a deep breath. He took a few full swings through the tense air, then calmly stepped back in.

Terryville's infielders, on the edge of the infield grass, urged their senior tri-captain on. Kosikowski came set. He pitched. Pete swung again and lofted a soft fly ball into shallow right field. Fortier turned, ran, and pointed up toward the ball.

Without enough time to think, my instincts kicked in. I told Joey to move down the line, as the sky ball didn't feel like one where Joey G. could tag and score standing up. Joey came down the line a few steps to see whether the ball would be dropped.

"Tag up!" shouted a guy in the stands behind us.

When Joey didn't tag, another fan screamed in disgust, "What are you doing?" The right fielder, Sirianni, caught the ball moving toward the infield. He threw a perfect one-bounce relay to the left-handed first baseman, Rogers, who turned while the ball was in flight. Anxious to throw a strike to the plate, Rogers caught the relay but held it when he saw Joey G. hadn't broke for home.

Although I believed a tag up was too risky in light of the score, to my dismay, some of our fans booed me for the split-second decision. Now I knew how Rick Nelson felt at Madison Square Garden. I couldn't believe it. I was simply a volunteer high school baseball coach trying my balls off to make the right call. Another fan behind me barked that I should have sent Joey G. But I knew what most of our fans didn't: Joey G. wouldn't have won any ribbons for Derby's track team if he wore loose shorts instead of baseball pants and was given a head start. More importantly, if Joey G. was out at the plate, I might as well have walked back to Derby, as the game would have ended on a meaningless play.

As Ben Bartone approached home plate, Coach Hunt asked for time. He huddled with Kosikowski and his infielders on the mound. Pete jogged back from first toward the outside edge of the gray home plate area. He changed direction toward Ben and stopped. Looking him in the eye, Pete gave Ben some words of encouragement. I was astounded. Most kids would just think about their failure and hustle back to the dugout to find a place to hide before the fans could remember their name. Some players might pout or take it out on the equipment, but not Pete. Here was a seventeen-year-old kid who had just failed at probably the most important at bat of his life, unselfishly giving his fellow captain a pep talk.

As Ben stepped into the batter's box, the public address announcer repeated his scripted announcement. "Ladies and gentlemen-*gentlemen,* at the conclusion-*clusion* of tonight's-*night's* game-*game,* please do not-*not* go-*go* onto the playing-*playing* field-*field.*" I squinted at the press box windows. The darkness before them, however, and the black netting above the backstop, wouldn't let me discern the announcer's identity through my glasses.

I couldn't believe the Bob Sheppard wannabe had repeated that thoughtless message again, just before what could be our final batter. I thought, *Doesn't that guy realize he could have an effect on the outcome of the game?* I hoped the fat lady would march into the stadium, climb the steps to the press box, and slap him silly. The Terryville fans, sitting above a banner that read "Terryville Rules," took the cue and began to stand, clap, scream, and stomp their feet, anything to help Kosikowski get the final out.

It was Ben versus Ben; number 16 versus number 16. Ben Kosikowski threw three straight balls to Ben Bartone, who now wore only a single red and white batting glove on his left hand. The crowd continued to cheer. Cow bells continued to clang. The next pitch looked outside and high for ball four, but the home plate umpire saw it different. The Derby fans booed. In anguish, D wrapped his head with his arms. Ben calmly stepped out the batter's box, banged both his red Nike cleats with his bat, and settled back in.

On the next pitch, Ben swung at an inside fastball, and I heard a lighter ping from his aluminum bat than I hoped for.

The ball rebounded off his bat just above the handle and flared over the shortstop Dan Matulis's head. Matulis turned and sped back to catch it, but with his back to the plate he was unable to put a glove on it. The charging left fielder, Mike Rogers, slowed to see whether his teammate was going to catch it, and it dropped into the outfield grass before him.

As soon as the ball blooped out, Joey G. sped toward the plate. I whirled my left arm and waved Richie C. on. "Run! Run! Run!" I screamed as loud as I could as he rounded third base and raced for home. With two outs, I wasn't going to hold him.

Matulis turned away from where the ball had dropped, allowing Rogers a shot to pick it up and throw it in. Even though neither Matulis nor Rogers had any real chance to catch the ball, I thought the charging Rogers had a chance to throw to the plate. He picked it up from the shadowed outfield grass but, for some reason, didn't throw it.

I pumped my right fist across my chest as Richie crossed home plate. Richie was mobbed by our entire team—still wearing their crazy rally caps.

Our fans went berserk. Horns blew, cow bells clanged, and rows of fans above our dugout screamed and high-fived each other. I looked up at my two brothers and my father in the front row of our stands. My brother Bob cheered and laughed in disbelief while Fred, camera on his right shoulder, taped the play like an ESPN cameraman as he sat beside my father, who smiled under his red hat at the fortunate turn of events.

Somebody yelled to me from the stands behind me. I realized it was Tom Lionetti, a friend of mine and D's. "Hey, Reilly, way to go," he shouted as he leaned over a guardrail on the stairway. "You made the right call not tagging Guion from third base on that fly ball. You needed two runs to tie it." At that moment I said to myself, *Thank you. At least somebody back there knows the freakin' game.*

We had a new ball game at 5–5, and Angelo DiRubba no longer had to kill himself. He was redeemed. The fans on the Terryville side were dead silent. They knew their team had only been one out, nay two pitches, away from having won a state championship.

D flashed me the hit-and-run sign. I relayed it to Ben at first and to Donny, who had his right foot in and his left foot out of the batter's box. Donny adjusted his Mizuno batting gloves and put his left foot back in the box. Ben took off on the pitch, and Donny ripped a laser beam that reached the outfield so fast it forced Ben to hold at second. As I watched Joe Lizza stride to the plate in his black high-top Nike spikes, I gazed at the starry night sky. *If only Joe could boom another one*, I thought, *we could take a three-run lead.* But it wasn't to be. Joe smacked the ball hard, but it reached Matulis at deep short on two hops. Matulis pivoted and snapped the ball to Fortier at second for the third out. Although we'd made a miracle comeback, we had to hold Terryville in the bottom of the seventh to send the game into extra innings or go home losers.

25

Extra Innings

In the bottom of the seventh, a determined and focused Ben Bartone blanked Terryville. The last batter hit a routine ground ball to short. Donny scooped it with soft hands, brought them into his gut, and fired a strike to first. We were on to extra innings.

Before the eighth inning began, D gathered our team together yet again. Tules was on the field side of the huddle, pointing to someone in our crowd. He clenched a fist with his right hand and pumped it hard. He flashed both hands up, then both fists up, and then both hands up again as the huddle ended with the scream. "*Win!*"

After the huddle broke, D was dying for a smoke. He approached Doug Martin on the right side of the dugout near the water fountain, where a quiet member of the press wearing a black blazer and jeans stood for the entire game with his telephoto lens atop its stand. "Doug, let me have my cigarettes," D said nonchalantly.

"No, Mr. D," Doug said, sensing the ploy. "You told me not to give them to you."

"I know, Doug, but I also never knew the game would go into extra innings either. I gotta have a smoke."

"No, Mr. D," Doug shot back. "You told me no matter what, don't give them to you."

"I know," D replied with his open hands vibrating near the sides of his troubled face, "but I just got to have a smoke. Give me the cigarettes."

"No, Mr. D. You told me not to."

D suddenly grabbed a fistful of Doug's multicolored shirt. "Give me those f—king cigarette's or I'll kill ya!" he shouted.

Doug tried to back up, but there was nowhere to run. Shaking, he took the packs of cigarettes and matches from the pockets of his black shorts, fumbled with them, and threw them up in the air, crying, "Take your f—king cigarettes!"

D crouched in a dark corner of the dugout behind the water fountain with his back to the field. He snapped a match across the matchbook cover and lit up. He took a few quick drags and left the cigarette lit on the cement floor. His urge satisfied, D returned to where he had been standing throughout the game in front of the opposite side of the dugout, closer to home plate.

In the eighth inning, Kosikowski continued to pitch well, despite giving up the two tying runs in the seventh with two outs. The kid just wouldn't quit. When the top half of the eighth inning ended and we didn't score, we knew even if Ben held Terryville in the bottom of the frame, we would be in serious trouble in the ninth. Because the Aquinas game had been played on Wednesday instead of Tuesday and Ben had pitched all seven innings of that game, the pitcher's rule limited him to only three innings, or a total of nine outs in this game. Even if Ben's arm was fine, the rule would force us to bring in someone else to pitch the ninth.

As Ben pitched his heart out, D, Tules, Jocko, and I deliberated in our dugout about the dilemma. We had three options. First, pitch Pete, a senior tri-captain who had only pitched a few innings this year and thrown batting practice with me but would give you everything he had. If we pitched Pete, we would have to put Massie or Romo in center field and put either Ben or Donny in left or right field, positions neither of them had ever played. Second, pitch Mike Massie, a junior who had pitched even fewer varsity innings than Pete but pitched in all of the JV games. Third, bring Donny back in and take our chances.

As we expected, Ben did his job again. In his third and final inning, he struck out two hitters, the last of which was Greg Fortier, Terryville's leadoff hitter. We had to hope we could give a lead to whoever we pitched in the last of the ninth.

In the top of the ninth, Pete beat out a slow roller in the soft infield grass for a hit. Ben faked a bunt. Mischke blinked and missed the pitch, allowing Pete to breeze down to second base unchallenged. Ben grounded to Matulis at short, and Pete dashed to third on the cross-diamond throw to first. Donny came through and knocked in Pete with a low line-drive single to left center. Squeezing a batting glove in each hand, Pete raised his arms as he touched home plate and raced toward our dug out. Everyone on the bench mobbed him. But the rally ended when Joe Lizza mashed an inside fastball into a Matulis to Fortier fielder's choice, and George Hay whiffed.

In the bottom of the ninth, somewhere between his head and his heart, D decided to take option three and bring Donny back in. He couldn't see putting in Pete. As he explained why, D imitated Pete's signature way of pitching by exaggerating the planting of his right foot after delivering a pitch. He didn't think

Massie was experienced enough to overcome the pressure of pitching in this game. "Donny's just got to pitch," he said. "That's it." Donny was reluctant to accept his chance at redemption, but he knew he had no choice but to do it.

Donny slogged toward the mound instead of his shortstop position. When he snatched up the ball to warm up, his return to the mound was not lost on the Derby crowd. D's mom rose from her seat, excused herself through the packed aisle, and descended to the landing on the steps, close to the home plate side of our dugout. With her thin left arm, she grasped the metal railing. "Johhhnie," she called out. D backed up to the side of our dugout below her.

"Yeah, Ma," D replied as he looked up, surprised but not annoyed.

"Whya youa takinga Ben out?" Lala was certainly right it would have been a stupid move for D to make if the pitching limitation rule hadn't been in effect. In Mr. D's coaching days, the dilemma wouldn't have arisen.

"I have to, Ma," D responded. "It's the rules. There is nothing I can do."

Her eyebrows lowered as she pulled the fingertips of her right hand together. "Johhhhhnnie, cheat!"

I turned around and for the first time in the game started to chuckle.

"That's stupid, Ma," D replied. "I can't. I'll get caught. Everybody in the park knows Ben can't pitch anymore."

I turned back to look at Lala again. As she turned around to return to her bench seat beside Nancy and the girls, I thought I caught a glimpse of a smile forming on the side of her mouth. As Lala navigated her way back to her seat through the crowded aisle, the voice behind the shadowy press box said, "Ladies and Gentlemen-*gentlemen*, due to the CIAC rule-*rule* prohibiting a pitcher-*pitcher* from pitching-*pitching* more than thirty innings-*innings* in any three-*three* calendar days-*days*, now pitching-*pitching* again for Derby-*Derby* is number nineteen-*teen*, Don-*Don* Shepard-*Shepard*."

While Donny threw his eight warm-up pitches, the public address announcer clicked on his microphone once again: "Your attention please-*please*, ladies and gentlemen-*gentlemen*, this is-*is* to remind you-*you* that at the conclusion-*clusion* of the game-*game*, there will be-*be* at the plate-*plate* an awards-*wards* ceremony-*mony*. We ask-*ask* that no one-*one* go-*go* onto the field-*field*. Thank you-*you*." The announcement didn't bother me as much this time, but I wondered whether it was bad luck to the team ahead. If its timing tormented me when we trailed, I suspected it crept its way into Coach Hunt's concentration.

Donny induced Matulis to chop a ground ball to Ben for an out, but with every pitch Donny raised his right arm, rolled his sleeve, and winced.

"D, go to the mound and talk to Donny," I said. "Something's seriously wrong." D hobbled to the mound and put his arm around our distraught pitcher. When D returned, I asked, "What did Donny say was wrong?"

"He said he had nothing left in his arm."

"What did you tell him?"

"I told him that's OK, as he wasn't pitching with his arm anymore but with his balls, and to suck it up and keep pitching."

Donny kept battling but walked Chris Rogers to put the tying run on. Coach Hunt put in T. J. Taylor to pinch run. Donny threw the next pitch fifty-eight feet into the gray dirt. Lizza dropped on his red shin guards and tucked his chin, but the spinning ball bounced past him to the backstop. The wild pitch advanced Taylor to second. Donny was clearly out of gas.

The next batter, Keith Nypert, ripped a base hit to right field. Romo attacked the ball. He thought about throwing it to home plate before he had it in his glove, and it zipped under his glove past him. The ball rolled toward the 322 sign on the right field fence. Terryville's bench players leaped and screamed at Nypert to keep running.

As Romo sped after the elusive ball like a squirrel running after an acorn, Taylor scored and Nypert rounded first.

Dave finally picked the ball up and threw it as hard as he could on a line toward Gino, standing on the edge of the outfield grass.

Nypert was already on his way to third. Coach Hunt was circling his left arm faster than a relay runner waiting for a baton.

Gino caught the relay. He turned and in one continuous motion slung it toward Joey G., straddling third.

Coach Hunt jumped, waved, and screamed at Nypert to hit the deck. Nypert started his headfirst slide into third when in one bounce the throw reached Joey G.'s extended glove.

Joey put the tag on the ground before the base with his left hand and then pumped his right fist into the night air.

With his right hand on top of the base and both knees on the ground—his right knee against the bag—the winded Nypert looked up at the third base umpire. The umpire pointed at the base with his extended left arm, quickly whirled his right arm, then pumped his clenched right fist. "You're out!" he yelled.

Coach Hunt stood right on top of the play and never argued the close call. We dodged a magnum bullet. Anguished, Terryville's first base coach wrapped his hands around his head. He knew as I did, if Nypert was safe, we might as well have turned the key to our number 7 school bus and packed the equipment, as we likely would've lost. Not only did Donny have nothing left, but, even if he did, there are some seventeen ways a man can score from third base with less than two outs, including on a wild pitch. With the bases empty, Donny got Ben Kosikowski to hit a comebacker to the mound, ending the inning.

After George Hay flipped the ball toward the mound, Donny ran into the dugout. Distraught, he dropped on the bench and leaned back like a beaten boxer saved by the bell. Grasping his right arm, he told me he didn't have anything left and couldn't pitch anymore. He wanted me to tell him he didn't have to go back out, but he knew our bullpen down the left field line was empty.

"It's not impossible, Donny," I said. "I already threw at least fifteen pitches to every hitter on our team twice today. Add it up."

Donny grabbed part of the dugout roof with his right hand, stretched his arm, and grimaced. "It's shot," he said. "I can't even reach the plate." He shook his head in disgust and started to walk away.

"If their pitcher can do it, you can," I added. "Just concentrate on your mechanics. Focus hard on Joey's mitt, and don't take as many warm-up pitches. You can do this."

In the top of the tenth, Romo worked a walk. D flashed his white glove, and I relayed the bunt sign to Massie. Mike pulled the bat back on an outside pitch. Mischke couldn't hold the ball in his mitt, and Romo dashed into second standing up. With Romo on second, D flashed the bunt sign again. After Kosikowski checked Romo's lead and kicked, Mike squared. Terryville's first baseman Rogers charged on the pitch. Mike leaned across the plate and stuck his bat out but tried to run before he bunted the ball. He popped it up to his right. Rogers dove and caught the ball in flight, as he hit the ground, his outstretched mitt slammed on the infield grass.

With one out, Joey G. pivoted and dropped his hand down the barrel of his bat as if to bunt but yanked the bat back. Again, the masked Mischke muffed the pitch and allowed Romo to beat the catcher's long-armed throw to third with a headfirst slide. Romo popped up, dusted himself off, and wiped his face with his sleeve. Joey G. then struck out again. Embarrassed, he grabbed his bat by the middle of the barrel and hurried into the dugout shadows.

Gino stepped to the plate with his bat on his shoulders. He dug in and bent his knees. With an 0–2 count, Kosikowski tried to sneak a fastball past him. Gino swung late and slapped a line drive down the right field line, scoring Romo to put us ahead 7–6, but that would be the end of the rally. After Gino hit the ball,

Tules jumped all 255 pounds of himself up and down with joy as Gino approached him at first, but the joy was again shortlived.

In the bottom of the tenth, Donny unraveled again. He plunked Mischke, who advanced to third base on a single by Crovo that sparked off Gino's glove. With nobody out, Paul LeClair hit a short fly ball to right. Romo snared it, crow hopped, and fired it all the way to the plate. Wisely, Mischke held at third. But Mike Rogers hit another fly ball to Romo long enough to knock in Mischke and tie the score once again. Terryville wouldn't give up.

In the top of the eleventh inning, we finally got rid of Ben Kosikowski on the mound, but not because of anything we did. Just as Ben was forced to leave the hill after pitching his third inning, Kosikowski was no longer eligible to pitch because of the CIAC pitching limitation rule. Kosikowski had pitched brilliantly, throwing 172 pitches in ten innings and holding us hitless for five innings after the first. The rubber-armed right-hander would still be battling us if not for the inflexible rule.

Terryville's shortstop, Dan Matulis, stepped to the mound to pitch to Lizza, Hay, and Anroman, our fourth, fifth, and sixth hitters. Lizza fouled a few off and worked the right-hander for a walk. Although Joe was no roadrunner, he ran the bases well. D decided not to try to bunt Hay. George had never been a good bunter and didn't like to bunt. Instead, George whiffed for out number one. Romo then flared a fastball to shallow right center. Joe hesitated in the baseline to make sure the ball dropped in safely and could only advance to second.

Massie popped the ball behind home plate. Like he was drilled, Mischke lifted his mask, turned his back to the plate, waited until the ball reached its maximum height, then chucked his metal mask aside. He backed up as the ball spun down in flight and took it in his brown mitt for out number two.

With two outs, Joey G. settled into the batter's box. Joey hadn't done anything all night. He was a dismal 0–5 wearing number 13 on his back, having already struck out twice on pitches above his eyes. Joey quickly fell behind 0–2, and we were one strike away from the bottom of the eleventh tied again.

But then Joey somehow fought off Matulis's pitches like a pinball flipper and worked the count to 3–2. At least with a full count and the runners going, if Joey put the ball in play on the ground, Terryville's infielders would not have the luxury of being able to get a force play at second or third. The throw would have to go to first base. If Joey could somehow earn a free pass, Gino would come up again. Despite Gino's batting average being less than his weight, he already had two hits on the night.

Matulis brought his hands to his chest. He kicked, and the runners took off in a dead sprint. Matulis slung a fastball. *Ping.* Joey fouled it straight back to the netting above the backstop. The fans behind the net in the first row of seats flinched. As he took the sign from Mischke, Matulis fiddled with the ball behind his right knee as he searched for the right grip. He brought his hands together again, paused, and pitched. The runners took off again. Joey fouled the ball straight back to the backstop. Matulis set again, pitched, and the runners took off once more. Joey fouled the ball straight back to the backstop. Another pitch with the runners going. The result: Groundhog Day and another foul ball back to the backstop. Matulis set again. He pitched. The runners took off again. Joey fouled it off—again.

Lizza gasped for air as he touched third base and turned around again to return to second. With each pitch, our super-sized freshman burst into a full sprint after he was certain the pitcher was delivering to home. I didn't worry about Romo. I knew the football team's 150-pound starting tailback wouldn't tire from five thirty-yard wind sprints.

On the sixth pitch from Matulis, after Joey G. had worked the count to 3–2, the runners ran again, and the same thing happened again: a foul ball straight back to the backstop. Like a skipping record, Matulis just kept throwing fastballs and Joey G. just kept fouling them off to the backstop.

On the seventh pitch, Joey fought off the pitch again into the netting behind home plate. Like two boxers standing toe to toe taking turns slugging each other with neither dropping to the canvas, neither player would give in. The desensitized fans in the front row knew the ball would head toward them again, but they still flinched. What I always thought was Joey's stubbornness turned into tenacity. Joey fouled back nine pitches and seven in a row with a 3–2 count.

After the last foul ball, Joey G. stepped out the box to take a deep breath and collect himself. D was close enough for Joey to hear him. "Will you please get a hit or strike out?" he implored. Joey nodded.

On the fourteenth and final pitch of Joey's at bat, Matulis focused on Mischke's fingers for the sign. He nodded and came set.

He started his delivery.

Joey Lizza took off again and headed toward me at third base in his sweat-stained shirt. Romo raced again toward second.

Matulis threw Joey yet another fastball, but the result was as different as the sound from his bat.

Bang.

The ball trampolined off Joey's thirty-three-inch aluminum bat high toward the left fielder. It just went and went and then went over the left fielder's outstretched glove and bounced toward the left field fence like a superball.

Lizza scored standing up and Romo, pumping his arms and ripping up gray dust from the ground, was heading toward me. I whirled my left arm while screaming, "Run your balls off!" Romo pushed off the inside corner of third base and headed to the pay dirt beyond home plate, stepping on the flat rubber base as he zoomed past it. He scored before the relay reached the infield.

When the third baseman finally caught the throw from the left fielder, Joey G. was already standing on second base. The Derby crowd was ecstatic. Our bench erupted on Joe Lizza and Romo as they approached the dugout. We now had a two-run cushion for Donny. Joey G., the same kid who had launched us into the tournament with his dramatic bottom of the seventh two-out home run against Cheshire, never quit. After five failed at bats, he miraculously did it again on a 3–2 pitch after fouling off seven consecutive pitches. But while I was glad Joey had blasted us a two-run lead, I feared it might not be enough to overcome the fact that Donny's arm was shot. Terryville still had the Hammer.

When the top of the eleventh ended, I peered at the scoreboard. Only designed for a ten-inning score, an orange-bulbed number 2 shined alone in the top of the first-inning column. When I entered the dugout before the bottom of the eleventh, I searched for my watch in my red bag. It was about eleven o'clock. "D, look at your Timex," I said, pointing to his left wrist.

"What for?"

"What are we going to do if this game goes past midnight?" D appeared puzzled, but then looked at me with wide eyes, as if awakened from a deep sleep. He realized the significance of what I asked.

If this battle carried on past midnight, was Ben eligible to pitch again? We knew a lot of innings were left in Ben's arm. If we could only return him to the hill, he would certainly put Terryville away. The CIAC rule specifically used calendar days, and, if we went past midnight, the calendar would flip over to a new day. The thought our pumpkin could turn into a carriage at midnight intrigued us. We wondered whether the CIAC officials in attendance were already considering an interpretation of the rigid rule.

When Donny warmed up in the bottom of the eleventh, he could barely reach home plate. If Terryville's hitters had the moxie to go up to the plate without bats, I feared they could win the game before Donny could get three outs.

The first batter up was the left-hand hitting Chris Rogers, who already pummeled one over Pete's head in center. Donny threw him three straight balls. I knew from the look on D's face that he wasn't changing his mind. He wasn't going to pull Donny out. Donny would have to find a way himself. I didn't think he could throw three strikes before he would throw one ball. Donny kicked and guided the fourth pitch right down the middle. To my surprise, Rogers swung and pulled it on the ground hard to Hay.

Donny bolted across the infield and up the line toward first. George scooped up the ball and pointed his first baseman's mitt at Donny. He stepped on first before Rogers, who sprinted down the line, got close.

Hay popped off the base. He fired the ball across the infield grass to Ben.

Ben snapped it to Gino, who shifted his red high-top spikes and slung it over to Joey G., who lobbed it back to Donny.

Ben turned and hustled back to his shortstop position. He pointed his right index finger high in the air. "One down!" he shouted. I was stunned. Terryville was chasing two runs with a 3–0 count and could have brought the tying run to the plate simply by standing there.

Donny lobbed another one down the middle to the fourth batter, Nypert, who roped the ball down the left field line. Massie moved on the crack of the bat. He backhanded the ball near the left field line, planted his right foot, and fired a rocket toward Ben's raised arms. Ben didn't cut the ball off, and on one bounce the ball reached Gino at second. Disappointed he couldn't stretch the hit into a double, Nypert returned to first. The strength of Mike's throw stunned me. I thought, *Perhaps D should've chosen option two.*

The five hitter, Kosikowski, didn't bite on any bad pitches and walked to put runners on first and second with only one out. I still couldn't get Chris Rogers turn at bat out of my head. If he had taken the walk, Terryville would have had the bases loaded with nobody out and only down two. I wondered whether Coach Hunt had given him the green light, or if the blank stare on Donny's face had convinced Rogers Donny could throw him two more strikes. I couldn't believe Coach Hunt would green light Rogers, down two runs, unless he knew something we didn't.

After Kosikowski walked, Mischke came to the plate. From the stretch, Donny threw the tall catcher two straight balls. Ben pounded his glove at shortstop and exhorted Donny to focus. He wished he could take the ball, but the rule prevented it. I again expected Mischke to at least take a strike before he swung at any pitch.

Donny brought his hands together. He kicked and threw a batting practice fastball. In years past, the pitch would have been called a meatball, but now it's sometimes referred to as a fatch—a hybrid pitch somewhere between a fastball and a changeup. To my astonishment again, Mischke swung at the tempting big ball, but too hard, and lifted a high pop in the infield. "I got it!" Ben shouted as he waved his arms.

The base umpires screamed, "Infield Fly!" The second out happened with the ball still in flight. The lights were friendly to us again, as Ben had no trouble seeing the ball, but it didn't matter. The batter was out even if Ben dropped it, and the runners couldn't risk trying to advance. I couldn't help think Terryville could have had, at worst, the bases loaded with one out, and, at best, if Donny couldn't throw two more strikes before throwing two balls, the bases loaded with one run in and nobody out.

With two outs and men on first and second base, I thought the Foxwood's odds might now be in our favor. Terryville wouldn't score two runs before we got one out. I tried to dismiss it from my mind so as not to jinx Donny. I knelt down on one knee beside D, who was doing the same in our gray on-deck batter's box. Together, we yelled words of encouragement to Donny.

In D's basement den, long before this season, we had once joked about what we would do if we ever won a state championship together. I tried to block the memory from my thoughts but couldn't. As he ironed his next day's dress shirt at midnight, D told me that if he ever won a state championship, despite his age, he would jump into the pile of players, wherever it formed on the field. He showed me a picture of himself at Quigley Stadium with his hands raised, running out to the pile near the mound after the 1977 team won. Tules once told me he would do the same. I began to think of what I might do if we won and again tried to block it from my mind so as not to jinx Donny.

With two outs, Donny faced A. J. Sirianni, Terryville's right fielder who Coach Hunt entered for the designated hitter Crovo. The tall, thin Sirianni stepped into the batter's box and took his closed stance. Joey crouched before the umpire and pulled his mask down like a gladiator. The umpire leaned behind Joey in a wide stance. Donny focused on Joey's mitt, more determined than I had ever seen him before. His eyes no longer displayed despair as he stood tall and confident. It was as if he had asked for and received a renewed inner strength. Where he was getting it from, I didn't know.

The players in our dugout and the fans above us continued their cheering, banging, and screaming. With outstretched arms, Jocko and Tules were doing everything they could to make sure the players didn't get too far outside the dugout. With the first fastball strike to Sirianni, our bench erupted. Joey pointed to Donny with the ball, then snapped it back.

Donny wasted no time. He brought his hands together, stopped, kicked, and threw another fastball.

"Steeeer-ike two!" shouted the umpire.

The bench went into a frenzy. Still pitching from the stretch, Donny took the single-digit sign from Joey. He fiddled with the ball, his fingers searching their way around the 216 red raised stitches until he found the perfect grip. He kicked high, whipped his arm, and let fly a high inside fastball toward Sirianni.

Sirianni swung at the pitch. The ball tipped off his bat, but not enough to affect its path straight into Lizza's raised mitt.

"Strike three!" yelled the umpire.

Joey flung his mask off to his right and his mitt and the ball to his left. He charged the mound with both fists raised above his head.

D pushed my arm, sprang up, and started to run toward the mound. Without saying it, he was telling me, "Let's go." Without thinking, I joined him. As Joey tackled Donny, the rest of the team rushed the mound.

A deafening roar shot out from our stands and overshadowed the nonstop fog horns, cow bells, and stadium horns. The emotion of an entire year of frustration erupted. I ran around toward the back of the pile that had already formed before I got there. D and Tules disappeared underneath the stack of bodies. I jumped on the back of the pile, and with my index finger in the air started screaming, "We did iiiiiiiiiiiit! We did iiiiiiit!"

Mike Massi raced in from left field and leaped onto the pile. Ben winged his glove three stories high and jumped straight up. Jocko jumped up and down with his red hat scrunched in his left hand. Waving his arms as if trying to draw angels' wings in the air, Jocko looked for somebody, anybody, to hug.

I spotted Ben. In a flash, the joy of what we had gone through together moistened my eyes. "Yeaaaaaaaaah!" I yelled as we embraced each other. My voice cracking, I told him, "I knew you could do it. I knew you had it in you." Pete jumped on top of us. Gino joined in, hugged Ben, and wrestled him to the infield grass as if Ben were a rodeo calf. Ben got up and leaped into Joe Lizza's arms and toppled over him headfirst to the ground. Joe Lizza spotted Tules, and they gave each other an extended hug.

Exhausted, I started toward our dugout water fountain. D found me and decided to walk with me. As we approached the dugout with an arm over each other's shoulders, the Derby crowd cheered us. In a moment of exuberance, we both pointed to the sky, while D bobbed his head to the raucous crowd. When we reached the dugout, I twisted my neck under the water fountain and pushed the button—for a moment, I relaxed.

Joe Lizza swaggered toward our third base side fans to their slow but loud chants of "Derrrrby! Derrrrby! Derrrrby!" The big freshman unclasped the black elastic straps of his red chest protector, flung it off, and pointed both index fingers to the sky as our fans continued their wild cheering.

While we celebrated our victory, two CIAC officials unfolded a white rectangular table on top of home plate for the presentation of medallions and plaques. After our on-the-field celebration ended, Terryville's distraught players were announced one by one. As each received a round silver medallion and a firm handshake, they were applauded by both sides of the stadium as well as by us. The officials presented Coach Hunt with the runner-up plaque, and again both sides of the stadium cheered.

Although I knew Terryville had nothing to be ashamed of, I also knew that, for now, nothing could console them. There was no joy in Terryville, but there was pride—pride in the fact that their players had been warriors just as we had for the last three hours and forty-four minutes, and had left everything they had on the field. Maybe nobody will remember they finished second, but anyone who saw the game will remember the way they played. They won the respect of every player, coach, and fan at Palmer Field. They never quit.

Each of our players and coaches were called to the table and given a round gold medallion and a firm handshake. When the officials motioned D to step forward and receive the championship plaque, D motioned the entire team and the rest of the coaches to step up to the plate with him to accept it. A silver metal plate stating "Baseball S Division Champs" and a cutout map of the state of Connecticut shined from the plaque's face; a metal baseball batter was affixed underneath. D took the plaque from the CIAC official and squeezed his hands tightly on its solid edges. His eyes began to tear. D raised it with the rest of the team and coaches touching it as the Derby crowd roared.

After the plaque was awarded, we lined up to exchange handshakes with our eleven-inning adversaries. After I shook the hand of every Terryville player and coach, I headed toward the stands above our dugout to accept congratulations from Sue, my brothers, and my dad, who were taking in every bit of the crazy scene.

I returned to the dugout to speak to Reegers. He was a true friend to the players and coaches and had profoundly influenced us. He shared in our joy. We might not have been at Palmer Field if he hadn't scouted Aquinas for us. I thanked Reegers and placed my gold medallion on his chair and told him I wanted him to have it.

After I guzzled down more water from the dugout fountain, Donny approached me and we embraced. "I knew you had it in you, kid," I said. "I knew it. You didn't get that arm blessed for nothing!"

"I didn't think I could do it," he replied with watery eyes. "My arm was shot. I had nothing. I could barely throw the ball. When D asked me to go out there again, I didn't know what I was gonna do."

"You didn't need your arm, Donny," I replied. "You pitched with your heart. I was proud of the way you fought. You just kept on battling. You battled all year. You never gave up. You got it done, kid. You got it done."

26

The Parade, the Clubhouse, and the Evergreen

The stadium staff opened the chain-link gate. I greeted Sue, my brothers, and my dad again. I learned Fred had start-stopped his camera as much as he could, but his two-hour battery had died in the ninth inning. We hoped somebody had caught Joey G.'s last at bat on tape.

A multitude of Derby fans, ex-players, friends, and fellow coaches from the Valley congratulated me as I stood before our dugout. Freshman players Steve Tilki and Chris Reuther approached me with their parents and talked about next year's team. While I waited for the team to regroup and board the bus back to Derby, Sue learned the CIAC was selling tournament T-shirts and hats at a card table near the front gate. We bought as many as we could for the players, moments before they sold out.

I returned to the field. Several tired reporters with small-ringed notebooks still surrounded D. Their hands hovered across their pads with each tidbit D chose to give them. From the grins on their faces, I knew they were satisfied their deadlines would be met with an entertaining sports story. D basked in the well-deserved glory. He found his niche, and he did it with his own hat. Tony D. would have been proud. But little did D know, he was already expected to repeat the feat.

Members of the press were also interviewing Donny, Ben, Gino, Joey G., and Joe Lizza. "Hey, what am I, chopped liver?" Romo jokingly asked, upset he wasn't getting more media attention. I glanced toward Terryville's dugout. Coach Hunt was still answering questions. As the interviews were ending, a sullen Coach Hunt walked past our empty dugout and again I told him, "Good game." After he passed me, I wondered whether he recognized me.

Before we climbed aboard our idling yellow bus, which was already adorned with red and white streamers, Ken Marcucio approached me. "Riles, I told D already, but with everything going on, I know he won't remember. Be sure to tell the bus driver to stop when you reach Derby's border. We're arranging for police cars to meet you at the town line and escort the bus through downtown and then back to the clubhouse."

"Sounds great, Ken," I replied as I wiped my face with a worn white towel I had pulled from my bag. "The kids will get a kick out of that, I'm sure."

"Also, there's a celebration waiting for the team at the Evergreen, so after the team gets to clubhouse and changes, they can head down there. They're supposed to have hot dogs, soda, and chips waiting for the players, parents and coaches."

"At the Evergreen?" I asked, surprised. The Evergreen was a bar as well as a restaurant at the former Howard Johnson's restaurant in east Derby across from St. Michael's Church. "That might not be such a great idea," I added. "Not that I have anything against the Evergreen, but it could send the wrong message to the kids. Somebody might complain."

"I know. I feel the same. But I'm told they're going to have an area sectioned off for us away from the bar. It's all been preordained by a member of the board of education."

"Who?"

"I shouldn't say."

"Only in Derby, Ken, can a team be denied by the board of education to have a morning practice on Mother's Day but be able to celebrate a state championship at a sports bar."

When we finally boarded the midnight bus, the celebration continued with the players constantly banging the walls inside. A few miles into our trek back toward Derby on Route 66, the driver pulled to the side of the road. A small red light on the dash warned him the diesel-powered bus was overheated. Few players noticed we had pulled over.

The driver thought he knew the reason for our problem. The bus door creaked open. Jocko jumped off the steps and went to the front of the bus. Somebody had tied the "D.H.S. Baseball We Believe" banner over the front grill, blocking the engine's cooling system. Jocko pulled it off and five seconds later was back on the bus. He sat across from D and I and chucked the wrinkled white and red banner on the bench seat behind him. The bus jerked and hissed its way back into the right lane.

"This all seems so unreal, D," I said. "Almost like a dream."

D laughed. "If this a dream, Riles, then I want to die now."

When we reached the intersection with Route 8, construction vehicles, mobile light towers, and equipment blocked the left lane exit ramp. Jocko declared he knew the detour route. As the bus driver followed Jocko's instructions, we ended up lost in a downtrodden section of Waterbury. Our players ducked as we passed each dark corner hangout. Ten minutes later, however, we found ourselves back onto Route 8 south toward Derby.

When we arrived at the Derby border, the bus stopped so we could line up behind several royal blue Crown Victoria police cars that waited for us. With blue lights flashing and sirens blazing, the police cars escorted us and a line of twenty-plus cars for two and a half miles through downtown Derby—all the way back to the clubhouse.

Throughout the slow, festive trip, our players screamed and shouted out the lowered windows and banged the outside of the bus as the cars behind us beeped their horns. Front door lights flicked on and doors opened. People in bathrobes, pajamas, and wrinkled T-shirts opened screen doors and stepped out on porches and sidewalks as they wiped their eyes or put on their glasses to see what was going on. When they did, the team screamed, "We're number one!" over and over again. Most people waved back; others looked at us like we were nuts.

When we finally reached the clubhouse, lights flickered from the second floor locker room and coaches' room windows. I asked if any team members wanted to take a victory lap with me around the track surrounding the football field. I recalled the 1977 championship team running the quarter mile when they returned to Ryan Field. I wanted to feel what it would have been like to run with them.

The players, Jocko, and I started to run on the dark oval track under the football moon. Donny bolted to the lead with the state championship plaque tucked under his right arm like a football he wouldn't fumble. We passed through our outfield, passed both dugouts, and ran in triumph in front of the empty football stands as the sharp smell of fertilizer burned my nose. I gasped for air as I reached the lightless scoreboard before turning for the home stretch before the clubhouse. At the lap's end, a number of players ran, dove, and slid through the automatic sprinklers coincidentally showering the dark football field.

Still short of breath, I greeted a number of Derby coaches in the crowded coaches' room. One of them had brought a bottle of champagne. After the white tin foil was unwrapped from the olive green bottle, the cork popped and shot across the room. The bottle was emptied into a row of six-ounce paper Gatorade cups. I didn't drink, but I decided to keep the featherweight tan cork as a memento.

Bill Pucci from the *Evening Sentinel* squeezed into the noisy room to get some additional quotes—the ones he knew D might not give to an out of the Valley reporter. While the coaches were deciding whether to attend the festivities at the Evergreen, Jocko opted to change out of his uniform and shower in the adjacent bathroom's stall. After steam drifted through the open door, Jocko dripped across the room. Oblivious to the crowd waiting outside the building, he toweled down before the bent, white plastic mini blinds hanging in front of the open coaches' room window with his ass sticking out. Only Jocko could turn a football moon into a full one.

"We are the Champions" by Queen blared from the locker room boom box. Like a World Series celebration, geysers from shaken soda cans streamed across the loud locker room. Players in soggy red and white uniforms stood atop the benches and whooped, clapped, and high-fived each other as fathers and friends offered congratulation. The championship plaque was passed around from player to player with each making sure it was kept dry.

After everyone finally left the clubhouse, I met Sue outside. I told her about the odd place for the postgame celebration but didn't think we could not show up. When the team entered the Evergreen, it was obvious that whatever hot dogs might have been piled on the empty trays had been devoured long before we walked in. Because of the delay in our arrival and since it was close to one o'clock in the morning, all that was left were a few warm half-empty liter-sized plastic soda bottles, some plastic cups, and a few open bags of broken potato chips. The players and their parents gathered in the room reserved for us.

The team surprised the coaches with gifts. The players presented me with a blown-up team picture on a white poster board with their autographs on it, the words "Class S State Champions" printed across its bottom in large red letters.

Despite our seclusion, we barely heard ourselves talk; the music in an adjoining room vibrated the walls. Some players decided to check it out. When I peeked into the dimly lit room, Ben was in the middle of the jammed crowd on a shiny wooden dance floor with a black wireless microphone in his right hand. Acting like Dick Clark, he welcomed everyone to the early morning celebration. He led the crowd while the DJ played "Jump" by Kris Kross. Donny and Gino, along with several other players, bounced up and down like pogo sticks to the song.

As they smiled and laughed, I couldn't help think about how different their futures would be because we had won. They weren't going to the White House or Disneyworld and weren't getting World Series bonus money, but in their victory they had achieved something more valuable—greater than redemption. They had battled beyond anyone's expectations of what was possible for them to accomplish. They had found out what it's like to dig deep into your soul and fight your way out of the obstacles life puts in front of you. It's what Big Lou had taught the school, it's what Big Lou had taught D and me, and it was what Big Lou had taught Derby. In a town where, six months ago Ben, Gino, and Donny were labeled losers forever, they were now not only winners—they were champions forever. Nobody could ever take that away from them. Like the rest of the players and coaches, they believed there was no I in team, tournament, or state champs. They never quit. D, Tules, Jocko, and I never quit. Derby never quit.

After a few hours of light sleep, I called D the next morning to see whether he wanted to return to Palmer Field to attend Seymour's late afternoon game against Tolland. Nancy told me D had spent the night in his BVDs on the carpeted hallway floor between their living room and bedroom—with the wooden state championship plaque clutched tightly in his bare arms. Although there were a lot of experiences that night I wanted to remember forever, the image that brought up was not one of them. Save that one for the fat lady who never sings anymore to Ben, Donny, Gino, and the rest of the 1992 Derby Red Raiders.

THE END

Acknowledgments

Thanks to assistant coaches George "Tules" DeTullio and Jacques "Jocko" Veillette, who made the ride with the team to the top a memorable one. Thanks to athletic director Ken Marcucio for his support of the team and his patience throughout the season.

Special thanks goes to all the parents, former players, coaches, Derby High students, alumni, friends, and fans who followed and supported the team's remarkable run and those who put up streamers, balloons, and signs, and cheered, roared, stomped their feet, sounded fog horns, and whacked cow bells for nearly four hours during all eleven innings of the championship game.

I would like to thank Mr. William Greenleaf for his most valuable assistance and advice with this book.

Thanks also to my friend and former player Rich Bruciati for his assistance.

I would also like to thank Janet Noddings and Sarie Whitson at IUniverse for their assistance and guidance with this book as well as their patience with me.

I also wish to thank Michael Regan, whose courage was an inspiration to the players and coaches and whose support of the players, his friendship, and his willingness to help will never be forgotten.

I am especially grateful to the members of the 1992 Derby High School baseball team for allowing me to be a part of their perseverance and triumph. I am also grateful to all the baseball players at Derby High School I have had the good fortune of being able to coach and who started and continued a tradition that made that night at Palmer Field possible.

Above all, I would like to thank my good friend John DeFrancisco for his willingness to allow me to assist him, for his friendship, and for his perseverance, which was an inspiration to me.

Endnotes

1. http://electronicvalley.org/Derby/Quiz/pages/Defillipo.htm; http://www.electronicvalley.org/derby/images/Defillipo/defilippo.htm; www.ctsportswriters.org/honorroll.html;

   New York Times, Obituary, 3/9/2000; Newsday, Obituaries, March 2000.
2. Connecticut High School Football Record Book, 2004 edition, p.38.
3. Barker, Sean. *The Evening Sentinel.* April 17, 1992, 11.
4. Wilson, Steve. *The New Haven Register.* April, 28, 1992, 21.
5. Wally Pipp was the New York Yankee's first baseman who in 1925 was replaced in the lineup by then rookie Lou Gehrig. Gehrig remained as the Yankee first baseman for the next 2,129 games.
6. Barker, Sean. *The Evening Sentinel*, May 14, 1992, 9.
7. Barker, Sean. *The Evening Sentinel*, May 16, 1992, 18.
8. Barker, Sean. *The Evening Sentinel*, May 16, 1992, 18.
9. Barker, Sean. *The Evening Sentinel*, June 4, 1992, 9.
10. Barker, Sean. *The Evening Sentinel*, June, 11, 1992, 9.
11. St. Onge, Peter. *The Waterbury Republican,* June 12, 1992, 1C, 6C.

978-0-595-39467-8
0-595-39467-1